Introduction to Cryptography

Introduction to Cryptography

Joey Holland

WILLFORD PRESS

www.willfordpress.com

Published by Willford Press,
118-35 Queens Blvd., Suite 400,
Forest Hills, NY 11375, USA

ISBN: 978-1-64728-031-4

Cataloging-in-Publication Data

Introduction to cryptography / Joey Holland.
p. cm.
Includes bibliographical references and index.
ISBN 978-1-64728-031-4
1. Cryptography. 2. Data encryption (Computer science). 3. Ciphers. I. Holland, Joey.
QA268 .I58 2022
003.54--dc23

For information on all Willford Press publications
visit our website at www.willfordpress.com

Contents

Preface

The practice and study of methods for secure communication in the presence of hostile third parties is known as cryptography. It consists of construction and analysis of protocols to prevent third parties from reading private messages. Some of the important aspects of cryptography are data integrity, data confidentiality, authentication and non-repudiation. There are several applications of this field of study such as digital currencies, military communications and electronic commerce. The field of cryptography consists of different areas of study like symmetric-key cryptography and public key cryptography. The sphere of study which seeks to detect insecurity or weakness in a cryptographic scheme is known as cryptanalysis. This book provides significant information of this discipline to help develop a good understanding of cryptography and related fields. Those in search of information to further their knowledge will be greatly assisted by this book. It will serve as a reference to a broad spectrum of readers.

A detailed account of the significant topics covered in this book is provided below:

Chapter 1- The branch of engineering which is involved in the development of techniques for secure communication in the presence of hostile third parties is known as cryptography engineering. Some of the major concepts related to this field are encryption, Kerchoff's principle and digital signatures. This is an introductory chapter which will provide a brief introduction to these concepts of cryptography engineering.

Chapter 2- The encryption method which uses a deterministic algorithm and a symmetric key to encrypt a block of text instead of one bit at a time is known as a block cipher. It plays a crucial role in designing secure cryptographic protocols. This chapter has been carefully written to provide an easy understanding of the varied facets of block ciphers and block cipher modes.

Chapter 3- The application of methods of digital encryption for the protection of messages is termed as message security. A secure channel refers to a way of transmitting data which is protected against overhearing or tampering. This chapter discusses the diverse aspects of message security and secure channels in detail.

Chapter 4- The protocols which are used to perform security related functions and apply cryptographic methods are known as cryptographic protocols. Some of the common protocols are key exchange protocols and identification protocols. The topics elaborated in this chapter will help in gaining a better perspective about these cryptographic protocols.

Chapter 5- The set of detailed and complex mathematical instructions which are used to encrypt or decrypt data are known as cryptographic algorithms. Some of its types are symmetric-key algorithms and asymmetric-key algorithms. The diverse aspects of these cryptographic algorithms have been thoroughly discussed in this chapter.

It gives me an immense pleasure to thank our entire team for their efforts. Finally in the end, I would like to thank my family and colleagues who have been a great source of inspiration and support.

Joey Holland

Understanding Cryptography Engineering

The branch of engineering which is involved in the development of techniques for secure communication in the presence of hostile third parties is known as cryptography engineering. Some of the major concepts related to this field are encryption, Kerchoff's principle and digital signatures. This is an introductory chapter which will provide a brief introduction to these concepts of cryptography engineering.

Cryptography

Cryptography is the study and practice of techniques for secure communication in the presence of third parties called adversaries. It deals with developing and analyzing protocols which prevents malicious third parties from retrieving information being shared between two entities thereby following the various aspects of information security.

Secure Communication refers to the scenario where the message or data shared between two parties can't be accessed by an adversary. In Cryptography, an Adversary is a malicious entity, which aims to retrieve precious information or data thereby undermining the principles of information security.

Data Confidentiality, Data Integrity, Authentication and Non-repudiation are core principles of modern-day cryptography:

1. Confidentiality refers to certain rules and guidelines usually executed under confidentiality agreements which ensure that the information is restricted to certain people or places.

2. Data integrity refers to maintaining and making sure that the data stays accurate and consistent over its entire life cycle.

3. Authentication is the process of making sure that the piece of data being claimed by the user belongs to it.

4. Non-repudiation refers to ability to make sure that a person or a party associated with a contract or a communication cannot deny the authenticity of their signature over their document or the sending of a message.

Consider two parties Alice and Bob. Now, Alice wants to send a message m to Bob over a secure channel. So, what happens is as follows. The sender's message or sometimes called the Plaintext, is converted into an unreadable form using a Key k. The resultant text obtained is called the Ciphertext. This process is known as Encryption. At the time of receival, the Ciphertext is converted back into the plaintext using the same Key k, so that it can be read by the receiver. This process is known as Decryption.

Alice (Sender) Bob (Receiver),

$$C = E\,(m,\,k) \longrightarrow m = D\,(C,\,k).$$

Here, C refers to the Ciphertext while E and D are the Encryption and Decryption algorithms respectively.

Let's consider the case of Caesar Cipher or Shift Cipher as an example. As the name suggests, in Caesar Cipher each character in a word is replaced by another character under some defined rules. Thus, if A is replaced by D, B by E and so on. Then, each character in the word would be shifted by a position of 3. For example:

Plaintext : Geeksforgeeks

Ciphertext : Jhhnvirujhhnv

Note that even if the adversary knows that the cipher is based on Caesar Cipher, it cannot predict the plaintext as it doesn't have the key in this case which is to shift the characters back by three places.

Encryption

Most search engines, regardless of if they track you, encrypt your search data. This is how search engines, including Google, Yahoo and Search Encrypt; all protect their users' information. Google, which collects tons of user data, is obligated to protect that information. SSL encryption is a standard for protecting sensitive information, for search engines and other websites.

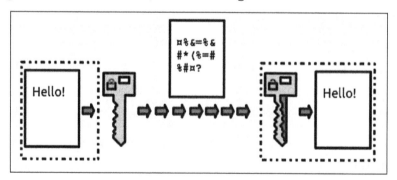

Encryption is a process that encodes a message or file so that it can be only be read by certain people. Encryption uses an algorithm to scramble, or encrypt, data and then uses a key for the receiving party to unscramble, or decrypt, the information. The message contained in an encrypted message is referred to as plaintext. In its encrypted, unreadable form it is referred to as ciphertext.

Basic forms of encryption may be as simple as switching letters. As cryptography advanced, cryptographers added more steps, and decryption became more difficult. Wheels and gears would be combined to create complex encryption systems. Computer algorithms have now replaced mechanical encryption.

Encryption Algorithm Performance

Many encryption algorithms exist, and they are all suited to different purposes—the two main characteristics that identify and differentiate one encryption algorithm from another are its ability to secure the protected data against attacks and its speed and efficiency in doing so.

As a good example of the speed difference between different types of encryption, you can use the benchmarking utility built into TrueCrypt's volume creation wizard—as you can see, AES is by far the fastest type of strong encryption.

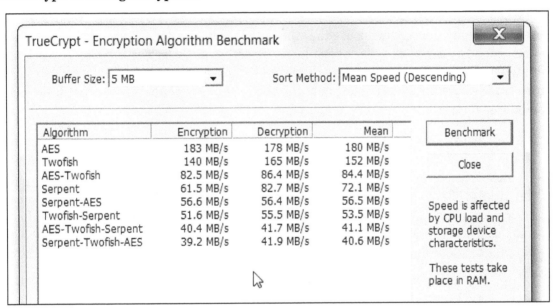

There are both slower and faster encryption methods, and they are all suited for different purposes. If you're simply trying to decrypt a tiny piece of data every so often, you can afford to use the strongest possible encryption, or even encrypt it twice with different types of encryption. If you require speed, you'd probably want to go with AES.

Types of Modern Encryption

All the fancy encryption algorithm that we have talked about earlier are mostly used for two different types of encryption:

- Symmetric key algorithms use related or identical encryption keys for both encryption and decryption.

- Asymmetric key algorithms use different keys for encryption and decryption—this is usually referred to as Public-key Cryptography.

Symmetric Key Encryption

Symmetric key encryption is defined as the type of encryption technique where only one secret key which is also the secret key is used for encryption and decryption of electronic messages.

These are the algorithms that are used in the case of cryptography and makes use of the same kind of keys for all kinds of encryption techniques which are related to both encryption of plaintext as well as decryption of the block ciphertext. The keys may be identical in shape and structure or there may be a simple kind of transformation that is involved when you go between keys. The keys as a whole, are used to represent a shared secret between one or two parties which can be effectively used to maintain an information link on a private basis. This construction where both parties have equal access over the secret key is a critical drawback of symmetry based encryption.

This is not the case with the asymmetric key encryption or the public key-based encryption technique. The symmetric keys can make use of either the block ciphers or stream ciphers. When you make use of this encryption, you ensure that the data is converted to an encrypted form that cannot be understood by anybody who doesn't have the access to the secret key for decryption. Once the intended recipient who has the access to that key possesses the message, we make sure that the algorithm reverses the action state such that the message is returned back to the original and understandable form.

- As we have already mentioned in the case of symmetric key encryption technique only a single key which is also known as the secret key is used for both the encryption and decryption of electronic information. Therefore both the entities which are participating in the process of symmetric key encryption must make sure that a single key is shared among both the groups of parties. This one is a less reliable method if compared with the asymmetric key encryption as this technique makes use of both the public as well as the private keys for the decryption and encryption purposes.

- In the case of symmetric key encryption, the secret key which is possessed by both the parties can be anything such as a passcode or a password or it can also be the random string of letters or numbers which have been generated by a secure random number generator (RNG). This RNG is used for critical applications such as banking based encryption where the symmetric keys must be developed by making use of RNG which is also an industry-wide standard such as FIPS 140-2.

S-DES is a simplified version of DES algorithm. It closely resembles the real thing, but it has smaller parameters, to facilitate operation by hand for pedagogical purposes. It was designed by Edward Schaefer as a teaching tool to understand DES. S-DES (and DES) are examples of a block cipher: the plain text is split into blocks of a certain size, in this case 8 bits.

$$\text{plaintext} = b_1 b_2 b_3 b_4 b_5 b_6 b_7 b_8$$
$$\text{key} = k_1 k_2 k_3 k_4 k_5 k_6 k_7 k_8 k_9 k_{10}$$

Subkey Generation

First, produce two subkeys K_1 and K_2:

$$K_1 = P8\left(LS_1\left(P10(\text{key})\right)\right)$$
$$K_2 = P8\left(LS_2\left(LS_1\left(P10(\text{key})\right)\right)\right)$$

Where P8, P10, LS1 and LS2 are bit substitution operators. For example, P10 takes 10 bits and returns the same 10 bits in a different order:

$$P10\left(k_1 k_2 k_3 k_4 k_5 k_6 k_7 k_8 k_9 k_{10}\right) = k_3 k_5 k_2 k_7 k_4 k_{10} k_1 k_9 k_8 k_6 \, .$$

It's convenient to write such bit substitution operators in this notation:

| P10 | 3 | 5 | 2 | 7 | 4 | 10 | 1 | 9 | 8 | 6 | 10 bits to 10 bits |

| P8 | 6 | 3 | 7 | 4 | 8 | 5 | 10 | 9 | 10 bits to 8 bits |

| LS_1 ("left shift 1 bit" on 5 bit words) | 2 | 3 | 4 | 5 | 1 | 7 | 8 | 9 | 10 | 6 | 10 bits to 10 bits |

| LS_2 ("left shift 2 bit" on 5 bit words) | 3 | 4 | 5 | 1 | 2 | 8 | 9 | 10 | 6 | 7 | 10 bits to 10 bits |

Encryption

The plain text is split into 8-bit blocks; each block is encrypted separately. Given a plaintext block, the cipher text is defined using the two subkeys K_1 and K_2, as follows:

$$\text{ciphertext} = IP^{-1}(f_{K_2}(SW(f_{K_1}(IP(plaintext)))))$$

where,

| IP ("initial permutation") | 2 | 6 | 3 | 1 | 4 | 8 | 5 | 7 | 8 bits to 8 bits |

| IP^{-1} | 4 | 1 | 3 | 5 | 7 | 2 | 8 | 6 | 8 bits to 8 bits |

| SW ("switch") | 5 | 6 | 7 | 8 | 1 | 2 | 3 | 4 | 8 bits to 8 bits |

and $f_K( )$ is computed as follows. We write exclusive-or (XOR) as (+).

$$f_K(L, R) = (L + F_K(R), R)$$

$$F_K(R) = P4 \ (S0(\ lhs(\ EP(R)+K)), \ S1(rhs(EP(R)+K)))$$

| EP ("expansion/permutation") | 4 | 1 | 2 | 3 | 2 | 3 | 4 | 1 | 4 bits to 8 bits |

| P4 | 2 | 4 | 3 | 1 | 4 bits to 4 bits |

| lhs | 1 | 2 | 3 | 4 | 8 bits to 4 bits |

| rhs | 5 | 6 | 7 | 8 | 8 bits to 4 bits |

So $(b_1b_2b_3b_4)$ = the [b_1b_4 , b_2b_3] cell from the "S-box" So below, and similarly for S1.

So

	0	1	2	3
0	1	0	3	2
1	3	2	1	0
2	0	2	1	3
3	3	1	0	3

S1

	0	1	2	3
0	0	1	2	3
1	2	0	1	3
2	3	0	1	0
3	2	1	0	3

Decryption

Decryption is a similar process:

$$plaintext = IP^{-1}\left(f_{K1}\left(SW\left(f_{K2}\left(IP\left(ciphertext \right) \right) \right) \right) \right)$$

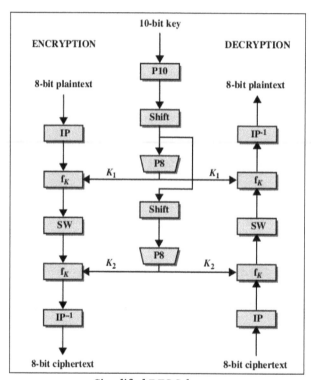

Simplified DES Scheme.

Relation with DES

SDES is a simplification of a real algorithm. DES operates on 64 bit blocks, and uses a key of 56 bits, from which sixteen 48-bit subkeys are generated. There is an initial permutation (IP) of 56 bits followed by a sequence of shifts and permutations of 48 bits. F acts on 32 bits:

$$ciphertext = IP^{-1}\left(f_{K16}\left(SW\left(f_{K15}\left(...\left(SW\left(f_{K1}\left(IP\left(plaintext \right) \right) \right) \right) \right) ... \right) \right) \right)$$

Analysis of SDES

DES (and SDES) do a lot of re-arranging of bits that makes it hard to analyse systematically. Additionally, the S-boxes mean that the output is not just a re-arrangement of the input bits, but is derived from the input bits in a non-linear way. This adds significantly to the security. For example, a known-plaintext attack (in which we attempt to calculate a key, given ciphertext and plaintext) involves solving 8 nonlinear equations in 10 unknowns in the case of SDES, which is hard; and many more equations in more unknowns for full DES.

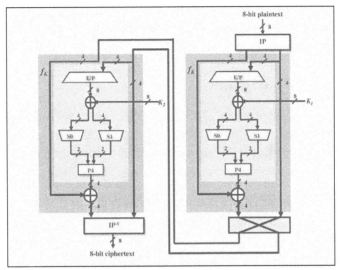

Simplified DES Encryption.

Brute-force Attacks

A brute-force attack consists of trying all the possible keys until the right one is found. The small key length for SDES makes it vulnerable to a brute force attack: there are only 1024 keys. For full DES, there are 7×10^{16} keys. This would take over 2000 years if you checked each key in one microsecond. Specialised designs might be able to achieve better performance than that. Michael Wiener designed a DES cracker with millions of specialised chips on specialised boards and racks. He concluded in 1995 that for $1 million, a machine could be built that would crack a 56-bit DES key in 7 hours. The cost of such a machine would be much less today (perhaps only tens of thousands of dollars). For these reasons, algorithms based on 56-bit keys, like DES, are no longer thought secure. Schneier: "insist on at least 112 bit keys."

Cryptanalysis

Cryptanalytic attacks are more subtle: they try to discover mathematical weaknesses in the algorithm that means a full brute force attack is not necessary. DES is vulnerable to "linear cryptanalysis" which can reduce the brute force search from 2^{56} to about 2^{43} operations; that is 2^{13} (about 8000) times easier.

Advanced Encryption Standard

DES is now considered to be insecure for many applications; this is chiefly due to the 56-bit key size being too small. The Advanced Encryption Standard (AES) is the result of a 5-year US government standardisation process to select a replacement for DES. The result, called Rijndael after its inventors Vincent Rijmen and Joan Daemen, is expected to be used worldwide and analysed extensively, as was the with DES. AES is quite a lot more complicated than DES. The main points about AES are:

- Longer key: Key size of 128, 192 or 256 bits.

- More elaborate key schedule.

- As well as S-boxes, AES uses operations in finite fields (roughly, modulo arithmetic) which makes things harder to cryptanalyse.

Other Symmetric Key Algorithms

- 3DES (which is DES then inverse-DES then DES again, with different keys). This has the effect of tripling the keylength of DES to 168 bits, which makes it much more secure; it also has a backwards-compatibility advantage (a 3DES algorithm can be made to compute DES, by supplying a key which repeats twice after the first 56 bits).

- IDEA, rated by Schneier as the best one partly because of its "impressive theoretical foundations". It mixes XOR, addition modulo 2^{16}, and multiplication modulo 2^{16}-1, and is based on a 128-bit key.

- Blowfish, invented by Schneier to be fast, compact, easy to implement, and to have variable key length (up to 448 bits).

Block Cipher Modes

Block ciphers can be used in different modes:

| Original | Encrypted using ECB mode. | Encrypted using a more secure mode, e.g. CBC. |

- ECB (Electronic codebook mode): In this mode, each block is encrypted individually, and the encrypted blocks are assembled in the same order as the plain text blocks. This is the regular usage, but it leaks some information (e.g., if blocks are repeated in the plain text, this is revealed by the cipher text), and it is vulnerable to block replays.

Here's a striking example of the degree to which ECB can reveal patterns in the plaintext. A pixel-map version of the image on the left was encrypted with ECB mode to create the center image.

- CBC (Cipher block chaining mode): Each block XOR'd with previous block; helps overcome replay attack. Suppose the plain text is B_1, B_2, ..., B_n. We write + for XOR. $C_1 = \text{encrypt}(B_1 + IV)$, where IV is a randomly chosen initialisation vector. $C_2 = \text{encrypt}(B_2 + C_1)$....$C_i = \text{encrypt}(B_i + C_{i-1})$. The following diagram shows how it works.

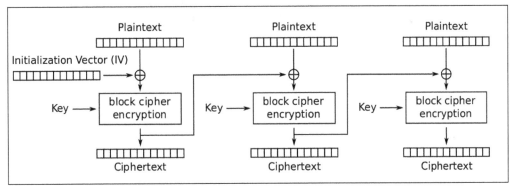

Cipher block chaining (CBC) mode encryption.

- CFB (Cipher feedback mode): It makes a block cipher into a *stream cipher*, by maintaining a queue block (initialised to some initial value). OFB (Output feedback mode) is similar. The following diagrams show how these modes work.

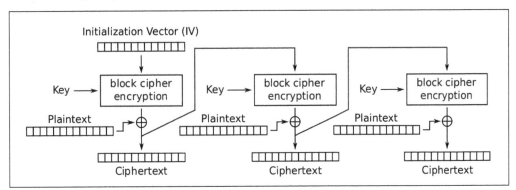

Cipher Feedback (CFB) mode encryption.

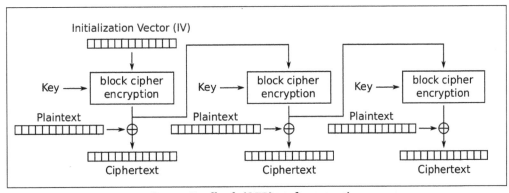

Output Feedback (OFB) mode encryption.

Stream Ciphers

Stream ciphers encrypt streams, e.g. a byte at a time, in cases that you can't wait for an entire block of text before starting the encyption. Typically, a stream is generated from the key, and the plaintext is XOR'd with the stream. Like a one-time pad generated on the fly (but without the security properties of one-time pads).

RC4 is a variable-key-size stream cipher developed in 1987 by Rivest. For seven years it was proprietary, but anonymously posted on the internet in 1994. It works in OFB: the keystream is independent of the plaintext. It maintains a vector S...S, whose entries are a permutation of the numbers 0...255. The following algorithm encrypts a stream:

```
// initialise S
for i = 0 ... 255
S[i] = i


for i = 0 ... 255 {
j = (j + S[i] + key[i mod key_length]) mod 256


swap (S[i],S[j])


}
i = 0
j = 0
while (still some bytes left to encrypt/decrypt) {

i = (i + 1) mod 256


j = (j + S[i]) mod 256


swap(S[i],S[j])


k = S[(S[i] + S[j]) mod 256]


output k XOR next_byte_of_input


}
```

The first part of the algorithm uses the key to randomise the byte array S. The second part produces the bytes to be XORed with the plain text. Each line has a distinct notional purpose.

- i = (i + 1) mod 256

It makes sure every array element is used once after 256 iterations.

- j = (j + S[i]) mod 256

It makes the output depend non-linearly on the array.

- swap(S[i],S[j])

It makes sure the array is evolved and modified as the iteration continues.

- k = S[(S[i] + S[j]) mod 256]

It makes sure the output sequence reveals little about the internal state of the array.

Public-key Encryption

Unlike symmetric key cryptography, we do not find historical use of public-key cryptography. It is a relatively new concept.

Symmetric cryptography was well suited for organizations such as governments, military, and big financial corporations were involved in the classified communication.

With the spread of more unsecure computer networks in last few decades, a genuine need was felt to use cryptography at larger scale. The symmetric key was found to be non-practical due to challenges it faced for key management. This gave rise to the public key cryptosystems.

The process of encryption and decryption is depicted in the following illustration:

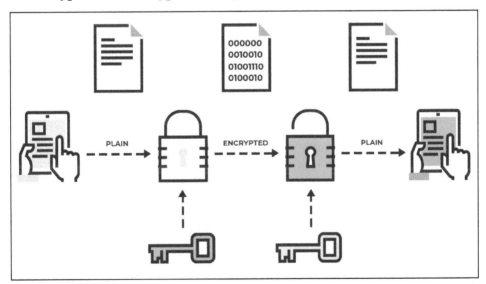

The most important properties of public key encryption scheme are:

- Different keys are used for encryption and decryption. This is a property which set this scheme different than symmetric encryption scheme.

- Each receiver possesses a unique decryption key, generally referred to as his private key.

- Receiver needs to publish an encryption key, referred to as his public key.

- Some assurance of the authenticity of a public key is needed in this scheme to avoid spoofing by adversary as the receiver. Generally, this type of cryptosystem involves trusted third party which certifies that a particular public key belongs to a specific person or entity only.

- Encryption algorithm is complex enough to prohibit attacker from deducing the plaintext from the ciphertext and the encryption (public) key.

- Though private and public keys are related mathematically, it is not be feasible to calculate the private key from the public key. In fact, intelligent part of any public-key cryptosystem is in designing a relationship between two keys.

There are three types of Public Key Encryption schemes. We discuss them in following sections:

RSA Cryptosystem

This cryptosystem is one the initial system. It remains most employed cryptosystem even today. The system was invented by three scholars Ron Rivest, Adi Shamir, and Len Adleman and hence, it is termed as RSA cryptosystem.

We can see two aspects of the RSA cryptosystem, firstly generation of key pair and secondly encryption-decryption algorithms.

Generation of RSA Key Pair

Each person or a party who desires to participate in communication using encryption needs to generate a pair of keys, namely public key and private key. The process followed in the generation of keys is described below:

- Generate the RSA Modulus (n):

    ○ Select two large primes, p and q.

    ○ Calculate n = p*q. For strong unbreakable encryption, let n be a large number, typically a minimum of 512 bits.

- Find Derived Number (e):

    ○ Number e must be greater than 1 and less than $(p - 1)(q - 1)$.

    ○ There must be no common factor for e and $(p - 1)(q - 1)$ except for 1. In other words two numbers e and $(p - 1)(q - 1)$ are coprime.

- Form the Public Key:

    ○ The pair of numbers (n, e) form the RSA public key and is made public.

- Interestingly, though n is part of the public key, difficulty in factorizing a large prime number ensures that attacker cannot find in finite time the two primes (p & q) used to obtain n. This is strength of RSA.

- Generate the Private Key:

  - Private Key d is calculated from p, q, and e. For given n and e, there is unique number d.

  - Number d is the inverse of e modulo $(p - 1)(q - 1)$. This means that d is the number less than $(p - 1)(q - 1)$ such that when multiplied by e, it is equal to 1 modulo $(p - 1)(q - 1)$.

  - This relationship is written mathematically as follows:

    $$ed = 1 \bmod (p - 1)(q - 1)$$

The Extended Euclidean Algorithm takes p, q, and e as input and gives d as output.

An example of generating RSA Key pair is given below. (For ease of understanding, the primes p & q taken here are small values. Practically, these values are very high).

- Let two primes be $p = 7$ and $q = 13$. Thus, modulus $n = pq = 7 \times 13 = 91$.

- Select $e = 5$, which is a valid choice since there is no number that is common factor of 5 and $(p - 1)(q - 1) = 6 \times 12 = 72$, except for 1.

- The pair of numbers $(n, e) = (91, 5)$ forms the public key and can be made available to anyone whom we wish to be able to send us encrypted messages.

- Input $p = 7$, $q = 13$, and $e = 5$ to the Extended Euclidean Algorithm. The output will be $d = 29$.

- Check that the d calculated is correct by computing:

  $$de = 29 \times 5 = 145 = 1 \bmod 72$$

- Hence, public key is $(91, 5)$ and private keys is $(91, 29)$.

Encryption and Decryption

Once the key pair has been generated, the process of encryption and decryption are relatively straightforward and computationally easy.

Interestingly, RSA does not directly operate on strings of bits as in case of symmetric key encryption. It operates on numbers modulo n. Hence, it is necessary to represent the plaintext as a series of numbers less than n.

RSA Encryption

- Suppose the sender wish to send some text message to someone whose public key is (n, e).

- The sender then represents the plaintext as a series of numbers less than n.

- To encrypt the first plaintext P, which is a number modulo n. The encryption process is simple mathematical step as:

  $C = P^e \bmod n$

- In other words, the ciphertext C is equal to the plaintext P multiplied by itself e times and then reduced modulo n. This means that C is also a number less than n.

- Returning to our Key Generation example with plaintext P = 10, we get ciphertext C:

  $C = 10^5 \bmod 91$

RSA Decryption

- The decryption process for RSA is also very straightforward. Suppose that the receiver of public-key pair (n, e) has received a ciphertext C.

- Receiver raises C to the power of his private key d. The result modulo n will be the plaintext P.

  $Plaintext = C^d \bmod n$

- Returning again to our numerical example, the ciphertext C = 82 would get decrypted to number 10 using private key 29:

  $Plaintext = 82^{29} \bmod 91 = 10$

RSA Analysis

The security of RSA depends on the strengths of two separate functions. The RSA cryptosystem is most popular public-key cryptosystem strength of which is based on the practical difficulty of factoring the very large numbers.

- Encryption Function: It is considered as a one-way function of converting plaintext into ciphertext and it can be reversed only with the knowledge of private key d.

- Key Generation: The difficulty of determining a private key from an RSA public key is equivalent to factoring the modulus n. An attacker thus cannot use knowledge of an RSA public key to determine an RSA private key unless he can factor n. It is also a one way function, going from p & q values to modulus n is easy but reverse is not possible.

If either of these two functions are proved non one-way, then RSA will be broken. In fact, if a technique for factoring efficiently is developed then RSA will no longer be safe.

The strength of RSA encryption drastically goes down against attacks if the number p and q are not large primes and chosen public key e is a small number.

ElGamal Cryptosystem

Along with RSA, there are other public-key cryptosystems proposed. Many of them are based on different versions of the Discrete Logarithm Problem.

ElGamal cryptosystem, called Elliptic Curve Variant, is based on the Discrete Logarithm Problem. It derives the strength from the assumption that the discrete logarithms cannot be found in practical time frame for a given number, while the inverse operation of the power can be computed efficiently.

Let us go through a simple version of ElGamal that works with numbers modulo p. In the case of elliptic curve variants, it is based on quite different number systems.

Generation of ElGamal Key Pair

Each user of ElGamal cryptosystem generates the key pair through as follows:

- Choosing a large prime p: Generally a prime number of 1024 to 2048 bits length is chosen.

- Choosing a generator element g.

  - This number must be between 1 and p − 1, but cannot be any number.

  - It is a generator of the multiplicative group of integers modulo p. This means for every integer m co-prime to p, there is an integer k such that $g^k = a \bmod n$.

For example, 3 is generator of group 5 ($Z_5 = \{1, 2, 3, 4\}$).

N	3^n	$3^n \bmod 5$
1	3	3
2	9	4
3	27	2
4	81	1

- Choosing the private key: The private key x is any number bigger than 1 and smaller than p−1.

- Computing part of the public key: The value y is computed from the parameters p, g and the private key x as follows:

$y = g^x \bmod p$

- Obtaining Public key: The ElGamal public key consists of the three parameters (p, g, y).

For example, suppose that p = 17 and that g = 6 (It can be confirmed that 6 is a generator of group Z_{17}). The private key x can be any number bigger than 1 and smaller than 71, so we choose x = 5. The value y is then computed as follows:

$y = 6^5 \bmod 17 = 7$

Thus the private key is 62 and the public key is (17, 6, 7).

Encryption and Decryption

The generation of an ElGamal key pair is comparatively simpler than the equivalent process for RSA. But the encryption and decryption are slightly more complex than RSA.

ElGamal Encryption

Suppose sender wishes to send a plaintext to someone whose ElGamal public key is (p, g, y), then:

- Sender represents the plaintext as a series of numbers modulo p.

- To encrypt the first plaintext P, which is represented as a number modulo p. The encryption process to obtain the ciphertext C is as follows:

  - Randomly generate a number k;

  - Compute two values C1 and C2.

Where,

$$C_1 = g^k \bmod p,$$

$$C_2 = (P^* y^k) \bmod p.$$

- Send the ciphertext C, consisting of the two separate values (C1, C2), sent together.

- Referring to our ElGamal key generation example given above, the plaintext P = 13 is encrypted as follows:

  - Randomly generate a number, say k = 10;

  - Compute the two values C1 and C2.

Where,

$$C_1 = 6^{10} \bmod 17,$$

$$C_2 = (13^* 7^{10}) \bmod 17 = 9,$$

Send the ciphertext C = (C1, C2) = (15, 9).

ElGamal Decryption

- To decrypt the ciphertext (C1, C2) using private key x, the following two steps are taken –

  - Compute the modular inverse of $(C_1)^x$ modulo p, which is $(C_1)^{-x}$, generally referred to as decryption factor.

  - Obtain the plaintext by using the following formula:

$$C_2 \times (C_1)^{-x} \bmod p = \text{Plaintext}$$

- In our example, to decrypt the ciphertext C = (C1, C2) = (15, 9) using private key x = 5, the decryption factor is:

$$15^{-5} \bmod 17 = 9$$

- Extract plaintext $P = (9 \times 9) \bmod 17 = 13$.

ElGamal Analysis

In ElGamal system, each user has a private key x. and has three components of public key – prime modulus p, generator g, and public $Y = g^x \bmod p$. The strength of the ElGamal is based on the difficulty of discrete logarithm problem.

The secure key size is generally > 1024 bits. Today even 2048 bits long key are used. On the processing speed front, Elgamal is quite slow, it is used mainly for key authentication protocols. Due to higher processing efficiency, Elliptic Curve variants of ElGamal are becoming increasingly popular.

Elliptic Curve Cryptography

Elliptic Curve Cryptography (ECC) is a term used to describe a suite of cryptographic tools and protocols whose security is based on special versions of the discrete logarithm problem. It does not use numbers modulo p.

ECC is based on sets of numbers that are associated with mathematical objects called elliptic curves. There are rules for adding and computing multiples of these numbers, just as there are for numbers modulo p. ECC includes a variants of many cryptographic schemes that were initially designed for modular numbers such as ElGamal encryption and Digital Signature Algorithm.

It is believed that the discrete logarithm problem is much harder when applied to points on an elliptic curve. This prompts switching from numbers modulo p to points on an elliptic curve. Also an equivalent security level can be obtained with shorter keys if we use elliptic curve-based variants.

The shorter keys result in two benefits:

- Ease of key management

- Efficient computation

These benefits make elliptic-curve-based variants of encryption scheme highly attractive for application where computing resources are constrained.

Let us briefly compare the RSA and ElGamal schemes on the various aspects.

RSA	ElGamal
It is more efficient for encryption.	It is more efficient for decryption.
It is less efficient for decryption.	It is more efficient for decryption.
For a particular security level, lengthy keys are required in RSA.	For the same level of security, very short keys are required.
It is widely accepted and used.	It is new and not very popular in market.

Kerckhoffs's Principle

Kerckhoffs's principle is one of the basic principles of modern cryptography. It was formulated in the end of the nineteenth century by Dutch cryptographer Auguste Kerckhoffs. The principle goes as follows: A cryptographic system should be secure even if everything about the system, except the key, is public knowledge.

In 1883, Auguste Kerckhoffs, stated that six axioms of cryptography. Some are no longer relevant given the ability of computers to perform complex encryption, but his second axiom, now known as Kerckhoffs' Principle, is still critically important:

> "The method must not need to be kept secret, and having it fall into the enemy's hands should not cause problems".

The same principle is also known as Shannon's Maxim after Claude Shannon who formulated it as "The enemy knows the system." That is, the security should depend only on the secrecy of the key, not on the secrecy of the methods employed. Keeping keys secret, and changing them from time to time, are reasonable propositions. Keeping your methods secret is more difficult, perhaps impossible in the long term against a determined enemy. Changing the methods once a system is deployed is also difficult, sometimes impossible. The solution is to design the system assuming the enemy will know how it works.

Any serious enemy — one with strong motives and plentiful resources — will learn all the internal details of any widely used system. In war, the enemy will capture some of your equipment and some of your people, and will use spies. If your method involves software, enemies can do memory dumps, run it under the control of a debugger, and so on. If it is hardware, they can buy or steal some of the devices and build whatever programs or gadgets they need to test them, or dismantle them and look at chip details with microscopes. They may bribe, blackmail or threaten your staff or your customers. One way or another, sooner or later they will know exactly how it all works.

Using secure cryptography is supposed to replace the difficult problem of keeping messages secure with a much more manageable one, keeping relatively small keys secure. A system that requires long-term secrecy for something large and complex — the whole design of a cryptographic system — obviously cannot achieve that goal. It only replaces one hard problem with another. However, if you can design a system that is secure even when the enemy knows everything except the key, then all you need to manage is keeping the keys secret.

Implications for Analysis

For purposes of analysing ciphers, Kerckhoffs' Principle neatly divides any design into two components. The key can be assumed to be secret for purposes of analysis; in practice various measures will be taken to protect it. Everything else is assumed to be knowable by the opponent, so everything except the key should be revealed to the analyst. Perhaps not all opponents will know everything, but the analyst should because the goal is to create a system that is secure against any enemy except one that learns the key:

> "That the security of a cipher system should depend on the key and not the algorithm has become a truism in the computer era, and this one is the best-remembered of Kerckhoff's dicta. Unlike a key, an algorithm can be studied and analyzed by experts to determine if it is likely to be secure. An algorithm that you have invented yourself and kept secret has not had the opportunity for such review".

Using this distinction is the only known method of building ciphers that it is reasonable to trust — everything except the key is published and analysed, so we can be reasonably confident that it is secure, and keys are carefully managed so we can reasonably hope they are secret.

Cryptographers will generally dismiss out-of-hand all security claims for a system whose internal details are kept secret. Without analysis, no system should be trusted, and without details, it cannot be properly analysed. Of course, there are some exceptions; if a major national intelligence agency claims that one of their secret systems is secure, the claim will be taken seriously because they have their own cipher-cracking experts. However, no-one else making such a claim is likely to be believed.

If you want your system trusted — or even just taken seriously — the first step is to publish all the internal details. Anyone who makes security claims for some system without providing complete details is showing that he is unaware of one of the basic principles of cryptography, so most experts will assume the system is worthless. Sensational claims about a system whose details are secret are one of the common indicators of cryptographic snake oil.

Security through Obscurity

It is moderately common for companies — and sometimes even standards bodies as in the case of the CSS encryption on DVDs — to keep the inner workings of a system secret. Some even claim this security by obscurity makes the product safer. Such claims are utterly bogus; of course keeping the innards secret may improve security in the short term, but in the long run only systems which have been published and analyzed should be trusted.

Steve Bellovin said that:

> The subject of security through obscurity comes up frequently. He thinks a lot of the debate happens because people misunderstand the issue.

> It helps, he thinks, to go back to Kerckhoffs' second principle, translated as "The system must not require secrecy and can be stolen by the enemy without causing trouble", per http://petit-colas.net/fabien/kerckhoffs/). Kerckhoffs said neither "publish everything" nor "keep everything secret"; rather, he said that the system should still be secure even if the enemy has a copy.

In other words - design your system assuming that your opponents know it in detail. A former official at NSA's National Computer Security Center told me that the standard assumption there was that serial number 1 of any new device was delivered to the Kremlin. After that, though, there's nothing wrong with trying to keep it secret - it's another hurdle factor the enemy has to overcome. One obstacle the British ran into when attacking the German Engima system was simple: they didn't know the unkeyed mapping between keyboard keys and the input to the rotor array.

That is, it is an error to rely on the secrecy of a system. In the long run, security through obscurity cannot possibly be an effective technique.

Authentication

In many environments, it is more important that communications be authenticated rather than encrypted. That is, both parties should be convinced of each others identity. We need to establish identity and verify identity before allowing access to resources.

There are three methods we can use to authenticate someone:

- Use something you have, for example, a key or a card. The problem is that these can be stolen.

- Use something you know. Passwords and PINs (personal ID numbers) fall into these categories. These can be guessed, shared, and stolen by snooping.

- Use something you are. This involves biometrics. For example, a system may examine a user's fingerprint or iris pattern. In general, these systems require hardware, can be costly, and are imprecise.

Authentication methods can be combined to strengthen the authentication. Using a single one of these methods is known as one-factor authentication. Using two techniques is two-factor authentication. Withdrawing cash at an ATM machine is an example of twofactor authentication. To authenticate, you present the ATM card (something you have) and enter PIN (something you know).

Most operating systems maintain a notion of a user identifier (user ID) which is a unique token that identifies each user on a system. Typically, systems employ a user name (a unique alphanumeric string that a user may use to identify himself/herself to the system) as well as well as a numeric user ID. The system uses the user ID to store and verify access permissions.

The most common method of authentication is with a simple password authentication scheme. The system prompts us for a user name and then for a password. It then looks up the name in a password table and sees if the passwords match. This is known as a reusable password since the same password is used for each login. One major weakness here is that if somebody manages to break into the system, she can steal the entire password file.

An enhancement to storing a password in plaintext on a system is to use a one-way hash function. We now have a password file that contains encrypted passwords that cannot be decrypted. How do we verify a password if we can't decrypt the one we have saved? When the system prompts for a password, it simply encrypts the string that you entered and compares it with the encrypted password. If they encrypt to the same string, then the system accepts the password. In recent years, passwords were moved from publicly readable files (/etc/passwd on UNIX) to files readable only by the administrator files. The reason behind this was that guessing passwords is often too easy and the system is vulnerable to dictionary attacks where a perpetrator would try every word in a dictionary with various modifications by adding numbers and symbols hoping to find a password that encrypts to the same value. A problem with passwords is that they can be stolen through observing a user's session (snooping on packets, for example). A stop-gap measure is to require users to change passwords frequently.

Another method of combating password theft is to turn to two-factor authentication systems or to use one-time passwords – a new password must be used for each login. Two-factor authentication generally involves using some form of "authenticator card". If we assume that the network is vulnerable to eavesdroppers, the card must be capable of doing some computation and cannot be a fixed set of bits as we find in a bank ATM card. One form of challenge/response authentication works like this: A user wants to login to a server and provides her user name. She is then given a challenge number from the server with a prompt for the response. This challenge number is entered into a challenge/response unit along with a PIN. This unit (that usually looks like a credit-card sized calculator) generates a response that is a function of the PIN, the challenge, and a key that is stored within the challenge/response unit. The response is copied back to the prompt from the server. The server maintains the user's PIN and the key inside the challenge/response unit and can perform the same calculation and thus verify the response. Any eavesdropper does not get to see two important ingredients: the key and user's PIN.

Another popular two-factor authentication scheme is through a SecureID card (from RSA, formerly Security Dynamics). This device maintains a clock and constantly generates a number that is a function of a seed number in the card and the current time. This number is permuted with the user's PIN and sent to the server along with a user name or ID. The server, having the seed of the card, the time, and the PIN can recreate this same number. Any eavesdropper has neither the seed nor the PIN.

Skey Authentication

The Skey authentication algorithm is used to provide one-time passwords. It relies on one-way functions (an example is x^a mod b). Suppose we wish to authenticate Alice for 100 logins. We will pick a random number, R. Then, using the one-way function $f(x)$, we will generate the following list:

$$x_1 = f(R)$$

$$x_2 = f(x_1) = f(f(R))$$

$$x_3 = f(x_2) = f(f(f(R)))$$

therefore,

$$x_{100} = f(x_{99}) = f(...f(f(R))...)$$

We will also compute $x_{101} = f(x_{100})$ and associate this value with Alice in some database (e.g. .password file). The list of numbers x_1 ... x_{100} is given to Alice.

When Alice wants to log in, she'll present the last number on her list (x_{100}) along with her name:

Alice to host: "alice", x_{100}

The host now computes $f(x_{100})$ and compares it with the value of x_{101} stored in its database. If the values match then Alice is authenticated. In that case, the value x_{101} in the database is replaced with the (x_{99}) provided by Alice. Alice must now cross out the last number from his list. Next time she logs in, she'll provide x_{99} along with her name. The system will compute (x_{99}) and compare it with the value of (x_{99}) in its database. Each number is used only once, so even if others see the authentication, there is nothing they can do with the data. When Alice uses x_1 she's out of logins and will have to see the system administrator to get a new list.

Skey authentication works only because $f(x)$ is a one way function and there is no known way to compute $f^{-1}(x)$. If somebody sees Alice enter x_{100}, there is no way that they can compute the x_{99} that is necessary for the next login.

Public Key Authentication

A basic form of authentication can be done with public keys. Suppose a host machine wants to know whether it's really Alice trying to log in. It can generate some random string, S, and present it to Alice. Alice then encrypts the string with her private key and sends it to the machine along with here name: {"Alice", $E_a(S)$}. The host looks up Alice's public key in a database, decrypts the message and compares it with S. If it matches, then the host knows that only someone with Alice's private key could have encrypted S such that it could be decrypted with Alice's public key. Authentication is complete. The random string, S, is called a nonce in cryptographic authentication parlance. It is simply a meaningless bunch of data that is different each time it is used (to prevent replay attacks).

SKID Authentication

SKID2 and SKID3 are authentication schemes that use symmetric cryptography and assume a shared secret (key) between two parties. SKID2 authenticates only one party. SKID3 has two final steps to provide mutual authentication. The principle of SKID is that you generate a random token and give it to the other party, which then returns the encrypted token to you. Since the key is shared between the two parties, you can decrypt the key and verify that the other party had the right key to encrypt it. The same protocol is done the other way around to enable the other party to authenticate you. SKID uses an encrypted hash of the random token and some other information instead of just simple encryption. We will denote this as $H_K(x)$, which means that a hash, $H(x)$ is computed from some message(s) x and the hash is encrypted with the symmetric key K.

Here's a scenario in which Alice and Bob mutually authenticate each other:

- Alice chooses a random number R_A and sends it to Bob.

- Bob chooses a random number R_B. He computes an encrypted hash of the random number he received, his own, and his name: $H_K(R_A, R_B, \text{"Bob"})$ and sends it to Alice along with R_B.

- Alice, having received R_B and already in possession of R_A can also compute the hash of { R_A, R_B, "Bob"} and encrypt it with K. By comparing the result with the value received from Bob, she can verify that Bob was indeed able to encrypt the data with K and hence possesses the shared key. Authentication is complete as far as Alice is concerned. This is where the SKID2 protocol ends. SKID3 provides mutual authentication, where Alice now has to convince Bob of her identity.

- Alice computes a hash of {R_B, "Alice"}, encrypts it and sends it to Bob.

- Bob computes the hash of {R_B, "Alice"} and compares it with the decryption of the value sent by Alice. This convinces Bob of Alice's identity and authentication is complete.

The essential point to note in the authentication sequence is that each party permutes data generated by the other. In effect, each party is challenging the other with data that will be different each time authentication is needed.

Combined Authentication and Key Exchange

SKID suffers from requiring the two parties to have a shared secret. If we can combine authentication with key exchange, then two parties across a network can exchange keys and be sure that they're communicating with each other.

Wide-mouth Frog

A protocol that accomplishes key exchange and authentication using symmetric cryptography is the Wide-mouth Frog algorithm. It uses an arbitrated protocol where one party encrypts a message for itself containing the key and sends it to the trusted third party. This third party decrypts the message and re-encrypts it for the recipient. The problem of having n(n-1)/2 keys is avoided because the secret keys are only for the third party. To prevent replay attacks (somebody snooping on the message and sending it at a later time), a timestamp is added to each message.

If Alice wants to talk to Bob, she sends a message to Trent (the third party) encrypted with her key (A):

> Alice to Trent: {"Alice", $E_A(T_A,$ "Bob", K)}

Trent receives the message and sees that it's from Alice. He looks up her key in his database and decrypts the rest of the message. He verifies the timestamp T_A to determine whether to accept the message. Seeing that it's for Bob, he looks up Bob's key and composes a new message (using A new timestamp T_T):

> Trent to Bob: {$E_B(T_T,$ "Alice", K)}

Diffie-Hellman Exponential Key Exchange

Diffie-Hellman is the first public key algorithm. Its use is different from RSA public-key cryptography in that it is only suitable for key exchange, not encryption. The publicly readable data is not really a key that will be used for encryption or decryption. The algorithm is based on the difficulty of calculating discrete logarithms in a finite field compared to the ease of calculating exponentiation.

Exponential key exchange allows us to negotiate a secret session key without the fear of eavesdroppers. To perform this algorithm, all arithmetic operations are performed in the field of integers modulo some large number (modulo means that we divide the results by and keep the remainder). Both parties then agree on some large prime number, p, and a number α, where $\alpha < p$ and α is a primitive root of p.

Each party then generates a public/private key pair. The private key for user i is X_i, which is just a random number less than q. The corresponding public key, Y_i, is computed as:

$$Y_i = \alpha_B{}^{Xi} \bmod p$$

Now, suppose that Alice and Bob wish to talk. Alice has a secret key X_A and a public key YA and Bob has a secret key X_B and a public key Y_B.

Alice sends Bob her public key, Y_A.

Bob sends Alice his public key, Y_B.

Alice computes:

$$K = (YB)^{XA} \bmod p$$

Bob computes:

$$K = (Y_A)^{X_B} \bmod p$$

Alice and Bob can now use symmetric encryption using the shared key K.

The essential point is that both Alice and Bob could generate a common shared key using their private key and the other's public key but nobody else could do so. The keys are equivalent because:

$$K = (Y_A)^{XB} \bmod p = (\alpha^{XA} \bmod p)^{XB} \bmod p = \alpha^{X_A X_B} \bmod p.$$

Now that two parties can derive a common conversation key (that only they can derive), one of them can pick a random token and send it to the other for encryption as was done in the SKID/2 or SKID/3 protocol.

UNIX Secure RPC and Exponential Key Exchange

By default Sun's Remote Procedure Call interface uses no security. As an option, it can use UNIX security, in which it passes machine name and user name to the remote procedure. Beyond that, a number of secure authentication schemes may be used. One of these is known as Secure RPC. Security data is stored in a credentials structure in the RPC handle.

In secure RPC, all encryption is via DES (Data Encryption Standard). The goal is secure authentication. If a covert conversation channel is needed, the user processes must encrypt their data. Secure RPC is based on the Diffie-Hellman exponential key exchange algorithm and generates a conversation key. We create a new random key each time we need a conversation channel. This decreases thee amount of data that we encrypt with our main keys and hence decreases an intruder's chance of collecting enough statistically significant data to decrypt the main keys. RPC relies on access to a database of private keys as well as to the user's private key.

Let's proceed with the authentication sequence. We will use a subscript notation to denote encryption. When we mention a user's name, we refer to a network name which is a union of the operating system name, user ID, and domain name. For this system to work properly, clocks on client and server must be synchronized (at least approximately).

- Client (A):

    ○ Generate the common key $C = (K_B)^{P_A}$.

    ○ Create a random conversation key for this session, CK.

    ○ Select a window value, W. This represents the lifetime of the credential.

    ○ Get the current time, T.

- Create the credentials structure: {user's network name, $CK_C \cdot W_{CK}$}. Note that CK, encrypted with the common key, C, means that the only other user that can decipher the value of CK is the server (B).

- Create a verifier structure: $\left\{ T_{CK} , (W+1)_{CK} \right\}$. The server won't be able to read any of these components unless it succeeded in deciphering the conversation key.

- Send the credentials and verifier to the server.

- Server (B):

  - Read the message: get network name; use that to find that user's public key; generate the common key $C = (K_A)^{P_B}$; decrypt CK. Use CK to decrypt the verifier.

  - vLook at the window value and see whether the window of valid time $(T + W)$ expired. If so, reject the request.

  - Use CK to decrypt W+1 and verify that the value really is the window plus one. This assures us (the server) that the user sending the request really does know the conversation key.

  - Send back a verifier containing a nickname to use for future requests between the two parties and $(T-1)_{CK}$. We subtract one from the time stamp that we received from the client and encrypt it with the conversation key. This way we get a different bit pattern than if we sent back the original encrypted time stamp (that would be useless) and allow for the client to verify that we really were able to decrypt the conversation key, CK.

- Client (A):

  - Get the verifier from the server. Decrypt the time stamp using CK and verify it. If the remote program was able to figure out the time stamp, then it was able to decrypt CK successfully and must therefore indeed be the desired server B.

  - Use the conversation key to authenticate all future messages. The client's credential contains the nickname (used to index into a table to find the window size on the server) and the client's verifier contains the current time encrypted with CK. The server sends back a verifier of that time stamp minus one encrypted with CK.

Kerberos

Another authentication scheme comes from Project Athena at MIT. Project Athena's goal was to create a computing environment around high-performance workstations with distributed servers. This scheme is based on trusted third party authentication. It assumes that the network is insecure (snoopable). To access a service you must be authenticated to use it and present an authentication ticket to the service. Since the network is insecure, passwords are never sent across in cleartext. Every user and every service has a password. Kerberos is a trusted third party that knows all the passwords. We'll take a look at a sample authentication scenario to get a feel for how this system performs authentication. Let's assume that Marge wishes to access the service Homer. Both Marge and Homer have passwords (or keys). For the purposes of this example, let's assume the following keys are assigned (we'll see where the session key and conversation key come from as we go along):

marge	18
homer	57
session key	28

- Marge contacts the Kerberos authentication server (AS), requesting a "ticket" to communicate with the Homer.

- The Kerberos Authentication Server looks up Marge and the service Homer to determine whether she is indeed allowed to access it. If she is, the Authentication Server generates a session key (28) and sends it back to Marge along with an identifier of Homer's service (e.g., IP address and port). The entire message is encrypted with Marge's key so that anybody else who sees this message will be unable to make sense of it: $\{homer\_service, 28\}_{18}$.

- The second message that Marge receives from the Kerberos Authentication server is the same session key and her identifier. This time, the message is encrypted with Homer's secret key, so she is unable to decode this: $\{marge, 28\}_{57}$. This message is known as a sealed envelope or ticket.

- Marge is now ready to establish communications with Homer. She first decodes the session key (28) and information on how to access the Homer service from the first message that she received (the one encrypted with her secret key). She then sends Homer the sealed envelope that she received from Kerberos along with a timestamp that she encrypted with the session key that she received from the Authentication Server.

- Homer gets the message and (if the service really is Homer), can decrypt the sealed envelope using his secret key. Doing so reveals the session key and an identifier for Marge. Because he was able to decrypt this message successfully, he knows that it must have been generated by a trusted party – one that has his password. Now that he has the session key, he decrypts the encrypted timestamp that he received from Marge and checks whether it is within a given time window. If it is within a valid range, he realizes that the message is not a replay attack and that the message must really have come from Marge because Kerberos would not have divulged the session key to anyone else.

- Homer now sends a message to Marge to prove to her that he really is homer. This message contains his identifier and the timestamp that he received from Marge. The message is encrypted with the session key: € $\{homer\_service, T\}_{28}$.

- When Marge receives this message, she decodes it using the session key. She is convinced that the remote party is Homer because only he would have been able to decode the ticket to extract the session key so that he could decrypt the timestamp she sent.

Now that authentication is ccmplete and both parties have the session key, they can communicate securely, encrypting each message with the session key.

A biometric authentication is a digitizing measurements of a physiological or behavioral characteristic for human. A biometric authentication systems can theoretically be used to distinguish one person from. However, many biometric authentication systems have been proposed which are categorized as; face detection authentication system, fingerprint authentication system, Iris authentication system, and voice authentication system.

1) Fingerprint recognition: A fingerprint system uses an electronic device to capture a digital image of the fingerprint pattern. This captured image in fingerprint system is called a live scan which is digitally processed to create a biometric template (finger features). The biometric features will be later stored and used for matching process.

2) Voice biometric authentication: Voice biometric authentication is the use of the voice pattern to recognize the identity of the person. Meanwhile, voice authentication is now considered as a fast wide deployed form of biometric authentication. However, it is one of the best methods of determining the biometric method efficacy. However, voice recognition is categorized into five types: speaker dependent system, speaker independent system, discrete speech recognition, continuous speech recognition, and natural language.

3) Face detection: Face detection and recognition systems are a two complementary scenarios. Face detection is as technology uses learning algorithms to allocate human faces in digital images. As shown by figure, face detection algorithm focuses and determines the facial features and ignores anything else in the digital images. Moreover, many face detection techniques have been presented such as; Viola and Jones face detection, face detection based Adaboost, semi-supervised learning for facial expression recognition, and etc.

Face detection.

Furthermore, face recognition technology is a natural biological authentication process according to the cognitive rule of human beings. This technology is used to identify any given face image using the main features of this face. Normally, face recognition process works after face detection process to identify the detected face by comparing the detected faces with the stored faces images. In general, different artificial neural network algorithms have been proposed such as; feed forward back propagation neural network (FFBPNN), cascade forward back propagation neural network (CFBPNN), function fitting neural network (FitNet), and pattern recognition neural network (PatternNet) algorithms. Since, Soon and Seiichi, While Volkan, Weihua and WeiFu are recognition systems applied on neural algorithms.

4) Iris Authentication: Actually, iris and fingerprints are parallel in their uniqueness technology. Worldly, the statistical result of the iris usage in authentication is presents that iris is one of the best ways of meeting high risk situations. Iris recognition software is currently in wide use at airport borders. As well as, it is also widely used at many other industries for doing authentication.

Digital Signatures

Digital signatures are the public-key primitives of message authentication. In the physical world, it is common to use handwritten signatures on handwritten or typed messages. They are used to bind signatory to the message.

Similarly, a digital signature is a technique that binds a person/entity to the digital data. This binding can be independently verified by receiver as well as any third party. Digital signature is a cryptographic value that is calculated from the data and a secret key known only by the signer.

In real world, the receiver of message needs assurance that the message belongs to the sender and he should not be able to repudiate the origination of that message. This requirement is very crucial in business applications, since likelihood of a dispute over exchanged data is very high.

Model of Digital Signature

As mentioned earlier, the digital signature scheme is based on public key cryptography. The model of digital signature scheme is depicted in the following illustration:

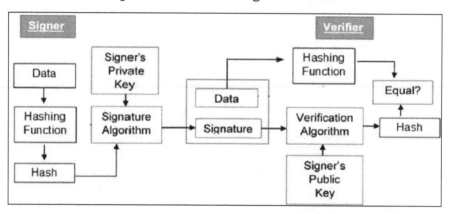

The following points explain the entire process in detail:

- Each person adopting this scheme has a public-private key pair.

- Generally, the key pairs used for encryption/decryption and signing/verifying are different. The private key used for signing is referred to as the signature key and the public key as the verification key.

- Signer feeds data to the hash function and generates hash of data.

- Hash value and signature key are then fed to the signature algorithm which produces the digital signature on given hash. Signature is appended to the data and then both are sent to the verifier.

- Verifier feeds the digital signature and the verification key into the verification algorithm. The verification algorithm gives some value as output.

- Verifier also runs same hash function on received data to generate hash value.

- For verification, this hash value and output of verification algorithm are compared. Based on the comparison result, verifier decides whether the digital signature is valid.

- Since digital signature is created by 'private' key of signer and no one else can have this key; the signer cannot repudiate signing the data in future.

It should be noticed that instead of signing data directly by signing algorithm, usually a hash of data is created. Since the hash of data is a unique representation of data, it is sufficient to sign the hash in place of data. The most important reason of using hash instead of data directly for signing is efficiency of the scheme.

Let us assume RSA is used as the signing algorithm. The encryption/signing process using RSA involves modular exponentiation.

Signing large data through modular exponentiation is computationally expensive and time consuming. The hash of the data is a relatively small digest of the data, hence signing a hash is more efficient than signing the entire data.

Importance of Digital Signature

Out of all cryptographic primitives, the digital signature using public key cryptography is considered as very important and useful tool to achieve information security.

Apart from ability to provide non-repudiation of message, the digital signature also provides message authentication and data integrity. Let us briefly see how this is achieved by the digital signature:

- Message authentication: When the verifier validates the digital signature using public key of a sender, he is assured that signature has been created only by sender who possess the corresponding secret private key and no one else.

- Data Integrity: In case an attacker has access to the data and modifies it, the digital signature verification at receiver end fails. The hash of modified data and the output provided by the verification algorithm will not match. Hence, receiver can safely deny the message assuming that data integrity has been breached.

- Non-repudiation: Since it is assumed that only the signer has the knowledge of the signature key, he can only create unique signature on a given data. Thus the receiver can present data and the digital signature to a third party as evidence if any dispute arises in the future.

By adding public-key encryption to digital signature scheme, we can create a cryptosystem that can provide the four essential elements of security namely – Privacy, Authentication, Integrity, and Non-repudiation.

Encryption with Digital Signature

In many digital communications, it is desirable to exchange an encrypted messages than plaintext to achieve confidentiality. In public key encryption scheme, a public (encryption) key of sender is available in open domain, and hence anyone can spoof his identity and send any encrypted message to the receiver.

This makes it essential for users employing PKC for encryption to seek digital signatures along with encrypted data to be assured of message authentication and non-repudiation. This can archived by combining digital signatures with encryption scheme. There are two possibilities, sign-then-encrypt and encrypt-then-sign.

However, the crypto system based on sign-then-encrypt can be exploited by receiver to spoof identity of sender and sent that data to third party. Hence, this method is not preferred. The process of encrypt-then-sign is more reliable and widely adopted. This is depicted in the following illustration

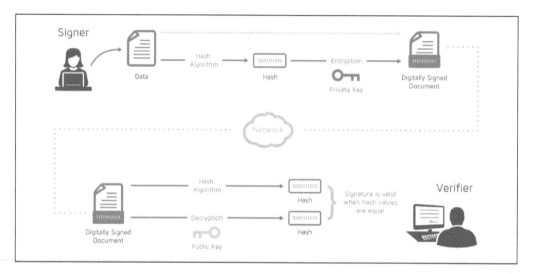

The receiver after receiving the encrypted data and signature on it, first verifies the signature using sender's public key. After ensuring the validity of the signature, he then retrieves the data through decryption using his private key.

Public Key Infrastructure

The comprehensive system required to provide public-key encryption and digital signature services is known as a public-key infrastructure (PKI). The purpose of a public-key infrastructure is to manage keys and certificates. By managing keys and certificates through a PKI, an organization establishes and maintains a trustworthy networking environment. A PKI enables the use of encryption and digital signature services across a wide variety of applications.

Effective Public-key Infrastructure

There are a number of requirements that businesses have with respect to implementing effective public-key infrastructures. First and foremost, if users cannot take advantage of encryption and digital signatures in applications, a PKI is not valuable. Consequently, the most important constraint on a PKI is transparency. The term transparency means that users do not have to understand how the PKI manages keys and certificates to take advantage of encryption and digital signature services. An effective PKI is transparent. In addition to user transparency, a business must implement the following items in a PKI to provide the required key and certificate management services:

- Public key certificates,

- A certificate repository,

- Certificate revocation,

- Key backup and recovery,

- Support for non-repudiation of digital signatures,

- Automatic update of key pairs and certificates,

- Management of key histories,

- Support for cross-certification,

- Client-side software interacting with all of the above in a secure, consistent, and trustworthy manner.

The term client-side refers to application clients and application servers. PKI requirements are the same for both application clients and servers, and both are "clients" of the infrastructure services.

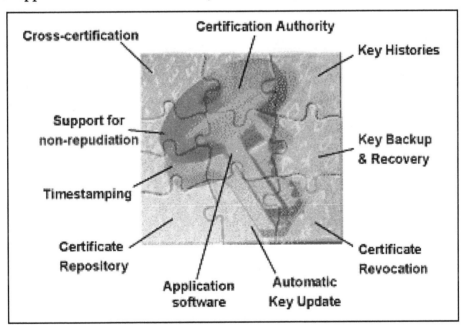

Certificates and Certification Authorities

For public-key cryptography to be valuable, users must be assured that the other parties with whom they communicate are "safe"—that is, their identities and keys are valid and trustworthy. To provide this assurance, all users of a PKI must have a registered identity. These identities are stored in a digital format known as a public key certificate. Certification Authorities (CAs) represent the people, processes, and tools to create digital certificates that securely bind the names of users to their public keys.In creating certificates, CAs act as agents of trust in a PKI.

As long as users trust a CA and its business policies for issuing and managing certificates, they can trust certificates issued by the CA. This is known as third-party trust.CAs create certificates for users by digitally signing a set of data that includes the following information (and additional items):

- The user's name in the format of a distinguished name (DN). The DN specifies the user's name and any additional attributes required to uniquely identify the user (for example, the DN could contain the user's employee number).

- A public key of the user: The public key is required so that others can encrypt for the user or verify the user's digital signature.

- The validity period (or lifetime) of the certificate (a start date and an end date).

- The specific operations for which the public key is to be used (whether for encrypting data, verifying digital signatures, or both).

The CA's signature on a certificate allows any tampering with the contents of the certificate to be easily detected. (The CA's signature on a certificate is like a tamper-detection seal on a bottle of pills—any tampering with the contents of a certificate is easily detected). As long as the CA's signature on a certificate can be verified, the certificate has integrity. Since the integrity of a certificate can be determined by verifying the CA's signature, certificates are inherently secure and can be distributed in a completely public manner (for example, through publicly-accessible directory systems).

Users retrieving a public key from a certificate can be assured that the public key is valid. That is, users can trust that the certificate and its associated public key belong to the entity specified by the distinguished name. Users also trust that the public key is still within its defined validity period. In addition, users are assured that the public key may be used safely in the manner for which it was certified by the CA.

Key Backup and Recovery

A business must be able to retrieve encrypted data when users lose their decryption keys. This means that the enterprise to which the user belongs requires a system for backing up and recovering the decryption keys. There are two reasons why key backup and recovery are so important to businesses.The first reasons are that users forget passwords. It is potentially catastrophic for a business to lose data when users forget the passwords required to access their decryption keys. Valuable information would be lost forever if there was no ability to securely recover those keys. Furthermore, unless users know they can always recover their encrypted data (even if they forget their passwords), some users will not encrypt their most valuable and sensitive information for fear of losing it—even though that information needs to be protected the most. The second reason is that users may lose, break, or corrupt the devices in which their decryption keys are stored. For instance, if a user's decryption keys are stored on a magnetic card, the magnetic field on the card can become corrupted. Again, permanent loss of those decryption keys can be disastrous.Users are prevented from recovering encrypted data unless their decryption keys are backed up.

Difference between Key Backup and Key Escrow

Commercial requirements for key backup and recovery can be completely separated from law enforcement requirements for "key escrow". Key escrow means that a third party (such as a federal agent) can obtain the decryption keys required to access encrypted information. The purpose of key escrow is to help with law enforcement, and key escrow is a heavily-debated topic because of the fine lines between issues of public interest (such as national security) and individual freedom and privacy. Key backup and recovery requirements, focus on fundamental commercial needs that exist regardless of law enforcement requirements.

Which Keys Require Backup?

The only keys requiring backup are users' decryption keys. As long as a trusted agent (for example, the CA) securely backs up users' decryption keys, security is not compromised and the user's data can always be recovered. However, signing keys have different requirements from decryption keys. In fact, backing up signing keys destroys a basic requirement of a PKI.

Support for Non-repudiation

Repudiation occurs when an individual denies involvement in a transaction. For instance, when someone claims a credit card is stolen, this means that he or she is repudiating liability for transactions that occur with that card any time after reporting the theft. Non-repudiation means that an individual cannot successfully deny involvement in a transaction. In the paper-world, individuals' signatures legally bind them to their transactions (for example, credit card charges, business contracts). The signature prevents repudiation of those transactions. In the electronic world, the replacement for the pen-based signature is a digital signature. All types of electronic commerce require digital signatures because electronic commerce makes traditional pen-based signatures obsolete.

Signing Private Key

The most basic requirement for non-repudiation is that the key used to create digital signatures can be generated and securely stored in a manner under the sole control of the user at all times. It is not acceptable to back up the signing key. Unlike encryption key pairs, there is no technical or business requirement to backup or restore previous signing key pairs when users forget their passwords or lose, break, or corrupt their signing keys. In such cases, it is acceptable for users to generate new signing key pairs and continue using them from that time forward.

Need for Two Key Pairs

It is difficult to simultaneously support key backup and recovery and non-repudiation. To support key backup and recovery the decryption keys must be backed up securely. To support non-repudiation, the keys used for digital signature cannot be backed up and must be under the sole control of the user at all times. To meet these requirements, a PKI must support two key pairs for each user. At any point in time, a user must have one current key pair for encryption and decryption, and a second key pair for digital signature and signature verification. Over time, users will have numerous key pairs that must be managed appropriately.

Key Update and Management of Key Histories

Cryptographic key pairs should not be used forever. They must be updated over time. As a result, every organization needs to consider two important issues:

- Updating users' key pairs, and

- Maintaining, where appropriate, the history of previous key pairs.

Updating users' Key Pairs

The process of updating keys pairs should be transparent to users. This transparency means users do not have to understand that key update needs to take place and they will never experience a "denial of service" because their keys are no longer valid. To ensure transparency and prevent denial of service, users' key pairs must be automatically updated before they expire.

Maintaining Histories of Key Pairs

When encryption key pairs are updated, the history of previous decryption keys must be maintained. This "key history" allows users to access any of their prior decryption keys to decrypt data. (When data is encrypted with a user's encryption key, only the corresponding decryption key—the paired key—can be used for decrypting). To ensure transparency, the client-side software must automatically manage users' histories of decryption keys.

The key history must also be securely managed by the key backup and recovery system. This allows encrypted data to be recovered securely, regardless of what encryption public key was used to originally encrypt the data (and, by extension, regardless of when the data was encrypted).

When a signing key pair is updated, the previous signing key be securely destroyed. This destruction prevents any other person from gaining access to the signing key and is acceptable because there is no need to retain previous signing keys.

Certificate Repositories and Certificate Distribution

The CA acts as a trusted third-party issuing certificates to users. Businesses also must distribute those certificates so they can be used by applications. Certificate repositories store certificates so that applications can retrieve them on behalf of users. The term repository refers to a network service that allows for distribution of certificates.Over the past few years, the consensus in the information technology industry is that the best technology for certificate repositories is provided by directory systems that are LDAP (Lightweight Directory Access Protocol)-compliant. LDAP defines the standard protocol to access directory systems. Several factors drive this consensus position:

- Storing certificates in directories and having applications retrieve certificates on behalf of users provides the transparency required for use in most businesses.

- Many directory technologies supporting LDAP can be scaled to:

    ◦ Support a very large number of entries,

○ Respond efficiently to search requests due to their information storage and retrieval methods,

○ Be distributed throughout the network to meet the requirements of even the most highly-distributed organizations.

In addition, the directories that support certificate distribution can store other organizational information. The PKI can also use the directory to distribute certificate revocation information.

Certificate Revocation

In addition to verifying the CA's signature on a certificate, the application software must also be sure that the certificate is still trustworthy at the time of use. Certificates that are no longer trustworthy must be revoked by the CA. There are numerous reasons why a certificate may need to be revoked prior to the end of its validity period. For instance, the private key (that is, either the signing key or the decryption key) corresponding to the public key in the certificate may be compromised. Alternatively, an organization's security policy may dictate that the certificates of employees leaving the organization must be revoked. In these situations, users in the system must be informed that continued use of the certificate is no longer considered secure. The revocation status of a certificate must be checked prior to each use. As a result, a PKI must incorporate a scalable certificate revocation system. The CA must be able to securely publish information regarding the status of each certificate in the system. Application software, on behalf of users, must then verify the revocation information prior to each use of a certificate. The combination of publishing and consistently using certificate revocation information constitutes a complete revocation system. The most popular means for distributing certificate revocation information is for the CA to create secure certificate revocation lists (CRLs) and publish these CRLs to a directory system. CRLs specify the unique serial numbers of all revoked certificates. Prior to using a certificate, the client-side application must check the appropriate CRL to determine if the certificate is still trustworthy. Client-side applications must check for revoked certificates consistently and transparently on behalf of users.

Cross-certification

Cross-certification extends third-party trust relationships between Certification Authority domains. For example, two trading partners, each with their own CA, may want to validate certificates issued by the other partner's CA. Alternatively, a large, distributed organization may require multiple CAs in various geographic regions. Cross-certification allows different CA domains to establish and maintain trustworthy electronic relationships. The term cross-certification refers to two operations. The first operation, which is generally executed infrequently, is the establishment of a trust relationship between two CAs. In the case of bilateral cross-certification, two CAs securely exchange their verification keys. These are the keys used to verify the CAs' signatures on certificates. To complete the operation, each CA signs the other CA's verification key in a certificate referred to as a "cross-certificate". The second operation is done by the client-side software. The operation, which is executed frequently, involves verifying the trustworthiness of a user certificate signed by a cross-certified CA. The operation is often referred to as "walking a chain of trust". The "chain" refers to a list of cross-certificate validations that are "walked" (or traced) from the CA key of the verifying user to the CA key required to validate the other user's certificate. When walking a chain of cross-certificates, each cross-certificate be checked to ensure that it is still trusted. User certificates must be able to be revoked; so must cross-certificates.

Client-side Software

When discussing requirements for PKIs, businesses often neglect the requirement for client-side software. (For instance, many people only focus on the CA component when discussing PKIs). Ultimately, however, the value of a PKI is tied to the ability of users to use encryption and digital signatures. For this reason, the PKI must include client-side software that operates consistently and transparently across applications on the desktop (for example, email, Web browsing, e-forms, file/folder encryption). A consistent, easy-to-use PKI implementation within client-side software lowers PKI operating costs. In addition, client-side software must be technologically enabled to support all of the elements of a PKI. The following list summarizes the requirements client-side software must meet to ensure that users in a business receive a usable, transparent (and thus, acceptable) PKI.

- Public key certificates: To provide third-party trust, all PKI-enabled applications must use certificates in a consistent, trustworthy manner. The client-side software must validate the CA's signature on certificates and ensure that the certificates are within their validity periods.

- Key backup and recovery: To ensure users are protected against loss of data, the PKI must support a system for backup and recovery of decryption keys. With respect to administrative costs, it is unacceptable for each application to provide its own key backup and recovery. Instead, all PKI-enabled client applications should interact with a single key backup and recovery system. The interactions between the client-side software and the key backup and recovery system must be secure, and the interaction method must be consistent across all PKI-enabled applications.

- Support for non-repudiation: To provide basic support for non-repudiation, the client-side software must generate the key pairs used for digital signature. In addition, the client-side software must ensure that the signing keys are never backed up and remain under the users' control at all times. This type of support must be consistent across all PKI-enabled applications.

- Automatic update of key pairs: To enable transparency, client-side applications must automatically initiate updating of users' key pairs. This activity must be done in accordance with the security policies of the organization. It is unacceptable for users to have to know that their key pairs require updating. To meet this requirement across all PKI-enabled applications, the client-side software must update key pairs transparently and consistently.

- Management of key histories: To enable users to easily access all data encrypted for them (regardless of when it was encrypted), PKI-enabled applications must have access to users' key histories. The client-side software must be able to securely recover users' key histories.

- A scalable certificate repository: To minimize the costs of distributing certificates, all PKI-enabled applications must use a common, scalable certificate repository.

Cryptographic Attacks

In cryptography, the goal of the attacker is to break the secrecy of the encryption and learn the secret message and, even better, the secret key. There are dozens of different types of attacks that have been developed against different types of cryptosystems with varying levels of effectiveness. Some are easily understandable while others may require an advanced degree in mathematics to comprehend.

The following attacks can refer to either of the two classes (all forms of attack assume the attacker knows the encryption algorithm):

- Ciphertext-only attack: In this attack the attacker knows only the ciphertext to be decoded. The attacker will try to find the key or decrypt one or more pieces of ciphertext (only relatively weak algorithms fail to withstand a ciphertext-only attack).

- Known plaintext attack: The attacker has a collection of plaintext-ciphertext pairs and is trying to find the key or to decrypt some other ciphertext that has been encrypted with the same key.

- Chosen Plaintext attack: This is a known plaintext attack in which the attacker can choose the plaintext to be encrypted and read the corresponding ciphertext.

- Chosen Ciphertext attack: The attacker has the able to select any ciphertext and study the plaintext produced by decrypting them.

- Chosen text attack: The attacker has the abilities required in the previous two attacks.

- An encryption scheme is unconditionally secure if the ciphertext generated does not contain enough information to determine uniquely the corresponding plaintext no matter how much ciphertext is available or how much computational power the attacker has. With the exception of the one time pad, no cipher is unconditionally secure.

- The security of a conditionally secure algorithm depends on the difficulty in reversing the underlying cryptographic problem such as how easy it is to factor large primes. All ciphers other than the one-time pad fall into this category.

- An encryption scheme is said to be computationally secure if:

  - The cost of breaking the cipher exceeds the value of the encrypted information.

  - The time required to break the cipher exceeds the useful lifetime of the information.

Brute force attacks are also available to the attacker. In 1977, Diffie and Hellman claimed that it would cost twenty million dollars to build a million chip machine that could find a DES key in twelve hours (given a plaintext-ciphertext pair). In 1995, it was estimated that advances in chip densities and speeds would permit a several thousand chip machine to do the same job at a cost of well under a million dollars. However in July 1998, a machine was build by EFF, cryptography research and Advanced wireless technologies that could search 90 billion keys per second which would take a little over 200 hours to search the entire key space. They managed however to find the key in 56 hours.

Cryptanalytic Attacks

All forms of cryptanalysis for symmetric encryption schemes are designed to exploit the fact that traces of structure or pattern in the plaintext may survive encryption and be discernible in the ciphertext. Cryptanalysis of public-key schemes proceeds from a fundamentally different premise, namely that the mathematical properties of the pair of keys may make it possible for one of the two keys to be deduced from the other. We will only be concerned with three main attacks. Two of them (Differential and Linear cryptanalysis) are used to attack block ciphers whereas the third (birthday attack) is used to attack hash functions.

Differential Cryptanalysis

One of the most significant advances in cryptanalysis in recent years is differential cryptanalysis. Although this appears to have been discovered at least 30 years ago it was not reported in the open literature until 1990. The first published effort appears to have been the cryptanalysis of a block cipher called FEAL. This was followed by Biham and Shamir, who demonstrated this form of attack on a variety of encryption algorithms and hash functions.

The most publicised results for this approach have been those that have application to DES. Differential cryptanalysis is the first published attack that is capable of breaking DES in less than 2^{55} complexity. The scheme can successfully cryptanalyse DES with an effort of 2^{47}, requiring 2^{47} chosen plaintext (hence it is a chosen plaintext attack). Although 2^{47} is certainly significantly less than 2^{55}, the need to find 2^{47} chosen plaintexts makes this attack of only theoretical interest. Apparently this attack was known at the time DES was being designed and played a large part in the design of DES.

The attack can be outlined as follows: consider the original plaintext block for DES m to consist of two halves m_0, m_1. Each round of DES maps the right-hand input into the left-hand output and sets the right-hand output to be a function of the left-hand input and the subkey for this round. So, at each round, only one new 32-bit block is created. If we label each new block $m_i \left(2 \leq i \leq 17 \right)$, then the intermediate message halves are related as follows:

$$m_{i+1} = m_{i-1} \oplus f\left(m_i, K_i\right), \ i = 1,2,...,16$$

In differential cryptanalysis, one starts with two messages, m and m', with a known XOR difference $\Delta m = m \oplus m'$, and considers the difference between the intermediate message halves: $\Delta m_i = m_i \oplus m_i'$. Then we have:

$$\Delta m_{i+1} = m_{i+1} \oplus m_{i+1}'$$
$$= [m_{i-1} \oplus f\left(m_i, K_i\right)] \oplus [m_{i-1}' \oplus f\left(m_i', K_i\right)]$$
$$= \Delta m_{i-1} \oplus [f\left(m_i, K_i\right) \oplus f\left(m_i', K_i\right)]$$

Now, suppose that many pairs of inputs to f with the same difference yield the same output difference if the same subkey is used. To put this more precisely, let us say that X may cause Y with probability p, if for a fraction p of the pairs in which the input XOR is X, the output XOR equals Y. We want to suppose that there are a number of values of X that have high probability of causing a particular output difference. Therefore, if we know Δm_{i-1} and Δm with high probability, then we know Δm_{i+1} with high probability. Furthermore, if a number of such differences are determined, it is feasible to determine the subkey used in the function f.

The overall strategy of differential cryptanalysis is based on these considerations for a single round. The procedure is to begin with two plaintext messages m and m' with a given difference and trace through a probable pattern of differences after each round to yield a probable difference for the ciphertext. Actually, there are two probable differences for the two 32-bit halves: $(\Delta m_{17} \| \Delta m_{16})$. Next, we submit m and m' for encryption to determine the actudifference under the unknown key and compare the result to the probable difference. If there is a match,

$$E_k(m) \oplus E_k(m') = (\Delta m_{17} \| \Delta m_{16})$$

then we suspect that all the probable patterns at all the intermediate rounds are correct. With that assumption, we can make some deductions about the key bits. This procedure must be repeated many times to determine all the key bits.

Linear Cryptanalysis

A more recent development is linear cryptanalysis that was presented by Mitsuru Mat- sui at Eurocrypt '93. This attack is based on finding linear approximations to describe the transformations performed in DES (and other block ciphers). This method can find a DES key given 2^{47} known plaintexts, as compared to 2^{47} chosen plaintexts for differential cryptanalysis (it is therefore a known plaintext attack although it can also work as a ciphertext only attack). Although this is a minor improvement (because it may be easier to acquire known plaintext rather than chosen plaintext) it still leaves linear cryptanalysis infeasible as an attack on DES. However it is useful for an understanding of other similar attacks and gives an insight into why the S-boxes are constructed the way they are.

To understand the attack we will define a few terms:

A Boolean function $h : Z_2^n \to Z_2$ in n variables $s_1, \ldots, s_n$ is linear if it can be represented as $h(s) = a_1 s_1 \oplus \ldots \oplus a_n s_n$ for some $a_i \in Z_2 = \{0, 1\}$, $i = 1, \ldots, n$. The set of all linear Boolean functions in n variables is denoted by,

$$L_n = \left\{ h : Z_2^n \to Z_2 \,\middle|\, h = a_1 s_1 \oplus \ldots \oplus a_n s_n \right\}$$

A Boolean function $f : Z_2^n \to Z_2$ is called affine if either $f(s) = h(s)$ or $f(s) = h(s) \oplus 1$, for some $h(s) \in L_n$. The set of all affine Boolean function in n variables is therefore:

$$A_n = L_n \cup \left\{ h \oplus 1 \mid h2L_n \right\} = L_n \cup \overline{L_n}$$

In other words, A_n consists of all linear functions and their negations.

For a cipher with n-bit plaintext and ciphertext blocks and an m-bit key, let the plaintext block be labelled $P[1], \ldots P[N]$, the cipher text block $C[1], \ldots C[n]$ and the key $K[1], \ldots K[m]$. Then define,

$$A[i, j, \ldots, k] = A[i] \oplus A[j] \oplus \ldots \oplus A[k]$$

The objective of linear cryptanalysis is to find an effective linear equation of the form that holds with probability p ≠ 0.5.

$$P[\alpha_1, \alpha_2, \ldots, \alpha_a] \oplus C[\beta_1, \beta_2, \ldots, \beta_b] = K[\gamma_1, \gamma_2, \ldots, \gamma_c]$$

Here we have, $x = 0, 1; 1 \leq a, b \leq n, 1 \leq c \leq m$, and where α, β and γ terms represent fixed, unique bit locations. The further p is from 0.5, the more effective the equation. Once a proposed relation is determined, the procedure is to compute the results of the left-hand side of the preceding equation for a large number of plaintext-ciphertext pairs. If the result is 0 more than half the time, assume $K[\gamma_1, \gamma_2, \ldots \gamma_c] = 0$. If it is 1 most of the time, assume $K[\gamma_1, \gamma_2, \ldots \gamma_c] = 1$. This gives us a linear equation on the key bits. Try to get more such relations so that we can solve for the key bits. Because we are dealing with linear equations, the problem can be approached one round of the cipher at a time, with the results combined.

The above explanation gives us an overview of the whole attack. Let us expand a little on some of the details. The fact that we desire equation $P[\alpha_1, \alpha_2, \ldots, \alpha_a] \oplus C[\beta_1, \beta_2, \ldots, \beta_b] = K[\gamma_1, \gamma_2, \ldots, \gamma_c]$ to hold with a probability p ≠ 0.5 implies that it can be $0 \geq p < 0.5$ or $0.5 < p \leq 1$. This leads us to the idea of a linear probability bias which is given by $\in = |p - 0.5|$. The larger this bias is (in other words the closer p is to 0 or 1) the better the applicability of linear cryptanalysis with fewer known plaintext. If $p = 1$ this implies that equation $P[\alpha_1, \alpha_2, \ldots, \alpha_a] \oplus C[\beta_1, \beta_2, \ldots, \beta_b] = K[\gamma_1, \gamma_2, \ldots, \gamma_c]$ is a perfect representation of the cipher behaviour and the cipher has a catastrophic weakness. If p = 0 then equation $P[\alpha_1, \alpha_2, \ldots, \alpha_a] \oplus C[\beta_1, \beta_2, \ldots, \beta_b] = K[\gamma_1, \gamma_2, \ldots, \gamma_c]$ represents an affine relationship in the cipher which is also a catastrophic weakness. Both linear and affine approximations, indicated by p > 0.5 and p < 0.5 respectively, are equally susceptible to linear cryptanalysis.

For an ideal cipher what we would like is that the plaintext be mapped to the ciphertext in such a way that the mapping is random. In other words there is no correlation between the plaintext and the ciphertext. By choosing a + b random values (number of plaintext plus ciphertext bits in equation $P[\alpha_1, \alpha_2, \ldots, \alpha_a] \oplus C[\beta_1, \beta_2, \ldots, \beta_b] = K[\gamma_1, \gamma_2, \ldots, \gamma_c]$ should hold with a probability of exactly 0.5. This would be the case if it were a perfect cipher. However as ciphers are not perfect the probability contains a bias $\in$. This bias not only exists for the overall cipher but also for each of the individual non-linear element (S-boxes in the case of DES). We can therefore find linear approximations for certain S-boxes and use what's known as the piling up lemma to concatenate the results to gain an expression for the whole cipher. With this expression, it is possible to take some plaintext andciphertext pairs and a target partial subkey (this is your guess at a part of the subkey) and deduce the target partial subkeys values.

Birthday Attack

The Birthday attack makes use of what's known as the Birthday paradox to try to attack cryptographic hash functions. The birthday paradox can be stated as follows: What is the minimum value of k such that the probability is greater than 0.5 that at least two people in a group of k people have the same birthday? It turns out that the answer is 23 which is quite a surprising result. In other words if there are 23 people in a room, the probability that two of them have the same birthday is approximately 0.5. If there is 100 people (i.e. k=100) then the probability is 0.9999997, i.e. you are almost guaranteed that there will be a duplicate. A graph of the probabilities against the value of k is shown in figure.

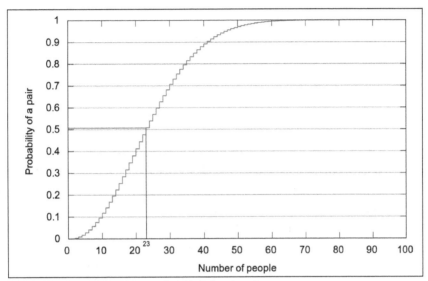

The Birthday Paradox.

Although this is the case for birthdays we can generalise it for n equally likely values (in the case of birthdays n = 365). So the problem can be stated like this: Given a random variable that is an integer with uniform distribution between 1 and n and a selection of k instances ($k \leq n$) of the random variable, what is the probability P(n, k), that there is at least one duplicate.

It turns out this value is,

$$P(n, k) = 1 - \frac{n!}{(n-k)!n^k}$$

$$= 1 - [(1 - \frac{1}{n}) \times (1 - \frac{2}{n}) \times \ldots \times (1 - \frac{k-1}{n})]$$

Take it that the following inequality holds:

$$(1 - x) \leq e^{-x}$$

then we have,

$$P(n, k) > 1 - \left[\left(e^{-1/n}\right) \times \left(e^{-2/n}\right) \times \ldots \times \left(e^{-(k-1)/n}\right) \right]$$

$$> 1 - e^{-\left[(e/n) + (2/n) + ((k-1)/n)\right]}$$

$$> 1 - e^{-(k \times (k-1))/2n}$$

We would like to know when $P(n, k) > 0.5$ so we set the right hand side of equation $P(n, k) .... 1 - e^{-(k \times (k-1))/2n}$ to 0.5:

$$0.5 = 1 - e^{-(k \times (k-1))/2n}$$

$$ln(2) = \frac{k \times (k-1)}{2n}$$

For large values of k we can replace $k \times (k-1)$ by k^2 giving,

$$k = \sqrt{2(ln2)n} = 1.18\sqrt{n} \approx \sqrt{n}$$

which can be seen to be almost equal to 23 for n = 365.

Now lets look at this in terms of hash codes. Remember a hash code is a function that takes a variable length message M and produces a fixed length message digest. Assuming the length of the digest is m then there are 2m possible message digests. Normally however, because the length of M will generally be greater than m this implies that more than one message will be mapped to the same digest. Of course the idea is to make it computationally infeasible to find two messages that map to the same digest. However if we apply k random messages to our hash code what must the value of k be so that there is the probability 0.5 that at least one duplicate (i.e. $H(x) = H(y)$ will occur for some inputs x, y)? This is the same as the question we asked about the birthday duplicates. Using equation $k = \sqrt{2(ln2)n} = 1.18\sqrt{n} \approx \sqrt{n}$ we have,

$$k = \sqrt{2m} = 2^{m/2}$$

Using this idea we can discuss the birthday attack as follows:

- The source, A is prepared to "sign" a message by appending the appropriate m-bit hash code and encrypting that hash code with A's private key.

- The opponent generates $2^{m/2}$ variations on the message, all of which convey essentially the same meaning. The opponent prepares an equal number of messages, all of which are variations of the fraudulent message to be substituted for the real one.

- The two sets of messages are compared to find a pair of messages that produce the same hash code. The probability of success is greater than 0.5. If no match is found, additional valid and fraudulent messages are generated until a match is made.

- The opponent offers the valid variation to A for signature. This signature can then be attached to the fraudulent variation for transmission to the intended recipient. Because the two variations have the same hash code, they will produce the same signature; the opponent is assured of success even though the encryption key is not known.

If we use a 64-bit hash code then the level of effort required is only on the order of which is clearly not sufficient to withstand today's computational systems.

The generation of many variations that convey the same meaning is not that difficult as figure shows.

Dear Anthony,

This letter is / I am writing — to introduce — you to / to you — Mr. / -- — Alfred — P. / --

Barton, the — new / newly appointed — chief / senior — jewellery buyer for — our / the

Northern — European / Europe — area / division . He — will take / has taken — over — the / --

responsibility for — all / the whole of — our interests in — watches and jewellery / jewellery and watches

in the — area / region . Please — afford / give — him — every / all the — help he — may need / needs

to — seek out / find — the most — modern / up to date — lines for the — top / high — end of the

market. He is — empowered / authorized — to receive on our behalf — samples / specimens — of the

latest / newest — watch and jewellery / jewellery and watch — products, — up / subject — to a — limit / maximum

of ten thousand dollars. He will — carry / hold — a signed copy of this — letter / document

as proof of identity. An order with his signature, which is — appended / attached

authorizes / allows — you to charge the cost to this company at the — above / head office

address. We — fully / -- — expect that our — level / volume — of orders will increase in

the — following / next — year and — trust / hope — that the new appointment will — be / prove

advantageous / an advantage — to both our companies.

A letter in 2^{37} variations.

Implementation Attacks

Implementation attacks take on a different approach to the above for discovering the secret key. Instead of attacking the mathematical properties of the algorithm these form of attacks (also known as side channel attacks) take advantage of the physical phenomena that occurs when a cryptographic algorithm is implemented in hardware. Four side channel attacks are listed in the FIPS standard 140-2 "Security Requirements for Cryptographic Modules", Power Analysis, Timing Analysis, Fault Induction and TEMPEST.

- Power Analysis: Attacks based on the analysis of power consumption can be divided into two categories, Simple Power Analysis (SPA) and Differential Power Analysis (DPA). SPA involves a direct (primarily visual) analysis of electrical power consumption patterns and timings derived from the execution of individual instructions carried out by a cryptographic module during a cryptographic process. The patterns are obtained through monitoring the variations in electrical power consumption of a cryptographic module for the purpose of revealing the features and implementations of cryptographic algorithms and subsequently values of cryptographic keys. DPA has the same goals but utilizes advanced statistical methods and other techniques to analyze the variations of the electrical power consumption of a cryptographic module. Cryptographic modules that utilize external power (direct current) sources appear to be at greatest risk. Methods that may reduce the overall risk of Power

Analysis attacks include the use of capacitors to level the power consumption, the use of internal power sources, and the manipulation of the individual operations of the algorithms or pro-cesses to level the rate of power consumption during cryptographic processing.

- Timing Analysis: Timing Analysis attacks rely on precisely measuring the time required by a cryptographic module to perform specific mathematical operations associated with a cryptographic algorithm or process. The timing information collected is analyzed to determine the relationship between the inputs to the module and the cryptographic keys used by the underlying algorithms or processes. The analysis of the relationship may be used to exploit the timing measurements to reveal the cryptographic key or CSPs (Cryptographic Security Parameters). Timing Analysis attacks assume that the attacker has knowledge of the design of the cryptographic module. Manipulation of the individual operations of the algorithms or processes to reduce timing fluctuations during processing is one method to reduce the risk of this attack.

- Fault Induction: Fault Induction attacks utilize external forces such as microwaves, temperature extremes, and voltage manipulation to cause processing errors within the cryptographic module. An analysis of these errors and their patterns can be used in an attempt to reverse engineer the cryptographic module, revealing certain features and implementations of cryptographic algorithms and subsequently revealing the values of cryptographic keys. Cryptographic modules with limited physical security appear to be at greatest risk. Proper selection of physical security features may be used to reduce the risk of this attack.

- TEMPEST: TEMPEST attacks involve the remote or external detection and collection of the electromagnetic signals emitted from a cryptographic module and associated equipment during processing. Such an attack can be used to obtain keystroke information, messages displayed on a video screen, and other forms of critical security information (e.g., cryptographic keys). Special shielding of all components, including network cabling, is the mechanism used to reduce the risk of such an attack. Shielding reduces and, in some cases, prevents the emission of electromagnetic signals. If a cryptographic module is designed to mitigate one or more specific attacks, then the modules security policy shall specify the security mechanisms employed by the module to mitigate the attack(s). The existence and proper functioning of the security mechanisms will be validated when requirements and associated tests are developed.

Here we will be interested mainly in Differential Power Analysis (DPA) as it applies to DES however we will have a brief look at Timing attacks.

Differential Power Analysis

Power Analysis is a relatively new concept but has proven to be quite effective in attacking smartcards and similar devices. It was first demonstrated by Ernst Bovelander in 1997, but a specific attack strategy was not given. A year later it was brought to the general public's attention by Paul Kocher and the Cryptographic Research team in San Francisco. Kocher et al. provided an attack strategy that would recover the secret key from cryptographic systems running the DES algorithm. This caused great concern amongst the smartcard community and a search for an effective countermeasure began. To date a limited number of countermeasures have been proposed and none are fully effective. The attacks work equally well on other cryptographic algorithms as shown by Thomas Messerges et al. who presented a great deal of supplementary research on the subject.

Power analysis involves an analysis of the pattern of power consumed by a cryptographic module as it performs its operations. The purpose of this pattern analysis is to acquire knowledge about causal operations that is not readily available through other sources. The power consumption will generally be different for each operation performed (and even for the same operations with different data values). One of the causes of these variations is the transistor technology used to implement the module. The transistors act as voltage controlled switches, and the power they consume varies with the type of instructions being processed. For example, a conditional branch instruction appears to cause a lot of noticeable fluctuations according to Kocher, and should therefore be avoided if possible where secret keys are concerned.

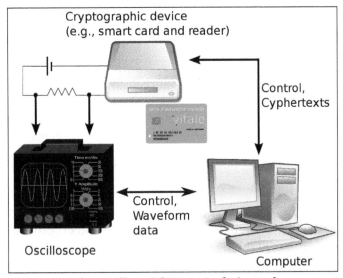

An example setup for a Differential Power Analysis attack on a smartcard.

An example of a setup for a power analysis attack is shown in figure above. For smartcards and similar devices, the power can be measured across a 10 – 50 resistor in series with the power or ground line of the specific device. It is better to put the resistor in series with the ground of the device as the oscilloscope measures voltages with reference to ground. Therefore the attacker only needs to measure one side of the resistor. If the power line is used then two scope probes would be needed and the resultant waveforms substracted.

Although the setup in figure above will suffice for a smartcard it will generally not be this simple for a complex cryptographic accelerator which probably draws its power from the peripheral component interconnect (PCI) backplane of a computer. Ideally, the attacker would wish to get as close as possible to the actual chip performing the operations if a high signal to noise ratio (SNR) is to be obtained. This might be more difficult than it first appears as information on which of the boards numerous chips is actually running the algorithm may not be readily available. Even if it were, the power pin of the chip would have to be physically separated from the board to perform the attack and then reattached once complete (if the attack were to go unnoticed). Most tamper resistant devices would not permit this from happening.

An example of a possible setup is shown in figure. In this case a PCI extender board is used to measure the power fluctuations. The actual cryptographic board slots into the extender board and therefore the power the cryptographic board draws from the PCI backplane has to flow through the extender board which can be fitted with some points that allow for measurement of the power. These can be homemade or easily purchased.

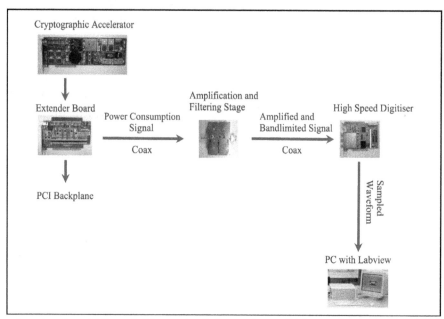

An example setup for a Differential Power Analysis attack on a high speed cryptographic accelerator.

Assuming a setup such as those in figures and in which the algorithm being executed is the Data Encryption Standard (DES) the attack can proceed as follows. A method must be devised to produce a random set of J plaintext inputs that can be sent to the cryptosystem for encryption. On receiving these plaintext inputs, pi_j, $1 \le j \le J$, the board will begin to run its algorithm and draw varying amounts of power. These power fluctuations can be sampled using a digital sampling oscilloscope which should be capable of sampling at about 20-30 times the clock frequency being used. There are two main reasons for this:

- Just because the clock frequency is a certain value, it is possible that we might have multiple operations occuring in each clock cycle. Also, the operation we are interested in might begin on the rising edge of a clock cycle but could only last a small fraction of the clock cycle itself.

- The more samples you have per cycle the less chance of noise caused by a misalignment of samples. Ideally what is required is that the samples at t = 0, (where t is the time of the sample) line up exactly with one another however, this may not be the case due to fluctuations in the triggering point of the waveform (when the samples are being acquired).

The waveforms observed for each pi_j can be represented as a matrix wf_{jk}, where $1 \le k \le K$. A second column matrix, co_j, can also be used to represent the ciphertext output. In practice, each row of wf_{jk} would probably be stored as a separate file for ease of processing. Having captured each power waveform and ciphertext output, a function known as a *partitioning function*, D(.), must now be defined. This function will allow division of the matrix wf_{jk} into two sub-matrices $wf0_{pk}$ and $wf1_{pk}$

containing P and Q rows respectively, with $1 \leq p \leq P$ and $1 \leq q \leq Q$ where $P + Q = J$. Provided that the inputs pi_j were randomly produced, then $P = Q = J/2$ as $J \to \infty$ (i.e. the waveforms will be divided equally between the two sets).

The partitioning function allows the division of wf_{jk} because it calculates the value of a particular bit, at particular times, during the operation of the algorithm. If the value of this bit is known, then it will also be known whether or not a power bias should have occurred in the captured waveform. For a 1, a bias should occur, and for a 0 it shouldn't. Separating the waveforms into two separate matrices (one in which the bias occurred and another in which it didn't) will allow averaging to reduce the noise and enhance the bias (if it occurred). For randomly chosen plaintexts, the output of the D(.) function will equal either a 1 or 0 with probability $\frac{1}{2}$ (this is just another statement of the fact that $P = Q = J/2$ as $J \to \infty$).

An example of a partitioning function is:

$$D(C_1, C_6, K_{16}) = C_1 \oplus SBOX1(C_6 \oplus K_{16})$$

where SBOX1(.) is a function that outputs the target bit of S-box 1 in the last round of DES (in this case it's the first bit), C_1 is the one bit of co_j that is exclusive OR'ed with this bit, C6 is the 6 bits of co_j that is exclusive OR'ed with the last rounds subkey and K_{16} is the 6 bits of the last round's subkey that is input into S-box 1.

The value of this partitioning function must be calculated at some point throughout the algorithm. So, if the values C_1, C_6 and K_{16} can be determined, it will be known whether or not a power bias occurred in each waveform. It is assumed that the values C_1 and C_6 can be determined and the value of the subkey K_{16} is the information sought. To find this, an exhaustive search needs to be carried out. As it is 6 bits long, a total of $2^6 = 64$ subkeys will need to be tested. The right one will produce the correct value of the partitioning bit for every plaintext input. However, the incorrect one will only produce the correct result with probability $\frac{1}{2}$. In this case, the two sets $wf0_{pk}$ and $wf1_{qk}$ will contain a randomly distributed collection of waveforms which will average out to the same result. The differential trace (discussed below) will thus show a power bias for the correct key only. Of course it means that 64 differential traces are needed but this is a vast improvement over a brute force search of the entire 56 bit key.

Mathematically, the partitioning of wf_{jk} can be represented as,

$$wf0_{pk} = \{ wf_{jk} \,|\, D(.) = 0 \}$$

and

$$wf1_{qk} = \{ wf_{jk} \,|\, D(.) = 1 \}$$

Once the matrices $wf0_{pk}$ and $wf1_{qk}$ have been set up, the average of each is then taken producing two waveforms $awf0_k$ and $awf1_k$ both consisting of K samples. By taking the averages of each, the noise gets reduced to very small levels but the power spikes in $wf1_{pk}$ will be reinforced. However, averaging will not reduce any periodic noise contained within the power waveforms and inherent to the operations on the cryptographic board. This can largely be eliminated by subtracting $awf0_{pk}$ from $awf1_{qk}$ (this can be thought of as demodulating a modulated signal to reveal the "baseband", where the periodic noise is the "carrier"). The only waveform remaining will be the one with a number of bias points identifying the positions where the target bit was manipulated. This trace is known as a *differential trace*, ΔD_k.

Again, in mathematical terms, the above can be stated as:

$$awf0_k = \frac{1}{p} \sum_{wf_{jk} \in wf1} wf_{jk} = \frac{1}{p} \sum_{p=1}^{p} wf0_{pk}$$

and

$$awf1_k = \frac{1}{Q} \sum_{wf_{jk} \in wf0} wf_{jk} = \frac{1}{Q} \sum_{q=1}^{Q} wf1_{pk}$$

The differential trace ΔD_k is then obtained as,

$$\Delta D_k = qwf1_k - qwf0_k$$

The last five equations can now be condensed into one:

$$\Delta D_k = \frac{\sum_{k=1}^{K} D(.) wf_{jk}}{\sum_{k=1}^{K} D(.)} - \frac{\sum_{k=1}^{K} (1 - D(.)) wf_{jk}}{\sum_{k=1}^{K} (1 - D(.))}$$

As $J \to \infty$, the power biases will average out to a value $\in$ which will occur at times k_D - each time the target bit D was manipulated. In this limit, the averages $awf0_k$ and $awf1_k$ will tend toward the expectation $E\{wf0_k\}$ and $E\{wf1_k\}$, and equations $\Delta D_k = qwf1_k - qwf0_k$ and

$$\Delta D_k = \frac{\sum_{k=1}^{K} D(.) wf_{jk}}{\sum_{k=1}^{K} D(.)} - \frac{\sum_{k=1}^{K} (1 - D(.)) wf_{jk}}{\sum_{k=1}^{K} (1 - D(.))}$$

It will converge to,

$$E\{wf1_k\} - E\{wf0_k\} \in, \qquad \text{at times} \quad k = k_D$$

and

$$E\{wf1_k\} - E\{wf0_k\} = 0 \qquad \text{at times} \quad k \neq k_D$$

Therefore, at times $k = k_D$, there will be a power bias $\in$ visible in the differential trace. At all other times, the power will be independent of the target bit and the differential trace will tend towards 0.

The above will only work if the subkey guess was correct. For all other guesses the partitioning function will separate the waveforms randomly, and equations,

$$E\{wf1_k\} - E\{wf0_k\} \in, \qquad \text{at times} \quad k = k_D$$

and

$$E\{wf1_k\} - E\{wf0_k\} = 0 \quad \text{at times} \quad k \neq k_D$$

It will condense to,

$$E\{wf1_k\} - E\{wf0_k\} = 0, \qquad \forall k$$

The 64 differential traces are needed to determine which key is the correct one. Theoretically, the one containing bias spikes will allow determination of the correct key however, in reality the other waveforms will contain small spikes due to factors such as non-random choices of plaintext inputs, statistical biases in the S-boxes and a non-infinite number of waveforms collected. Generally however, the correct key will show the largest bias spikes and can still be determined quite easily.

The other 42 bits from the last round's subkey can be determined by applying the same method to the other 7 S-boxes. A brute force search can then be used to obtain the remaining 8 bits of the 56 bit key.

Mitigation Techniques

The following could be used as mitigation techniques for power attacks in general:

- Timing Randomisation: This involves placing random time delays into the software so that a power analysis will not be possible. With random delays introduced, a steady trigger will not be sufficient to allow the averaging to work and will therefore act as a countermeasure.

- Internal power supplies/power supply filtering: This would be another method that could be used to reduce the possibility of a power attack. For example, Adi Shamir proposes building a simple capacitance network into each smartcard to allow the fluctuations to be contained within the smartcard itself thereby preventing power attacks.

- Data masking: One of the methods proposed consists of *masking* the intermediate data (i.e. mask the input data and key before executing the algorithm). This would make the power fluctuations independent of the actual data.

- Tamper Resistance: This involves placing some detection/prevention system around the device to stop intruders gaining access to the power fluctuations.

- Fail Counters: A differential power analysis attack requires the attacker to obtain a significant number of power waveforms. In order to do this the attacker must have the ability to run quite a few encryptions on the system under attack. If the number of encryptions were limited to a certain number then the attacks would become increasingly difficult.

- Removal of conditional elements: One of the main features used to attack the square and multiply algorithm is the fact that it has a conditional multiplication that depends on the value of the exponent bit being operated upon. One suggested countermeasure is to implement this multiplication in every round (regardless of the value of the bit) and to only do a register update when the bit is a 1.

Timing Attacks

A timing attack is somewhat analogous to a burglar guessing the combination of a safe by observing how long it takes for someone to turn the dial from number to number. We can explain the attack using the modular exponentiation algorithm shown in the code below, but the attack can be adapted to work with any implementation that does not run in fixed time. In this algorithm, modular exponentiation is accomplished bit by bit, with one modular multiplication performed at each iteration and an additional modular multiplication performed for each 1 bit.

The attack is simplest to understand in an extreme case. Suppose the target system uses a modular multiplication function that is very fast in almost all cases but in a few cases takes musch more time than an entire average modular exponentiation. The attack proceeds bit by bit starting with the leftmost bit $e[N-1]$. Suppose that the first j bits are known (to obtain the entire exponent, start with $j = 0$ and repeat the attack until the entire exponent is known). For a given ciphertext, the attacker can complete the first j iterations of the for loop. The operation of the subsequent steps depends on the unkown exponent bit. If the bit is set $d = (d \times b)$ mod m will be executed. For a few values of b and d, the modular multiplication will be extremely slow, and the attacker knows which these are. Therefore, if the observed time to execute the decryption algorithm is always slow when this particular iteration is slow with a 1 bit, then this bit is assumed to be 1. If a number of observed execution times for the entire algorithm are fast, then this bit is assumed to be 0.

```
Square_and_mul(b, e, m)

{

d = 1;

for (k = N-1 downto 0)

{

d = (d × d) mod m;

if (e[k] == 1)

{

d = (d × b) mod m;

}

Return d;

}
```

The code on the previous page represents square and multiply algorithm for computing be mod (m) where (e) is N bits long.

In practice, modular exponentiation implementations do not have such extreme timing variations, in which the execution time of a single iteration can exceed the mean execution time of the entire algorithm. Nevertheless, there is enough variation to make this attack practical.

Although the timing attack is a serious threat, there are simple counter measures that can be used including the following:

- Constant exponentiation time: Ensure that all exponentiations take the same amount of time before returning a result. This is a simple fix but does degrade performance.

- Random delay: Better performance could be achieved by adding a random delay to the exponentiation algorithm to confuse the timing attack. Kocher point out that if defenders don't add enough noise, attackers could still succeed by collecting additional measurements to compensate for the random delays.

- Blinding: Multiply the ciphertext by a random number before performing exponentiation. This process prevents the attacker from knowing what ciphertext bits are being processed inside the computer and therefore prevents the bit-by-bit analsys essential to the timing attack.

RSA Data Security incorportates a blinding feature into some of its products. The private-key operation $M = C^d$ mod n is implemented as follows:

- Generate a secret random number r between 0 and n – 1.

- Compute $C' = C\left(r^e\right) \bmod n$, where e is the public exponent.

- Compute $M' = \left(C'\right)d \bmod n$ with the ordinary RSA implementation.

- Compute $M = M'r^{-1} \bmod n$ (where r^{-1} is the multiplicative inverse of r mod n). It can be demonstrated that this is the correct result by observing that $r^{ed} \bmod n = r \bmod n$.

Cryptography Hash Functions

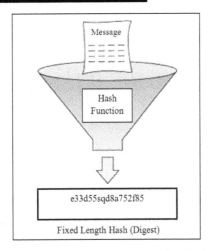

Hash functions are extremely useful and appear in almost all information security applications. A hash function is a mathematical function that converts a numerical input value into another compressed numerical value. The input to the hash function is of arbitrary length but output is always of fixed length. Values returned by a hash function are called message digest or simply hash values. The following picture illustrated hash function:

Features of Hash Functions

The typical features of hash functions are:

- Fixed Length Output (Hash Value):
  - Hash function coverts data of arbitrary length to a fixed length. This process is often referred to as hashing the data.
  - In general, the hash is much smaller than the input data, hence hash functions are sometimes called compression functions.
  - Since a hash is a smaller representation of a larger data, it is also referred to as a digest.
  - Hash function with n bit output is referred to as an n-bit hash function. Popular hash functions generate values between 160 and 512 bits.
- Efficiency of Operation:
  - Generally for any hash function h with input x, computation of h(x) is a fast operation.
  - Computationally hash functions are much faster than a symmetric encryption.

Properties of Hash Functions

In order to be an effective cryptographic tool, the hash function is desired to possess following properties:

- Pre-image Resistance:
  - This property means that it should be computationally hard to reverse a hash function.
  - In other words, if a hash function h produced a hash value z, then it should be a difficult process to find any input value x that hashes to z.
  - This property protects against an attacker who only has a hash value and is trying to find the input.
- Second Pre-image Resistance:
  - This property means given an input and its hash, it should be hard to find a different input with the same hash.
  - In other words, if a hash function h for an input x produces hash value h(x), then it should be difficult to find any other input value y such that h(y) = h(x).
  - This property of hash function protects against an attacker who has an input value and its hash, and wants to substitute different value as legitimate value in place of original input value.

- Collision Resistance:

    - This property means it should be hard to find two different inputs of any length that result in the same hash. This property is also referred to as collision free hash function.

    - In other words, for a hash function h, it is hard to find any two different inputs x and y such that h(x) = h(y).

    - Since, hash function is compressing function with fixed hash length, it is impossible for a hash function not to have collisions. This property of collision free only confirms that these collisions should be hard to find.

    - This property makes it very difficult for an attacker to find two input values with the same hash.

    - Also, if a hash function is collision-resistant then it is second pre-image resistant.

Design of Hashing Algorithms

At the heart of a hashing is a mathematical function that operates on two fixed-size blocks of data to create a hash code. This hash function forms the part of the hashing algorithm.

The size of each data block varies depending on the algorithm. Typically the block sizes are from 128 bits to 512 bits. The following illustration demonstrates hash function:

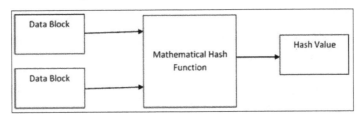

Hashing algorithm involves rounds of above hash function like a block cipher. Each round takes an input of a fixed size, typically a combination of the most recent message block and the output of the last round.

This process is repeated for as many rounds as are required to hash the entire message. Schematic of hashing algorithm is depicted in the following illustration:

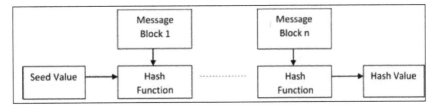

Since, the hash value of first message block becomes an input to the second hash operation, output of which alters the result of the third operation, and so on. This effect, known as an avalanche effect of hashing.

Avalanche effect results in substantially different hash values for two messages that differ by even a single bit of data.

Understand the difference between hash function and algorithm correctly. The hash function generates a hash code by operating on two blocks of fixed-length binary data.

Hashing algorithm is a process for using the hash function, specifying how the message will be broken up and how the results from previous message blocks are chained together.

Popular Hash Functions

Message Digest

MD5 was most popular and widely used hash function for quite some years:

- The MD family comprises of hash functions MD2, MD4, MD5 and MD6. It was adopted as Internet Standard RFC 1321. It is a 128-bit hash function.

- MD5 digests have been widely used in the software world to provide assurance about integrity of transferred file. For example, file servers often provide a pre-computed MD5 checksum for the files, so that a user can compare the checksum of the downloaded file to it.

- In 2004, collisions were found in MD5. An analytical attack was reported to be successful only in an hour by using computer cluster. This collision attack resulted in compromised MD5 and hence it is no longer recommended for use.

Secure Hash Function

Family of SHA comprise of four SHA algorithms: SHA-0, SHA-1, SHA-2, and SHA-3. Though from same family, there are structurally different:

- The original version is SHA-0, a 160-bit hash function, was published by the National Institute of Standards and Technology (NIST) in 1993. It had few weaknesses and did not become very popular. Later in 1995, SHA-1 was designed to correct alleged weaknesses of SHA-0.

- SHA-1 is the most widely used of the existing SHA hash functions. It is employed in several widely used applications and protocols including Secure Socket Layer (SSL) security.

- In 2005, a method was found for uncovering collisions for SHA-1 within practical time frame making long-term employability of SHA-1 doubtful.

- SHA-2 family has four further SHA variants, SHA-224, SHA-256, SHA-384, and SHA-512 depending up on number of bits in their hash value. No successful attacks have yet been reported on SHA-2 hash function.

- Though SHA-2 is a strong hash function. Though significantly different, its basic design is still follows design of SHA-1. Hence, NIST called for new competitive hash function designs.

- In October 2012, the NIST chose the Keccak algorithm as the new SHA-3 standard. Keccak offers many benefits, such as efficient performance and good resistance for attacks.

RIPEMD

The RIPEND is an acronym for RACE Integrity Primitives Evaluation Message Digest. This set of hash functions was designed by open research community and generally known as a family of European hash functions.

- The set includes RIPEND, RIPEMD-128, and RIPEMD-160. There also exist 256, and 320-bit versions of this algorithm.

- Original RIPEMD (128 bit) is based upon the design principles used in MD4 and found to provide questionable security. RIPEMD 128-bit version came as a quick fix replacement to overcome vulnerabilities on the original RIPEMD.

- RIPEMD-160 is an improved version and the most widely used version in the family. The 256 and 320-bit versions reduce the chance of accidental collision, but do not have higher levels of security as compared to RIPEMD-128 and RIPEMD-160 respectively.

Whirlpool

This is a 512-bit hash function:

- It is derived from the modified version of Advanced Encryption Standard (AES). One of the designer was Vincent Rijmen, a co-creator of the AES.

- Three versions of Whirlpool have been released; namely WHIRLPOOL-0, WHIRLPOOL-T, and WHIRLPOOL.

Applications of Hash Functions

There are two direct applications of hash function based on its cryptographic properties.

Password Storage

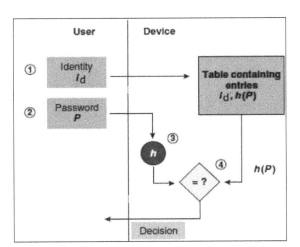

Hash functions provide protection to password storage:

- Instead of storing password in clear, mostly all logon processes store the hash values of passwords in the file.

- The Password file consists of a table of pairs which are in the form (user id, h(P)).

- An intruder can only see the hashes of passwords, even if he accessed the password. He can neither logon using hash nor can he derive the password from hash value since hash function possesses the property of pre-image resistance.

Data Integrity Check

Data integrity check is a most common application of the hash functions. It is used to generate the checksums on data files. This application provides assurance to the user about correctness of the data.

The process is depicted in the following illustration:

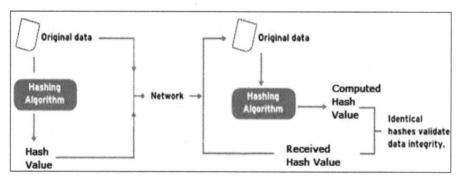

The integrity check helps the user to detect any changes made to original file. It however, does not provide any assurance about originality. The attacker, instead of modifying file data, can change the entire file and compute all together new hash and send to the receiver. This integrity check application is useful only if the user is sure about the originality of file.

References

- Computer-network-cryptography-introduction: geeksforgeeks.org, Retrieved 31 March, 2019

- What-is-encryption-how-does-it-work, searchencrypt: medium.com, Retrieved 14 July, 2019

- Htg-explains-what-is-encryption-and-how-does-it-work, how to: howtogeek.com, Retrieved 17 May, 2019

- Symmetric-key-encryption: educba.com, Retrieved 19 April, 2019

- Public-key-encryption, cryptography: tutorialspoint.com, Retrieved 5 February, 2019

- Attacks-on-cryptosystems: iitkgp.ac.in, Retrieved 26 July, 2019

- Cryptography-hash-functions, cryptography: tutorialspoint.com, Retrieved 21 May, 2019

2

Block Cipher

The encryption method which uses a deterministic algorithm and a symmetric key to encrypt a block of text instead of one bit at a time is known as a block cipher. It plays a crucial role in designing secure cryptographic protocols. This chapter has been carefully written to provide an easy understanding of the varied facets of block ciphers and block cipher modes.

In cryptography, block ciphers are one of the two main types of symmetric cipher; they operate on fixed-size blocks of plaintext, giving a block of ciphertext for each. The other main type are stream ciphers, which generate a continuous stream of keying material to be mixed with messages.

The basic function of block ciphers is to keep messages or stored data secret; the intent is that an unauthorised person be completely unable to read the enciphered material. Block ciphers therefore use a key and are designed to be hard to read without that key. Of course an attacker's intent is exactly the opposite; he wants to read the material without authorisation, and often without the key.

Among the best-known and most widely used block ciphers are two US government standards. The Data Encryption Standard (DES) from the 1970s is now considered obsolete; the Advanced Encryption Standard (AES) replaced it in 2002. To choose the new standard, the National Institute of Standards and Technology ran an AES competition. Fifteen ciphers were entered, five finalists selected, and eventually AES chosen.

These standards greatly influenced the design of other block ciphers. DES and alternatives describes 20th century block ciphers, all with the 64-bit block size of DES. The AES generation describes the next generation, the first 21st century ciphers, all with the 128-bit block size of AES. Large-block ciphers covers a few special cases that do not fit in the other sections.

Block ciphers are essential components in many security systems. However, just having a good block cipher does not give you security, much as just having good tires does not give you transportation. It may not even help; good tires are of little use if you need a boat. Even in systems where block ciphers are needed, they are never the whole story.

Any cipher is worthless without a good key. Keys must be kept secure, they should be random so they are difficult to guess, and in any application which encrypts large volumes of data, the key must be changed from time to time.

It is hard to design any system that must withstand adversaries; see cryptography is difficult. In particular, block ciphers must withstand cryptanalysis; it is impossible to design a good block cipher, or to evaluate the security of one, without a thorough understanding of the available attack methods. Also, Kerckhoffs' Principle applies to block ciphers; no cipher can be considered secure unless it can resist an attacker who knows all its details except the key in use.

A block cipher defines how a single block is encrypted; a mode of operation defines how multiple block encryptions are combined to achieve some larger goal. Using a mode that is inappropriate for the application at hand may lead to insecurity, even if the cipher itself is secure. A block cipher can be used to build another cryptographic function such as a random number generator, a stream cipher, or a cryptographic hash. These are largely just a matter of choosing the correct mode, but there are some overall design issues as well.

Block ciphers are often used as components in hybrid cryptosystems; these combine public key (asymmetric) cryptography with secret key (symmetric) techniques such as block ciphers or stream ciphers. Typically, the symmetric cipher is the workhorse that encrypts large amounts of data; the public key mechanism manages keys for the symmetric cipher and provides authentication. Generally other components such as cryptographic hashes and a cryptographically strong random number generator are required as well. Such a system can only be as strong as its weakest link, and it may not even be that strong. Using secure components including good block ciphers is certainly necessary, but just having good components does not guarantee that the system will be secure.

Size Parameters

One could say there are only three things to worry about in designing a block cipher:

- Make the block size large enough that an enemy cannot create a code book, collecting so many known plaintext/ciphertext pairs that the cipher is broken.

- Make the key size large enough that he cannot use a brute force attack, trying all possible keys.

- Then design the cipher well enough that no other attack is effective.

Getting adequate block size and key size is the easy part; just choose large enough numbers. This section describes how those choices are made. Making ciphers that resist attacks that are cleverer than brute force is far more difficult.

Later on, we describe two generations of actual ciphers. The 20th century ciphers use 64-bit blocks and key sizes from 56 bits up. The 21st century ciphers use 128-bit blocks and 128-bit or larger keys.

If two or more ciphers use the same block and key sizes, they are effectively interchangeable. One can replace another in almost any application without requiring any other change to the application. This might be done to comply with a particular government's standards, to replace a cipher against which some new attack had been discovered, to provide efficiency in a particular environment, or simply to suit a preference.

Nearly all cryptographic libraries give a developer a choice of components, and some protocols such as IPsec allow a network administrator to select ciphers. This may be a good idea if all the available ciphers are strong, but if some are weak it just gives the developer or administrator, neither of whom is likely to be an expert on ciphers, an opportunity to get it wrong. There is an argument that supporting multiple ciphers is an unnecessary complication. On the other hand, being able to change ciphers easily if one is broken provides a valuable safety mechanism. Striking some sort of balance with a few strong ciphers is probably the best policy.

Block Size

The block size of a cipher is chosen partly for implementation convenience; using a multiple of 32 bits makes software implementations simpler. However, it must also be large enough to guard against code book attacks.

DES and the generation of ciphers that followed it all used a 64-bit block size. To weaken such a cipher significantly the attacker must build up a code book with 2^{32} blocks, 32 gigabytes of data, all encrypted with the same key, As long as the cipher user changes keys reasonably often, a code book attack is not a threat. Procedures and protocols for block cipher usage therefore always include a re-keying policy.

However, with Moore's Law making larger code books more practical, NIST chose to play it safe in their AES specifications; they used a 128-bit block size. This was a somewhat controversial innovation at the time (1998), since it meant changes to a number of applications and it was not absolutely clear that the larger size was necessary. However, it has since become common practice; later ciphers such as Camellia and SEED also use 128 bits.

There are also a few ciphers which either support variable block size or have a large fixed block size.

Key Size

In theory, any cipher except a one-time pad can be broken by a brute force attack; the enemy just has to try keys until he finds the right one. However, the attack is practical only if the cipher's key size is inadequate. If the key uses n bits, there are 2^n possible keys and on average the attacker must test half of them, so the average cost of the attack is 2^{n-1} encryptions.

Current block ciphers all use at least 128-bit keys to protect against brute force attacks. Suppose an attacker has a billion machines each testing a billion keys a second; he can then test about 2^{60} keys a second, so he needs 2^{67} seconds against a 128-bit key. There are about 2^{25} seconds in a year, so that is about 2^{42} years, over 4 trillion years; the cipher is secure against brute force. Many ciphers support larger keys as well.

Key size is critical in stream ciphers as well as block ciphers, for the same reasons. In many applications of cryptographic hash algorithms, no key is used. However in applications where a key is used, such as hashed message authentication codes, key size is naturally an issue.

Principles and Techniques

This topic introduces the main principles of block cipher design, defines standard terms, and describes common techniques.

All of the principles and many of the terms and techniques discussed here for block ciphers also apply to other cryptographic primitives such as stream ciphers and cryptographic hash algorithms.

Iterated Block Ciphers

Nearly all block ciphers are iterated block ciphers; they have multiple rounds, each applying the same transformation to the output of the previous round. At setup time, a number of round keys are computed from the primary key; the method used is called the cipher's key schedule. In the actual encryption or decryption, each round uses its own round key. This allows the designer to define some relatively simple transformation, called a round function, and apply it repeatedly to create a cipher with enough overall complexity to thwart attacks.

Three common ways to design iterated block ciphers — SP networks, Feistel structures and the Lai-Massey construction — and two important ways to look at the complexity requirements — avalanche and nonlinearity.

Any iterated cipher can be made more secure by increasing the number of rounds or made faster by reducing the number. In choosing the number of rounds, the cipher designer tries to strike a balance that achieves both security and efficiency simultaneously. Often a safety margin is applied; if the cipher appears to be secure after a certain number of rounds, the designer specifies a somewhat larger number for actual use.

There is a trade-off that can be made in the design. With a simple fast round function, many rounds may be required to achieve adequate security; for example, GOST and TEA both use 32 rounds. A more complex round function might allow fewer rounds; for example, IDEA uses only 8 rounds. Since the ciphers with fast round functions generally need more rounds and the ones with few rounds generally need slower round functions, neither strategy is clearly better. Secure and reasonably efficient ciphers can be designed either way, and compromises are common.

In cryptanalysis it is common to attack reduced round versions of a cipher. For example, in attacking a 16-round cipher, the analyst might start by trying to break a two-round or four-round version. Such attacks are much easier. Success against the reduced round version may lead to insights that are useful in work against the full cipher, or even to an attack that can be extended to break the full cipher.

Whitening and Tweaking

Nearly all block ciphers use the same basic design, an iterated block cipher with multiple rounds. However, some have additional things outside that basic structure.

Whitening involves mixing additional material derived from the key into the plaintext before the first round, or into the ciphertext after the last round or both. The technique was introduced by Ron Rivest in DES-X and has since been used in other ciphers such as RC6, Blowfish and Twofish. If the whitening material uses additional key bits, as in DES-X, then this greatly increases resistance to brute force attacks because of the larger key. If the whitening material is derived from the primary key during key scheduling, then resistance to brute force is not increased since the primary key remains the same size. However, using whitening is generally much cheaper than adding a round, and it does increase resistance to other attacks.

A recent development is the tweakable block cipher. Where a normal block cipher has only two inputs, plaintext and key, a tweakable block cipher has a third input called the tweak. The tweak, along with the key, controls the operation of the cipher. Whitening can be seen as one form of tweaking, but many others are possible.

If changing tweaks is sufficiently lightweight, compared to the key scheduling operation which is often fairly expensive, then some new modes of operation become possible. Unlike the key, the tweak need not always be secret, though it should be somewhat random and in some applications it should change from block to block. Tweakable ciphers and the associated modes are an active area of current research.

The Hasty Pudding Cipher was one of the first tweakable ciphers, pre-dating the Tweakable Block Ciphers paper and referring to what would now be called the tweak as "spice".

Avalanche

The designer wants changes to quickly propagate through the cipher. This was named the avalanche effect in a paper by Horst Feistel. The idea is that changes should build up like an avalanche, so that a tiny initial change quickly creates large effects. The term and its exact application were new, but the basic concept was not; avalanche is a variant of Claude Shannon's diffusion and that in turn is a formalisation of ideas that were already in use.

If a single bit of input or of the round key is changed at round n, that should affect all bits of the ciphertext by round $n + x$ for some reasonably small x. Ideally, x would be 1, but this is not generally achieved in practice. Certainly x must be much less than the total number of rounds; if x is large, then the cipher will need more rounds to be secure.

The strict avalanche criterion is a strong version of the requirement for good avalanche properties. Complementing any single bit of the input or the key should give exactly a 50% chance of a change in any given bit of output.

Cipher Structures

In Claude Shannon's terms, a cipher needs both confusion and diffusion, and a general design principle is that of the product cipher which combines several operations to achieve both goals. This goes back to the combination of substitution and transposition in various classical ciphers from before the advent of computers. All modern block ciphers are product ciphers.

Two structures are very commonly used in building block ciphers — SP networks and the Feistel structure. The Lai-Massey construction is a third alternative, less common than the other two. In Shannon's terms, all of these are product ciphers. Any of these structures is a known quantity for a cipher designer, part of the toolkit. He or she gets big chunks of a design — an overall cipher structure with a well-defined hole for the round function to fit into — from the structure, This leaves him or her free to concentrate on the hard part, designing the actual round function. None of these structures gives ideal avalanche in a single round but, with any reasonable round function, all give excellent avalanche after a few rounds.

SP Networks

A substitution-permutation network or SP network or SPN is Shannon's own design for a product cipher. It uses two layers in each round: a substitution layer provides confusion, then a permutation layer provides diffusion.

The S-layer typically uses look-up tables called substitution boxes or S-boxes, though other mechanisms are also possible. The input is XOR-ed with a round key, split into parts and each part used as an index into an S-box. The S-box output then replaces that part so the combined S-box outputs become the S-layer output. The P-layer permutes the resulting bits, providing diffusion or in Feistel's terms helping to ensure avalanche.

A single round of an SP network does not provide ideal avalanche; output bits are affected only by inputs to their S-box, not by all input bits. However, the P-layer ensures that the output of one S-box in one round will affect several S-boxes in the next round so, after a few rounds, overall avalanche properties can be very good.

Feistel Structure

Another way to build an iterated block cipher is to use the Feistel structure. This technique was devised by Horst Feistel of IBM and used in DES. Such ciphers are known as Feistel ciphers or Feistel networks. In Shannon's terms, they are another class of product cipher.

Feistel ciphers are sometimes referred to as Luby-Rackoff ciphers after the authors of a theoretical paper analyzing some of their properties. Later work based on that shows that a Feistel cipher with seven rounds can be secure.

In a Feistel cipher, each round uses an operation called the F-function whose input is half a block and a round key; the output is a half-block of scrambled data which is XOR-ed into the other half-block of text. The rounds alternate direction — in one data from the left half-block is input and the right half-block is changed, and in the next round that is reversed.

Showing the half-blocks as left and right, bitwise XOR as $\oplus$ (each bit of the output word is the XOR of the corresponding bits of the two input words) and round key for round n as k_n, even numbered rounds are then:

$$\text{left}_n = \text{left}_{n-1} \oplus F\left(\text{right}_{n-1}, k_n\right)$$

$$\text{right}_n = \text{right}_{n-1}$$

and odd-numbered rounds are,

$$\text{right}_n = \text{right}_{n-1} \oplus F\left(\text{right}_{n-1}, k_n\right)$$

$$\text{left}_n = \text{left}_{n-1}$$

Since XOR is its own inverse ($a \oplus b \oplus b = a$ for any a,b) and the half-block that is used as input to the F-function is unchanged in each round, reversing a Feistel round is straightforward. Just calculate the F-function again with the same inputs and XOR the result into the ciphertext to cancel out the previous XOR. For example, the decryption step matching the first example above is:

$$\text{left}_{n-1} + \text{left}_n \oplus \left(\text{right}_n, k_n\right)$$

$$\text{right}_{n-1} = \text{right}_n$$

In some ciphers, including those based on SP networks, all operations must be reversible so that decryption can work. The main advantage of a Feistel cipher over an SP network is that the F-function itself need not be reversible, only repeatable. This gives the designer extra flexibility; almost any operation he can think up can be used in the F-function. On the other hand, in the Feistel construction, only half the output changes in each round while an SP network can change all of it in a single round.

A single round in a Feistel cipher has less than ideal avalanche properties; only half the output is changed. However, the other half is changed in the next round so, with a good F-function, a Feistel cipher can have excellent overall avalanche properties within a few rounds.

There is a variant called an unbalanced Feistel cipher in which the block is split into two unequal-sized pieces rather than two equal halves. Skipjack was a well-known example. There are also variations which treat the text as four blocks rather than just two; MARS and CAST-256 are examples.

The hard part of Feistel cipher design is of course the F-function. Design goals include efficiency, easy implementation, and good avalanche properties. Also, it is critically important that the F-function be highly nonlinear. All other operations in a Feistel cipher are linear and a cipher without enough nonlinearity is weak.

Lai-Massey Scheme

This structure was introduced in a thesis by Xuejia Lai, supervised by James Massey, in a cipher which later became the International Data Encryption Algorithm, IDEA. It has since been used in other ciphers such as FOX, later renamed IDEA NXT. Perhaps the best-known analysis is by Serge Vaudenay, one of the designers of FOX.

One Study proposes a general class of "quasi-Feistel networks", with the Lai-Massey scheme as one instance, and shows that several of the well-known results on Feistel networks can be generalised to the whole class. Another gives some specific results for the Lai-Massey scheme.

Nonlinearity

To be secure, every cipher must contain nonlinear operations. If all operations in a cipher were linear then the cipher could be reduced to a system of linear equations and be broken by an algebraic attack. The attacker can choose which algebraic system to use; for example, against one cipher he might treat the text as a vector of bits and use Boolean algebra while for another he might choose to treat it as a vector of bytes and use arithmetic modulo 2^8. The attacker can also try linear cryptanalysis. If he can find a good enough linear approximation for the round function and has enough known plaintext/ciphertext pairs, then this will break the cipher. Defining "enough" in the two places where it occurs in the previous sentence is tricky.

What makes these attacks impractical is a combination of the sheer size of the system of equations used (large block size, whitening, and more rounds all increase this) and nonlinearity in the relations involved. In any algebra, solving a system of *linear* equations is more-or-less straightforward provided there are more equations than variables. However, solving *nonlinear* systems of equations is far harder, so the cipher designer strives to introduce nonlinearity to the system, preferably to have at least some components that are not even close to linear. Combined with good avalanche properties and enough rounds, this makes both direct algebraic analysis and linear cryptanalysis prohibitively difficult.

There are several ways to add nonlinearity; some ciphers rely on only one while others use several. One method is mixing operations from different algebras. If the cipher relies only on Boolean operations, the cryptanalyst can try to attack using Boolean algebra; if it uses only arithmetic operations, he can try normal algebra. If it uses both, he has a problem. Of course arithmetic operations can be expressed in Boolean algebra or vice versa, but the expressions are inconveniently (for the cryptanalyst) complex and nonlinear whichever way he tries it.

For example, in the Blowfish F-function, it is necessary to combine four 32-bit words into one. This is not done with just addition, x = a+b+c+d or just Boolean operations x = a $\oplus$ b $\oplus$ c $\oplus$ d but instead with a mixture, x = ((a+b) $\oplus$ c)+d. On most computers this costs no more, but it makes the analyst's job harder.

Other operations can also be used, albeit at higher costs. IDEA uses multiplication modulo $2^{16}+1$ and AES does matrix multiplications with polynomials in a Galois field.

Rotations, also called circular shifts, on words or registers are nonlinear in normal algebra, though they are easily described in Boolean algebra. GOST uses rotations by a constant amount, CAST-128 and CAST-256 use a key-dependent rotation in the F-function, and RC5, RC6 and MARS all use data-dependent rotations. A general operation for introducing nonlinearity is the substitution box or S-box.

Nonlinearity is also an important consideration in the design of stream ciphers and cryptographic hash algorithms. For hashes, much of the mathematics and many of the techniques used are similar to those for block ciphers. For stream ciphers, rather different mathematics and methods apply, but the basic principle is the same.

S-boxes

S-boxes or substitution boxes are look-up tables. The basic operation involved is a = sbox[b] which, at least for reasonable sizes of a and b, is easily done on any computer.

S-boxes are described as m by n, with m representing the number of input bits and n the number of output bits. For example, DES uses 6 by 4 S-boxes. The storage requirement for an m by n S-box is $2^m n$ bits, so large values of m (many input bits) are problematic. Values up to eight are common and MARS has a 9 by 32 S-box; going much beyond that would be expensive. Large values of n (many output bits) are not a problem; 32 is common and at least one system, the Tiger hash algorithm, uses 64.

S-boxes are often used in the S-layer of an SP Network. In this application, the S-box must have an inverse to be used in decryption. It must therefore have the same number of bits for input and output; only n by n S-boxes can be used. For example, AES is an SP network with a single 8 by 8 S-box and Serpent is one with eight 4 by 4 S-boxes. Another common application is in the F-function of a Feistel cipher. Since the F-function need not be reversible, there is no need to construct an inverse S-box for decryption and S-boxes of any size may be used. With either an SP network or a Feistel construction, nonlinear S-boxes and enough rounds give a highly nonlinear cipher.

Large S-boxes

The first generation of Feistel ciphers used relatively small S-boxes, 6 by 4 for DES and 4 by 4 for GOST. In these ciphers the F-function is essentially one round of an SP Network. The eight S-boxes give 32 bits of S-box output. Those bits, reordered by a simple transformation, become the 32-bit output of the F-function. Avalanche properties are less than ideal since each output bit depends only on the inputs to one S-box. The output transformation (a bit permutation in DES, a rotation in GOST) compensates for this, ensuring that the output from one S-box in one round affects several S-boxes in the next round so that good avalanche is achieved after a few rounds.

Later Feistel ciphers use larger S-boxes, 8 by 32 in both CAST and Blowfish. They do not use S-box bits directly as F-function output. Instead, they take a 32-bit word from each S-box, then combine them to form a 32-bit output. This gives an F-function with ideal avalanche properties — every output bit depends on all S-box output words, and therefore on all input bits and all key bits. With the Feistel structure and such an F-function, complete avalanche — all 64 output bits depend on all 64 input bits — is achieved in three rounds. No output transformation is required in such an F-function, but one may be used anyway; CAST-128 has a key-dependent rotation.

These ciphers are primarily designed for software implementation, rather than the 1970s hardware DES was designed for, so looking up a full computer word at a time makes sense. An 8 by 32 S-box takes one K byte of storage; several can be used on a modern machine without difficulty. They need only four S-box lookups, rather than the eight in DES or GOST, so the F-function and therefore the whole cipher can be reasonably efficient.

S-box Design

There is an extensive literature on the design of good S-boxes, much of it emphasizing achieving high nonlinearity though other criteria are also used.

The CAST S-boxes use bent functions (the most highly nonlinear Boolean functions) as their columns. That is, the mapping from all the input bits to any single output bit is a bent function. Such S-boxes meet the strict avalanche criterion; not only does every every bit of round input and every bit of round key affect every bit of round output, but complementing any input bit has exactly a 50% chance of changing any given output bit. A paper on generating the S-boxes is Mister & Adams "Practical S-box Design". Bent functions are combined to get additional desirable traits — a balanced S-box (equal probability of 0 and 1 output), miniumum correlation among output bits, and high overall S-box nonlinearity.

Blowfish uses a different approach, generating random S-boxes as part of the key scheduling operation at cipher setup time. Such S-boxes are not as nonlinear as the carefully constructed CAST ones, but they are nonlinear enough and, unlike the CAST S-boxes, they are unknown to an attacker.

In perfectly nonlinear S-boxes, not only are all columns bent functions (the most nonlinear possible Boolean functions), but all linear combinations of columns are bent functions as well.

This is possible only if $m \geq 2n$, there are at least twice as many input bits as output bits. Such S-boxes are therefore not much used.

S-boxes in Analysis

S-boxes are sometimes used as an analytic tool even for operations that are not actually implemented as S-boxes. Any operation whose output is fully determined by its inputs can be described by an S-box; concatenate all inputs into an index, look that index up, get the output. For example, the IDEA cipher uses a multiplication operation with two 16-bit inputs and one 16-bit output; it can be modeled as a 32 by 16 S-box. One might use such a model in order to apply standard tools for measuring S-box nonlinearity. A well-funded cryptanalyst might actually build the S-box (8 gigabytes of memory) either to use in his analysis or to speed up an attack.

Resisting Linear and Differential Attacks

Two very powerful cryptanalytic methods of attacking block ciphers are linear cryptanalysis and differential cryptanalysis. The former works by finding linear approximations for the nonlinear components of a cipher, then combining them using the piling-up lemma to attack the whole cipher. The latter looks at how small changes in the input affect the output, and how such changes propagate through multiple rounds. These are the only known attacks that break DES with less effort than brute force, and they are completely general attacks that apply to any block cipher.

Both these attacks, however, require large numbers of known or chosen plaintexts, so a simple defense against them is to re-key often enough that the enemy cannot collect sufficient texts.

Techniques introduced for CAST go further, building a cipher that is provably immune to linear or differential analysis with any number of texts. The method, taking linear cryptanalysis as our example and abbreviating it LC, is as follows:

- Start from properties of the round function (for CAST, from bent functions in the S-boxes).

- Derive a limit m, the maximum possible quality of any linear approximation to a single round.

- Consider the number of rounds, r, as a variable.

- Derive an expression for e, the effort required to break the cipher by LC, in terms of r and m.

- Find the minimum r such that e exceeds the effort required for brute force, making LC impractical.

- Derive an expression for c, the number of chosen plaintexts required for LC, also in terms of r and m (LC with only known plaintext requires more texts, so it can be ignored).

- Find the minimum r such that c exceeds the number of possible plaintexts, $2^{blocksize}$, making LC impossible.

A similar approach applied to differentials gives values for r that make differential cryptanalysis impractical or impossible. Choose the actual number of rounds so that, at a minimum, both attacks are impractical. Ideally, make both impossible, then add a safety factor. This type of analysis is now a standard part of the cryptographer's toolkit. Many of the AES candidates, for example, included proofs along these lines in their design documentation, and AES itself uses such a calculation to determine the number of rounds required for various key sizes.

There are other methods of constructing ciphers provably immune to these attacks. Serge Vaudenay's work on decorrelation theory gives one and Knudsen-Nyberg ciphers are another.

Large-block Ciphers

For most applications a 64-bit or 128-bit block size is a fine choice; nearly all common block ciphers use one or the other. Such ciphers can be used to encrypt objects larger than their block size; just choose an appropriate mode of operation.

For nearly all ciphers, the block size is a power of two. Joan Daemen's thesis, though, had two exceptions: 3-Way uses 96 bits and BaseKing 192. Neither cipher was widely used, but they did influence later designs.

A block cipher with larger blocks may be more efficient; it takes fewer block operations to encrypt a given amount of data. It may also be more secure in some ways; diffusion takes place across a larger block size, so data is more thoroughly mixed, and large blocks make a code book attack more difficult. On the other hand, great care must be taken to ensure adequate diffusion within a block so a large-block cipher may need more rounds, larger blocks require more padding, and there is not a great deal of literature on designing and attacking such ciphers so it is hard to know if one is secure. Large-block ciphers are inconvenient for some applications and simply do not fit in some protocols.

Some block ciphers, such as Block TEA and Hasty Pudding, support variable block sizes. They may therefore be both efficient and convenient in applications that need to encrypt many items of a fixed size, for example disk blocks or database records. However, just using the cipher in ECB mode to encrypt each block under the same key is unwise, especially if encrypting many objects. With ECB mode, identical blocks will encrypt to the same ciphertext and give the enemy some information. One solution is to use a tweakable cipher such as Hasty Pudding with the block number or other object identifier as the tweak. Another is to use CBC mode with an initialisation vector derived from an object identifier.

Cryptographic hash algorithms can be built using a block cipher as a component. There are general-purpose methods for this that can use existing block ciphers; Applied Cryptography gives a long list and describes weaknesses in many of them. However, some hashes include a specific-purpose block cipher as part of the hash design. One example is Whirlpool, a 512-bit hash using a block cipher similar in design to AES but with 512-bit blocks and a 512-bit key. Another is the Advanced Hash Standard candidate Skein which uses a tweakable block cipher called Threefish. Threefish has 256-bit, 512-bit and 1024-bit versions; in each version block size and key size are both that number of bits.

It is possible to go the other way and use any cryptographic hash to build a block cipher; again Applied Cryptography has a list of techniques and describes weaknesses. The simplest method is to make a Feistel cipher with double the hash's block size; the F-function is then just to hash text and round key together. This technique is rarely used, partly because a hash makes a rather expensive round function and partly because the block cipher block size would have to be inconveniently large; for example using a 160-bit bit hash such as SHA-1 would give a 320-bit block cipher.

The hash-to-cipher technique was, however, important in one legal proceeding, the Bernstein case. At the time, US law strictly controlled export of cryptography because of its possible military uses, but hash functions were allowed because they are designed to provide authentication rather than secrecy. Bernstein's code built a block cipher from a hash, effectively circumventing those regulations. Moreover, he sued the government over his right to publish his work, claiming the export regulations were an unconstitutional restriction on freedom of speech. The courts agreed, effectively striking down the export controls.

It is also possible to use a public key operation as a block cipher. For example, one might use the RSA algorithm with 1024-bit keys as a block cipher with 1024-bit blocks. Since the round function is itself cryptographically secure, only one round is needed. However, this is rarely done; public key techniques are expensive so this would give a very slow block cipher. A much more common practice is to use public key methods, block ciphers, and cryptographic hashes together in a hybrid cryptosystem.

Data Encryption Standard

The Data Encryption Standard (DES) is a symmetric-key block cipher published by the National Institute of Standards and Technology (NIST).

DES is an implementation of a Feistel Cipher. It uses 16 round Feistel structure. The block size is 64-bit. Though, key length is 64-bit, DES has an effective key length of 56 bits, since 8 of the 64 bits of the key are not used by the encryption algorithm (function as check bits only). General Structure of DES is depicted in the following illustration:

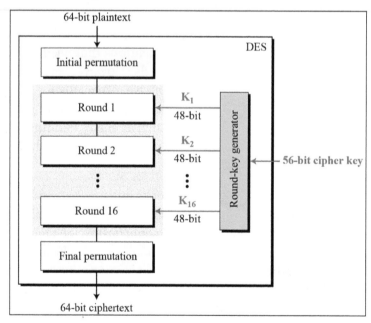

Since DES is based on the Feistel Cipher, all that is required to specify DES is:

- Round function,

- Key schedule,

- Any additional processing: Initial and final permutation.

Initial and Final Permutation

The initial and final permutations are straight Permutation boxes (P-boxes) that are inverses of each other. They have no cryptography significance in DES. The initial and final permutations are shown as follows:

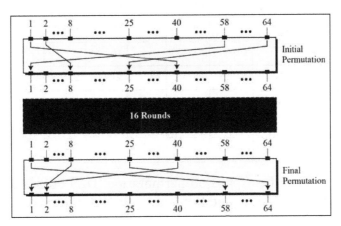

Round Function

The heart of this cipher is the DES function, f. The DES function applies a 48-bit key to the right-most 32 bits to produce a 32-bit output.

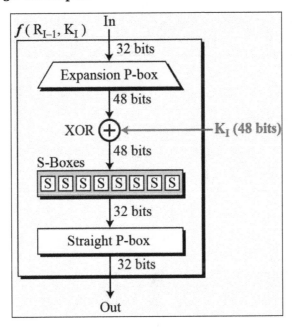

- Expansion Permutation Box: Since right input is 32-bit and round key is a 48-bit, we first need to expand right input to 48 bits. Permutation logic is graphically depicted in the following illustration:

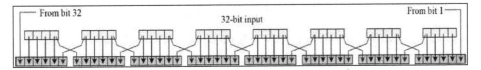

The graphically depicted permutation logic is generally described as table in DES specification illustrated as shown:

32	01	02	03	04	05
04	05	06	07	08	09
08	09	10	11	12	13
12	13	14	15	16	17
16	17	18	19	20	21
20	21	22	23	24	25
24	25	26	27	28	29
28	29	31	31	32	01

- XOR (Whitener): After the expansion permutation, DES does XOR operation on the expanded right section and the round key. The round key is used only in this operation.

- Substitution Boxes: The S-boxes carry out the real mixing (confusion). DES uses 8 S-boxes, each with a 6-bit input and a 4-bit output. Refer the following illustration:

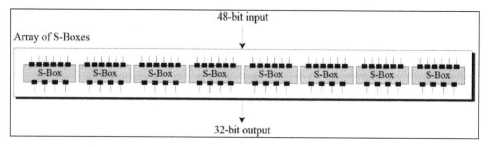

The S-box rule is illustrated below:

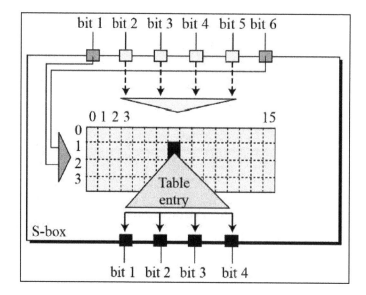

- There are a total of eight S-box tables: The output of all eight s-boxes is then combined in to 32 bit section.

- Straight Permutation: The 32 bit output of S-boxes is then subjected to the straight permutation with rule shown in the following illustration:

16	07	20	21	29	12	28	17
01	15	23	26	05	18	31	10
02	08	24	14	32	27	03	09
19	13	30	06	22	11	04	25

Key Generation

The round-key generator creates sixteen 48-bit keys out of a 56-bit cipher key. The process of key generation is depicted in the following illustration:

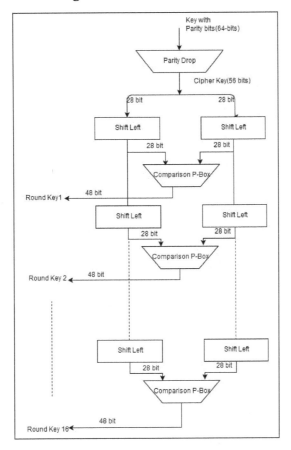

DES Analysis

The DES satisfies both the desired properties of block cipher. These two properties make cipher very strong:

- Avalanche effect: A small change in plaintext results in the very great change in the ciphertext.

- Completeness: Each bit of ciphertext depends on many bits of plaintext.

During the last few years, cryptanalysis have found some weaknesses in DES when key selected are weak keys. These keys shall be avoided.

DES has proved to be a very well designed block cipher. There have been no significant cryptanalytic attacks on DES other than exhaustive key search.

Advanced Encryption Standard

The more popular and widely adopted symmetric encryption algorithm likely to be encountered nowadays is the Advanced Encryption Standard (AES). It is found at least six time faster than triple DES.

A replacement for DES was needed as its key size was too small. With increasing computing power, it was considered vulnerable against exhaustive key search attack. Triple DES was designed to overcome this drawback but it was found slow.

The features of AES are as follows:

- Symmetric key symmetric block cipher.

- 128-bit data, 128/192/256-bit keys.

- Stronger and faster than Triple-DES.

- Provide full specification and design details.

- Software implementable in C and Java.

Operation of AES

AES is an iterative rather than Feistel cipher. It is based on 'substitution–permutation network'. It comprises of a series of linked operations, some of which involve replacing inputs by specific outputs (substitutions) and others involve shuffling bits around (permutations).

Interestingly, AES performs all its computations on bytes rather than bits. Hence, AES treats the 128 bits of a plaintext block as 16 bytes. These 16 bytes are arranged in four columns and four rows for processing as a matrix.

Unlike DES, the number of rounds in AES is variable and depends on the length of the key. AES uses 10 rounds for 128-bit keys, 12 rounds for 192-bit keys and 14 rounds for 256-bit keys. Each of these rounds uses a different 128-bit round key, which is calculated from the original AES key.

The schematic of AES structure is given in the following illustration:

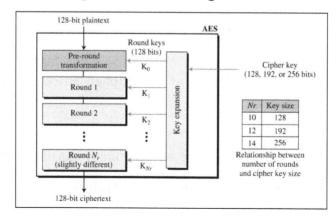

Encryption Process

Here, we restrict to description of a typical round of AES encryption. Each round comprise of four sub-processes. The first round process is depicted below:

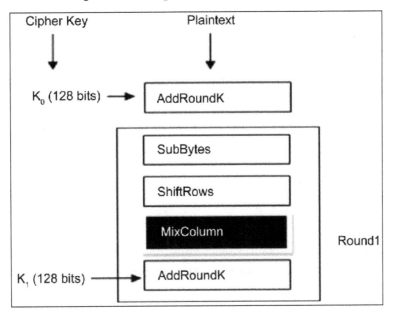

Byte Substitution

The 16 input bytes are substituted by looking up a fixed table (S-box) given in design. The result is in a matrix of four rows and four columns.

Shiftrows

Each of the four rows of the matrix is shifted to the left. Any entries that 'fall off' are re-inserted on the right side of row. Shift is carried out as follows:

- First row is not shifted.

- Second row is shifted one (byte) position to the left.

- Third row is shifted two positions to the left.

- Fourth row is shifted three positions to the left.

- The result is a new matrix consisting of the same 16 bytes but shifted with respect to each other.

MixColumns

Each column of four bytes is now transformed using a special mathematical function. This function takes as input the four bytes of one column and outputs four completely new bytes, which replace the original column. The result is another new matrix consisting of 16 new bytes. It should be noted that this step is not performed in the last round.

Addroundkey

The 16 bytes of the matrix are now considered as 128 bits and are XORed to the 128 bits of the round key. If this is the last round then the output is the ciphertext. Otherwise, the resulting 128 bits are interpreted as 16 bytes and we begin another similar round.

Decryption Process

The process of decryption of an AES ciphertext is similar to the encryption process in the reverse order. Each round consists of the four processes conducted in the reverse order:

- Add round key,

- Mix columns,

- Shift rows,

- Byte substitution.

Since sub-processes in each round are in reverse manner, unlike for a Feistel Cipher, the encryption and decryption algorithms needs to be separately implemented, although they are very closely related.

AES Analysis

In present day cryptography, AES is widely adopted and supported in both hardware and software. Till date, no practical cryptanalytic attacks against AES has been discovered. Additionally, AES has built-in flexibility of key length, which allows a degree of 'future-proofing' against progress in the ability to perform exhaustive key searches.

However, just as for DES, the AES security is assured only if it is correctly implemented and good key management is employed.

The Ideal Block Cipher

In an ideal block cipher, the relationship between the input blocks and the output block is completely random. But it must be invertible for decryption to work. Therefore, it has to be one-to-one, meaning that each input block is mapped to a unique output block.

The mapping from the input bit blocks to the output bit blocks can also be construed as a mapping from the integers corresponding to the input bit blocks to the integers corresponding to the output bit blocks. The encryption key for the ideal block cipher is the codebook itself, meaning the table that shows the relationship between the input blocks and the output blocks.

Problems with Ideal Block Cipher

- There is a practical problem with the ideal block cipher.

- If a small block size, such as $n = 4$, is used, then the system is equivalent to a classical substitution cipher.

  - Such systems are vulnerable to a statistical analysis of the plaintext.

  - This weakness is not inherent in the use of a substitution cipher but rather results from the use of a small block size.

- If n is sufficiently large and an arbitrary reversible substitution between plaintext and ciphertext is allowed, then the statistical characteristics of the source plaintext are masked to such an extent that this type of cryptanalysis is infeasible.

- However, an arbitrary reversible substitution cipher (the ideal block cipher) for a large block size is not practical from an implementation and performance point of view.

- $n = 4$, required key length: $(4 \text{ bits}) \times (16 \text{ rows}) = 64$ bits.

  - In general, for an n-bit ideal block cipher, the length of the key defined in this fashion is $n \times 2^n$ bits.

- For a 64-bit block, which is a desirable length to thwart statistical attacks, the required key length is $64 \times 2^{64} = 2^{70} = 10^{21}$ bits.

- The size of the encryption key would make the ideal block cipher an impractical idea.

  - Think of the logistical issues related to the transmission, storage, and processing of such large keys.

- Considering these difficulties, what we need to do is make an approximation for large value of n so that it is easily realizable.

Block Cipher Modes

The modes of operation of block ciphers are configuration methods that allow those ciphers to work with large data streams, without the risk of compromising the provided security.

It is not recommended, however it is possible while working with block ciphers, to use the same secret key bits for encrypting the same plaintext parts. Using one deterministic algorithm for a number of identical input data, results in some number of identical ciphertext blocks.

This is a very dangerous situation for the cipher's users. An intruder would be able to get much information by knowing the distribution of identical message parts, even if he would not be able to break the cipher and discover the original messages.

Luckily, there exist ways to blur the cipher output. The idea is to mix the plaintext blocks (which are known) with the ciphertext blocks (which have been just created), and to use the result as the cipher input for the next blocks. As a result, the user avoids creating identical output ciphertext blocks from identical plaintext data. These modifications are called the block cipher modes of operations.

Electronic Codebook Mode

It is the simplest mode of encryption. Each plaintext block is encrypted separately. Similarly, each ciphertext block is decrypted separately. Thus, it is possible to encrypt and decrypt by using many threads simultaneously. However, in this mode the created ciphertext is not blurred.

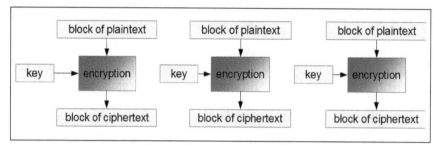

Encryption in the ECB mode.

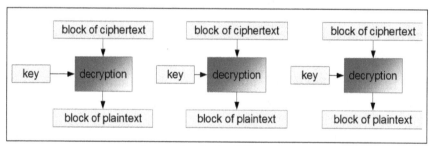

Decryption in the ECB mode.

A typical example of weakness of encryption using electronic codebook mode (ECB) mode is encoding a bitmap image (for example a .bmp file). Even a strong encryption algorithm used in ECB mode cannot blur efficiently the plaintext.

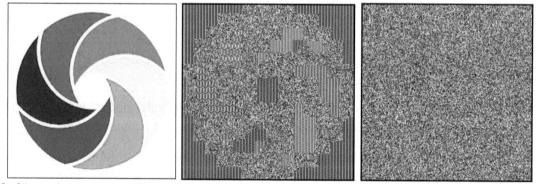

The bitmap image encrypted using DES and the same secret key. The ECB mode was used for the left image and the more complicated CBC mode was used for the right image.

A message that is encrypted using the ECB mode should be extended until a size that is equal to an integer multiple of the single block length. A popular method of aligning the length of the last block is about appending an additional bit equal to 1 and then filling the rest of the block with bits equal to 0. It allows to determine precisely the end of the original message. There exist more methods of aligning the message size.

Apart from revealing the hints regarding the content of plaintext, the ciphers that are used in ECB mode are also more vulnerable to replay attacks.

Cipher-block Chaining Mode

The cipher-block chaining mode (CBC) encryption mode was invented in IBM in 1976. This mode is about adding XOR each plaintext block to the ciphertext block that was previously produced. The result is then encrypted using the cipher algorithm in the usual way. As a result, every subsequent ciphertext block depends on the previous one. The first plaintext block is added XOR to a random initialization vector (commonly referred to as IV). The vector has the same size as a plaintext block.

Encryption in CBC mode can only be performed by using one thread. Despite this disadvantage, this is a very popular way of using block ciphers. CBC mode is used in many applications.

During decrypting of a ciphertext block, one should add XOR the output data received from the decryption algorithm to the previous ciphertext block. Because the receiver knows all the ciphertext blocks just after obtaining the encrypted message, he can decrypt the message using many threads simultaneously.

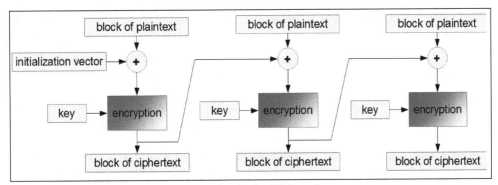

Encryption in the CBC mode.

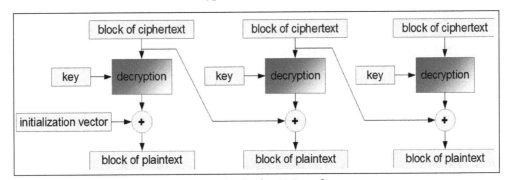

Decryption in the CBC mode.

If one bit of a plaintext message is damaged (for example because of some earlier transmission error), all subsequent ciphertext blocks will be damaged and it will be never possible to decrypt the ciphertext received from this plaintext. As opposed to that, if one ciphertext bit is damaged, only two received plaintext blocks will be damaged. It might be possible to recover the data.

A message that is to be encrypted using the CBC mode, should be extended till the size that is equal to an integer multiple of a single block length (similarly, as in the case of using the ECB mode).

Security of the CBC Mode

The initialization vector IV should be created randomly by the sender. During transmission it should be concatenated with ciphertext blocks, to allow decryption of the message by the receiver. If an intruder could predict what vector would be used, then the encryption would not be resistant to chosen-plaintext attacks:

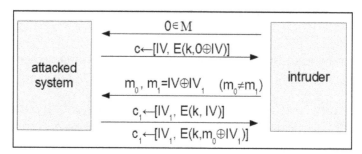

In the example presented above, if the intruder is able to predict that the vector IV_1 will be used by the attacked system to produce the response c_1, they can guess which one of the two encrypted messages m_0 or m_1 is carried by the response c_1. This situation breaks the rule that the intruder shouldn't be able to distinguish between two ciphertexts even if they have chosen both plaintexts. Therefore, the attacked system is vulnerable to chosen-plaintext attacks.

If the vector IV is generated based on non-random data, for example the user password, it should be encrypted before use. One should use a separate secret key for this activity.

The initialization vector IV should be changed after using the secret key a number of times. It can be shown that even properly created IV used too many times, makes the system vulnerable to chosen-plaintext attacks. For AES cipher it is estimated to be 2^{48} blocks, while for 3DES it is about 2^{16} plaintext blocks.

Plaintext Cipher-block Chaining Mode

The Propagating or Plaintext Cipher-block Chaining (PCBC) mode is similar to the previously described CBC mode. It also mixes bits from the previous and current plaintext blocks, before encrypting them. In contrast to the CBC mode, if one ciphertext bit is damaged, the next plaintext block and all subsequent blocks will be damaged and unable to be decrypted correctly.

In the PCBC mode both encryption and decryption can be performed using only one thread at a time.

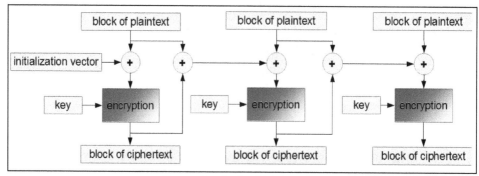

Encryption in the PCBC mode.

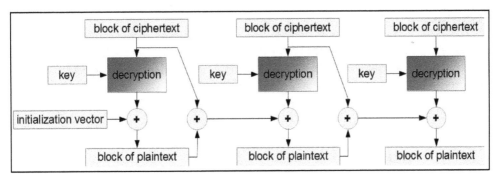

Decryption in the PCBC mode.

Cipher Feedback Mode

The Cipher Feedback (CFB) mode is similar to the CBC mode described earlier. The main difference is that one should encrypt ciphertext data from the previous round (so not the plaintext block) and then add the output to the plaintext bits. It does not affect the cipher security but it results in the fact that the same encryption algorithm (as was used for encrypting plaintext data) should be used during the decryption process.

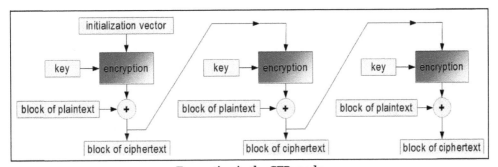

Encryption in the CFB mode.

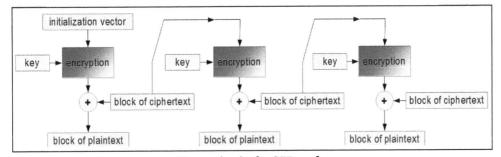

Decryption in the CFB mode.

If one bit of a plaintext message is damaged, the corresponding ciphertext block and all subsequent ciphertext blocks will be damaged. Encryption in CFB mode can be performed only by using one thread.

On the other hand, as in CBC mode, one can decrypt ciphertext blocks using many threads simultaneously. Similarly, if one ciphertext bit is damaged, only two received plaintext blocks will be damaged. As opposed to the previous block cipher modes, the encrypted message doesn't need to be extended till the size that is equal to an integer multiple of a single block length.

Output Feedback Mode

Algorithms that work in the Output Feedback (OFB) mode create keystream bits that are used for encryption subsequent data blocks. In this regard, the way of working of the block cipher becomes similar to the way of working of a typical stream cipher.

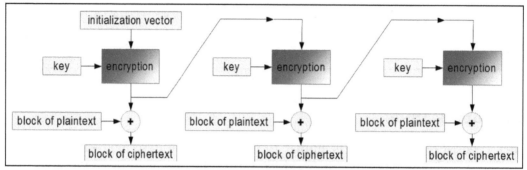

Encryption in the OFB mode.

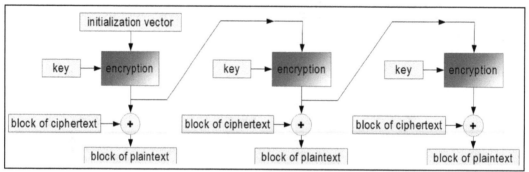

Decryption in the OFB mode.

Because of the continuous creation of keystream bits, both encryption and decryption can be performed using only one thread at a time. Similarly, as in the CFB mode, both data encryption and decryption uses the same cipher encryption algorithm.

If one bit of a plaintext or ciphertext message is damaged (for example because of a transmission error), only one corresponding ciphertext or respectively plaintext bit is damaged as well. It is possible to use various correction algorithms to restore the previous value of damaged parts of the received message.

The biggest drawback of OFB is that the repetition of encrypting the initialization vector may produce the same state that has occurred before. It is an unlikely situation but in such a case the plaintext will start to be encrypted by the same data as previously.

Counter Mode

Using the Counter (CTR) mode makes block cipher way of working similar to a stream cipher. As in the OFB mode, keystream bits are created regardless of content of encrypting data blocks. In this mode, subsequent values of an increasing counter are added to a *nonce* value (the nonce means a number that is unique: *number used once*) and the results are encrypted as usual. The nonce plays the same role as initialization vectors in the previous modes.

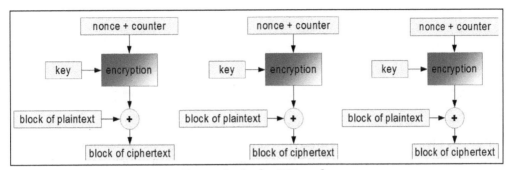

Encryption in the CTR mode.

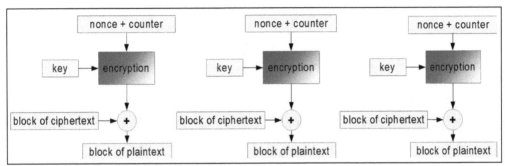

Decryption in the CTR mode.

It is one of the most popular block ciphers modes of operation. Both encryption and decryption can be performed using many threads at the same time. If one bit of a plaintext or ciphertext message is damaged, only one corresponding output bit is damaged as well. Thus, it is possible to use various correction algorithms to restore the previous value of damaged parts of received messages. The CTR mode is also known as the SIC mode (Segment Integer Counter).

Security of the CTR Mode

As in the case of the CBC mode, one should change the secret key after using it for encrypting a number of sent messages. It can be proved that the CTR mode generally provides quite good security and that the secret key needs to be changed less often than in the CBC mode.

References

- Block-cipher: knowino.org, Retrieved 8 January, 2019

- Data-encryption-standard, cryptography: tutorialspoint.com, Retrieved 13 May, 2019

- Advanced-encryption-standard, cryptography: tutorialspoint.com, Retrieved 25 February, 2019

- Cryptography-ideal-block-cipher: blogspot.com, Retrieved 16 January, 2019

- Modes-of-block-ciphers, theory, eng: crypto-it.net, Retrieved 29 March, 2019

Message Security and Secure Channel

The application of methods of digital encryption for the protection of messages is termed as message security. A secure channel refers to a way of transmitting data which is protected against overhearing or tampering. This chapter discusses the diverse aspects of message security and secure channels in detail.

Message Security

Message security applies techniques of digital encryption to protect the contents of individual messages. Using these techniques, an individual message can be signed, or encrypted or both.

Security Systems

Various systems exist for securing messages. Thunderbird has built-in support for a Internet standard called S/MIME. In other security systems the concepts are very similar.

Thunderbird supports RFC 3851 (S/MIME version 3.1). The new features of RFC 5757 are not supported. You can add support for other security systems by installing extensions. For example, the Enigmail extension adds support for PGP.

Whether to choose S/MIME or Enigmail depends mainly upon what your recipients will support, not technical details. However, one reason for Enigmail's popularity is its much easier to figure out how to set it up than S/MIME. It's also got much better documentation and a dedicated support forum. Long term, the Thunderbird developers are planning on adding support for p≡p (Pretty Easy Privacy) once the Enigmail add-on is compatible with it. It's an attempt to make end-to-end encryption much easier to use.

SSL/TLS is also supported, but it is only used to temporarily encrypt data as it is being send/received between a email client and server. Neither S/MIME nor OpenPGP protect your email password, as that is not part of the message. SSL/TLS works well in combination with S/MIME or OpenPGP.

Signed Messages

A signed message is an ordinary message with a digital signature added by the sender. The signature has two purposes: it identifies the sender, and it verifies that the content of the message has not been altered since the message was sent.

Anyone can read a signed message, because it is just an ordinary message. There is nothing different about the message content. The signature is part of the message, but separate from the content.

A signed message can identify the sender in two ways. You might have received other signed messages from this sender in the past. In this case Thunderbird recognizes the signature in the message. Alternatively, the signature in the message might itself be signed by an authority that Thunderbird recognizes.

If the content of the message changes after it is signed by the sender, then Thunderbird warns you. The content might change while the message is being transmitted, or it might change while it is stored on your computer. For example, security software on your computer might change it, or you might edit the content yourself. Any of these changes invalidate the signed content. A signature does not apply to any of the message headers, not even to the subject or date.

Encrypted Messages

An encrypted message has content that is unreadable. However, the message identifies certain people who can decrypt and read the message. If you are one of those people, then Thunderbird automatically decrypts the message when you display it. The message stored on your computer remains encrypted.

Some drawbacks of not being able to permanently decrypt messages is that you can't search them, and if you archive them they can't be accessed using other applications. Both S/MIME and the Enigmail extension can have problems with HTML messages. If the message is going to be both signed and encrypted its recommended you create a plain text message to help avoid signature failures. If you're using the Enigmail extension use PGP/MIME instead of inline PGP if you want to send HTML messages.

Components of the System

The S/MIME system in Thunderbird has various components. Four of these are known as certificates. Each certificate identifies a person, organization, or web site as follows:

Certificate Authorities (CAs)	Trusted organizations (or more rarely, people) that sign other certificates to assure you that those other certificates are genuine.
Web sites	Thunderbird uses web sites to download extensions and for RSS feeds.
Other people	People who send you messages.
You	The identities that you use to send messages.

Thunderbird can also use certificates to verify signed extensions, but this feature is rarely used, and Thunderbird does not have a separate list of certificates for this purpose. Another (optional) component of the system is your master password.

Table: Three further components are beyond the scope.

Certificate revocation lists (CRLs)	Online services for identifying certificates that are no longer valid (removed in 24.0 and later).
Online Certificate Status Protocol (OCSP)	Online services for identifying certificates that are no longer valid.
Security devices	Additional software and perhaps hardware for the security system—for example, a smart card device.

Certificates

A certificate is a file containing data used for encryption (known as *keys*) together with other information. Thunderbird imports certificate files and stores them together in your profile, not as separate files.

To work with the lists of certificates, choose: Tools → Options (Preferences) → Advanced → Certificates → View Certificates. In the Certificate Manager window, you can view, edit, import and delete certificates.

The other information in certificates includes, for example:

- The name and other information about the person or organization the certificate identifies.

- The dates when the certificate becomes valid and expires.

- The purposes that the certificate can be used for.

You can view any certificate to see this information, and you can edit it to make limited changes to the purposes. Some of the purposes are:

SSL Certificate Authority	Able to sign other certificates
SSL Server Certificate	Able to identify web sites
Email Signer Certificate	Able to sign e-mail messages
Email Recipient Certificate	Able to decrypt encrypted messages

To use your own certificate there are usually three steps:

- Get or create the certificate file.

- Import the certificate into Thunderbird.

- Associate the certificate with an identity.

Certificate files for your own identities normally contain their own password-protection. File name extensions for them are: .p12 and .pfx.

Create your own certificates and import them into Thunderbird. When you import your own certificate, you normally need to supply the password that protects the file.

You can export your own certificates for separate backup. When you export a certificate to back up, the exported .p12 file is protected by its own password. Do not share your certificates with any other person because it contain both private (must be kept secret) and public keys.

Probably you want export your public key certificate (.cer) to share it with friends or to publish it on your website allowing people to send you encrypted emails. Thunderbird has no built-in function for this. However it can be easily done with the Firefox Add-on Key Manager. First you need to export your .p12 certificate from Thunderbird and import it into Firefox. Second open Key Manager (Tools → Key Manager Toolbox → Key Manager → Your Keys), select your key, export and choose X.509 as file format.

Certificates and Identities

Associating a certificate with an identity for sending messages is a separate step. In Account Settings, on an account's Security page, choose the certificates for the account's default identity. You can use the same certificate for both signing and encryption, if the certificate allows this.

Thunderbird has no user interface for choosing a certificate for other identities (this is bug 252250). To work around it, choose the certificate for an account's default identity. Close Thunderbird and go to your profile. Back up and edit the file prefs.js there, and search in the file for the four certificate settings:

> mail.identity.idnn.signing_cert_name
>
> mail.identity.idnn.sign_mail
>
> mail.identity.idnn.encryption_cert_name
>
> mail.identity.idnn.encryptionpolicy

Change the identity number in these settings from the account's default identity number to the identity number you want. You will have to look around the file to discover which number it is. The order of settings within the file is not important, so there is no need to move them.

You can associate certificates with other identities by copying these four settings and changing the identity numbers and values.

Set Master Password

You are asked to set a master password to protect your own certificates stored in Thunderbird. If you do not set a master password, then someone who has access to your computer might be able steal and use your certificates.

You might choose different security measures to protect your stored certificates instead of a master password—for example, if you work in an environment where you could be observed typing a master password. However, leaving your stored certificates unprotected is probably a bad idea.

Certificates for other People and Organizations

Certificate files for other people and organizations can have various file name extensions: .crt, .cert, .cer, .pem and .der. Thunderbird imports certificates automatically from signed messages that you open, if the certificates are themselves signed by trusted certificate authorities (CAs).

When you import certificate files for other people and organizations, you specify the purposes that you allow the certificate to be used for. You do not normally have to do anything else to use the certificates.

You cannot export certificates for other people and organizations unless you use a separate program to export them. This are bugs 161275 and 315871. A workaround is to use the add-on Cert Viewer Plus. If you have set a master password, it does not apply to these certificates (because all the information in them is public).

Expired Certificate

Eventually the S/MIME certificate will expire (usually within a year). You need to keep an expired S/MIME certificate in order to read any messages that were encrypted and signed with it. Don't delete it when Thunderbird complains about an expired certificate, just add the new certificate.

You typically get a new S/MIME certificate for yourself in Firefox, export it using. Tools → Options → Advanced → Encryption → View Certificates → Your Certificates → Backup, and then import it into Thunderbird. It is recommended that you backup your expired certificate in the browser and then delete it before getting a new certificate for yourself.

Sending Mail

When you write a message, choose Options – Security to choose whether to sign it, encrypt it or both. To sign a message, you must have a certificate (.p12 because the private key is used) for the identity that you are using to send the message. The certificate must be stored in Thunderbird, and associated with your identity. Specify the identity by choosing the message's From address before you choose to sign the message. If you change the From address, the message will not be signed unless you again choose to sign it.

To encrypt a message, you must have a certificate (.cer because the public key is used) for each person who will receive the message, and also your own certificate for the identity that you are using to send the message (this is because the message will be encrypted so that only these people, including you, the sender, can decrypt it). All these certificates must be stored in Thunderbird, and your own certificate must be associated with your identity.

Icons in the status bar at the bottom of the message indicate whether it will be signed or encrypted when sent. The icons are smaller versions of those in the section below. To see information about the message's security, click one of the icons or choose: View → Message Security Info (in the default theme it is not obvious that the icons are clickable).

The message is signed or encrypted when you send it or save it as a draft. If you edit the draft, you must set the message's security features again.

Invalid Certificate

When trying to send a digitally signed or encrypted message, the certificate used for signing/encryption will be validated. It is possible that you receive an error at this stage that prevents you from sending or storing a draft of this message. This error occurs, if the certificate you are using is not fully trusted. In Thunderbird, you will receive the following error message:

Sending of message failed. Unable to sign message. Please check that the certificates specified in Mail & Newsgroups Account Settings for this mail account are valid and trusted.

To resolve this issue follow these steps:

- Go to the security preferences and view the certificate you were about to use for signing/encryption.

- Change to the details tab and look at the certificate hierarchy: you will see your certificate at the lowest node in the tree. The node at the top is the root CA.

- Verify whether all parent nodes of the certificate are in your list of trusted CAs, and whether they can be used to identify mail users.

Receiving Mail

When you receive a signed or encrypted message, you see one or two icons in the message's header area (but only if the header area is not collapsed).

In the default theme in Thunderbird 2, the icons are:

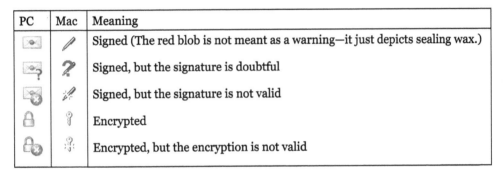

PC	Mac	Meaning
		Signed (The red blob is not meant as a warning—it just depicts sealing wax.)
		Signed, but the signature is doubtful
		Signed, but the signature is not valid
		Encrypted
		Encrypted, but the encryption is not valid

Message Authentication Code

MAC is used as a proof in symmetric key cryptography, which then is added to the end of the cryto messgae. At the receiver point, the receiver decrypt the message, generate a MAC from it and compare with the received MAC one. The integrity of the message can be guarrated practically in the case of the same recieved and computed MACs. A good illustration:

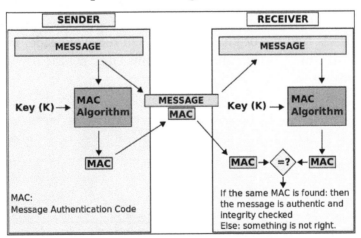

MAC description.

Based on the name, the MAC is used for authentication. Moreover, it is used to check the integrity and to become sure regarding non-repudiation of the message.

- MAC has a lower length in comparison with the plaintext. Thus, it is not unique like hash function. In other words, two different plaintexts may have the same MAC values. However, the likelihood of this occurrence is very low and thus it can be used for authentication and integrity.

- In comparison with checksum, a private key is used to generate MAC. So it cannot be regenerated by an imaginary intruder, who has an oracle who decrypts the crypt massage.

- A good comparion between cryptography hash functions and MAC:

```
Cryptographic primitive | Hash |   MAC   | Digital
Security Goal           |      |         | signature
------------------------+------+---------+-------------
Integrity               | Yes  |   Yes   |   Yes
Authentication          | No   |   Yes   |   Yes
Non-repudiation         | No   |   No    |   Yes
------------------------+------+---------+-------------
Kind of keys            | none | symmetric| asymmetric
                        |      |   keys   |   keys
```

Comparion of hash, MAC and digital signature.

Apart from intruders, the transfer of message between two people also faces other external problems like noise, which may alter the original message constructed by the sender. To ensure that the message is not altered there's this cool method MAC.

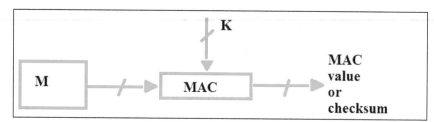

MAC stands for Message Authentication Code. Here in MAC, sender and receiver share same key where sender generates a fixed size output called Cryptographic checksum or Message Authentication code and appends it to the original message. On receiver's side, receiver also generates the code and compares it with what he/she received thus ensuring the originality of the message. These are components:

- Message,

- Key,

- MAC algorithm,

- MAC value.

There are different types of models of Message Authentication Code (MAC) as following below:

- MAC without encryption: This model can provide authentication but not confidentiality as anyone can see the message.

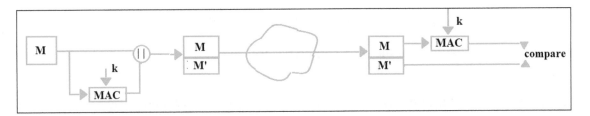

- Internal Error Code: In this model of MAC, sender encrypts the content before sending it through network for confidentiality. Thus this model provides confidentiality as well as authentication.

M' = MAC(M, k)

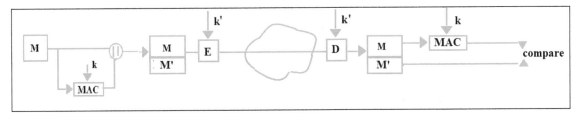

- External Error Code: For cases when there is an alteration in message, we decrypt it for waste, to overcome that problem, we opt for external error code. Here we first apply MAC on the encrypted message 'c' and compare it with received MAC value on the receiver's side and then decrypt 'c' if they both are same, else we simply discard the content received. Thus it saves time.

c = E(M, k')

M' = MAC(c, k)

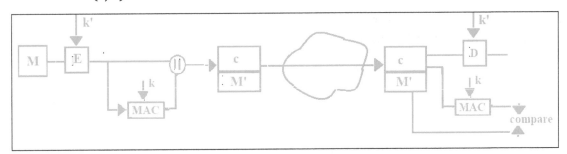

Problems in MAC: If we do reverse engineering we can reach plain text or even the key. Here we have mapped input to output, to overcome this we move on to hash functions which are "One way".

MAC Algorithms based on PRF

It is possible to create secure MAC algorithms using a secure pseudorandom function (PRF).

Having a pseudorandom function F: (K x X) $\rightarrow$ Y one can define a pair of secure MAC algorithms (S, V) as:

$$S(k, m) := F(k, m)$$

- $V(k, m, t)$: returns a value true if $t = F(k, m)$ or false otherwise.

- One should consider that the set Y should be large enough that a probability of guessing the result of the F function would be negligible.

For example, to encrypt a 16 byte long message one can use the AES encryption algorithm or any other similar symmetric cipher that operates on data blocks of size of 16 bytes.

CBC MAC

CBC MAC is based on a pseudorandom function (for convenience called F). It works similarly to encryption performed in the CBC mode, with a difference that intermediate values are not returned. Moreover, after encryption of the last data block, one additional encryption of the current result is performed using the second secret key.

The additional encryption is performed to protect the calculated code. The whole process, including the last additional step, is often referred to as ECBC MAC (Encrypted MAC), in contrast to the previous algorithm steps called Raw CBC MAC.

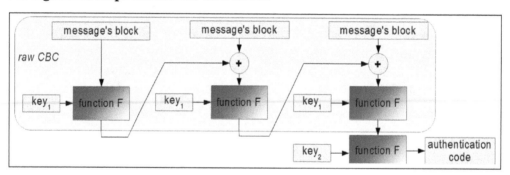

Without the last algorithm step (that is, without encryption using the second key), an intruder could attack CBC MAC security using a chosen-plaintext attack:

- The intruder chooses a message m of size of one block.

- The intruder obtains a value of authentication code of the message from the attacked system: $t = F(k, m)$.

- At this moment, the attacker can determine a value of authentication code of the message m_1 of the size of two blocks $m_1 = (m, t \text{ XOR } m)$:

$$\text{awCBC}(k, m_1) = \text{rawCBC}(k, (m, t \text{ XOR } m)) = F(k, F(k, m) \text{ XOR } (t \text{ XOR } m))$$
$$= F(k, t \text{ XOR } (t \text{ XOR } m)) = t$$

CBC MAC can protect a message of any length, from one to many blocks. To ensure security, while using CBC MAC one should change the secret key every some time. It can be proved that after sending the number of messages that is equal roughly to the square of the number of all possible values of data blocks, the key is no longer safe.

The last data block should be filled up to the full length using previously agreed bits. The additional bits should clearly determine the end of the original message to prevent attackers from using a potential ambiguity. A popular method of aligning the length of the last block is to append an additional bit equal to 1 and then filling the rest of the block up with bits equal to 0. If there is not enough free space in the last block, one should add one more extra block and fill it with the additional padding bits.

For comparison, adding only zeros would cause ambiguity where is the last bit of the broadcast message (because the original message may have zeros as last bits of data). Furthermore, a lot of messages with different contents that only differ in the number of zeros at the end, would have the same authentication codes. This situation would break safety rules of message encoding.

ECBC MAC is used in various applications, for example in banking systems. It is often based on the AES algorithm, that is used as F function.

NMAC

The NMAC algorithm (*Nested MAC*) is similar to the CBC MAC algorithm. It uses a slightly different pseudorandom function F. The function F returns numbers that are correct values of secret keys (thus, not the values of data blocks).

As in the case of CBC MAC, after encryption of the last data block, one additional encryption of the result is performed, using the second secret encryption key. Because the previous result of encryption of the last data block consists of the same amount of bits as the secret key, an additional sequence of bits (a fix pad) should be append, to assure that the result has the same size as data blocks. NMAC is usually used in systems, where the length of data blocks is much bigger than the size of secret keys.

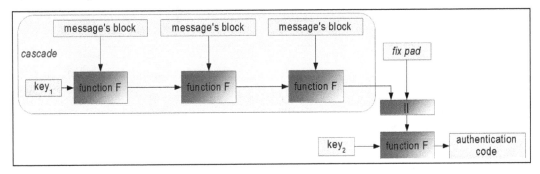

The last additional encryption is performed to protect the calculated code, as in the case of CBC MAC. During encryption the subsequent blocks without the last step of NMAC, the algorithm is commonly referred to as a Cascade.

Without the last step of the algorithm (that is, without encryption using the second key), an intruder would be able to append any number of blocks to the intercepted message with the correctly calculated authentication code. Then, he could calculate a new authentication code and attach it to the modified message. As input to the first new added function F, the attacker would use the original authentication code of the original message.

To ensure NMAC security, one should change the secret key from time to time. It can be proved that after sending the number of messages equal roughly to the square of the number of all possible values of secret keys, the key is no longer safe.

The NMAC algorithm uses the same methods for adding padding bits to the end of the last incomplete message block, as the CBC MAC algorithm.

CMAC

The CMAC algorithm is similar to the previously described CBC MAC algorithm. Is uses the same pseudorandom function F, which returns numbers that are elements of the set of all possible values of data blocks.

Instead of the last additional encryption that uses a second key, CMAC uses two additional keys that are added to input bits to the last block of F function. Depending on whether the last message block is completely filled up with data bits, or it must be filled up with a previously determined sequence of padding characters, the corresponding encryption key should be used.

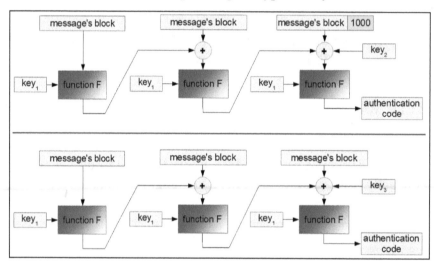

Adding the additional key in the last encryption step protects against appending new blocks of modified messages by a potential intruder. It is not necessary to use an additional encryption by the F function, unlike in other MAC algorithms. Thanks to this solution, there is no need to add an additional block to make room for padding (it is enough to choose the correct additional key).

CMAC is considered to be secure. It provides a safe way for message authentication. It is certified for example by the American institute NIST.

PMAC

The PMAC algorithm (*Parallel MAC*) can be performed using many threads at time (that require sequential processing of data blocks).

PMAC uses two secret encryption keys. The first secret key is used in P functions. All P functions receive also the subsequent numbers of the additional counter. Output bits of P functions are added XOR to data blocks. The result is encrypted by a pseudorandom function F, that uses the second secret key. The P function should be uncomplicated and it should work much faster than F functions.

Output bits from all F functions and output bits from the last data block (which is not encrypted by the F function) are added XOR together, then the result is encrypted using the F function algorithm, with the second secret encryption key.

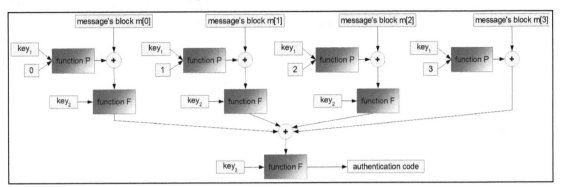

As usual, it can be proved that PMAC is secure, if the secret key is changed from time to time. A new key should be created after sending the number of messages that is equal roughly to the square of the number of all possible values of data blocks.

PMAC allows to update authentication codes easily and quickly, in a case when one of the message block was replaced by a new one. For example, if a block m[x] is replaced by m'[x], then the following calculations should be performed:

$$\text{tag'} = F(k_2, (F^{-1}(k_2, \text{tag}) \text{ XOR } F(k_2, m[x] \text{ XOR } P(k_1, x)) \text{ XOR } F(k_2, m'[x] \text{ XOR } P(k_1, x)))$$

One-time MAC

Similar to one-time encryption, one can define a one-time MAC algorithm, which provides security against potential attacks and it is generally faster than other message authentication algorithms based on PFR functions.

One-time MAC is a pair of algorithms (S, V):

- $S(m, k_1, k_2) := P(m, k_1) + k_2 \pmod q$: returns an authentication code t.

- $V(m, k_1, k_2, t)$: returns a value true or false depending on the correctness of the examined authentication code t.

where,

- q is a large prime (about 2^{128}),

- m is a message that contains L blocks of size of 128 bits,

- k_1, k_2 are two secret keys; each of them has value from the interval [1, q],

- $P(m, x) = m[L] \times x^L + ... + m[1] \times x$ *is a polynomial of degree L.*

It can be proved that two messages secured by using the same keys are indistinguishable for potential observers.

Carter-Wegman MAC

The construction of Carter-Wegman MAC is based on the idea of one-time MAC. It is extended by a pseudorandom function to allow using one secret key many times for subsequent messages.

Having a secure one-time MAC (S, V) defined over sets (M, K_J, T) and a secure pseudorandom function F: $K_F \ x\{0,1\}^n \rightarrow \{0,1\}^n$, one can define a pair of algorithms Carter-Wegman MAC.

- $S_{C-W}\left(m, k_F, k_J\right) := \left(r, F\left(k_F, r\right) \ XOR \ S\left(m, k_J\right)\right)$: returns an authentication code that is a pair $\left(r, t_{C-W}\right)$.

- $V_{C-W}\left(m, k_J, F\left(k_F, r\right) \ XOR \ t_{C-W}\right)$: returns true or false depending on the correctness of the examined authentication code $\left(r, t_{C-W}\right)$.

where,

- k_J, k_F are two secret keys of sets k_J and k_F,

- T is a set of all possible values of authentication codes of the one-time MAC algorithm (of length of n bits),

- r is a random number of length of n bits,

- $\left(r, t_{C-W}\right)$ is a value of an authentication code of the Carter-Wegman algorithm (of length of 2n bits).

HMAC

HMAC is a popular system of checking message integrity, which is quite similar to NMAC. The HMAC algorithm uses one-way hash functions to produce unique mac values.

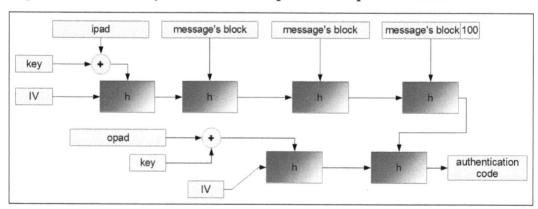

The input parameters ipad and opad are used to modify the secret key. They may have various values assigned. It is recommended to choose the values that would make both inputs to the hash functions look as dissimilar as possible (that is, that modify the secret key in two different ways). Using a secure hash function (that means the function which doesn't produce the same outputs for different input data) guarantees the security of the HMAC algorithm.

Secure Channel

A secure channel provides a secure communication path between the following security principals:

- A workstation or member server and a domain controller (DC) in the same domain.

- DCs in the same domain.

- DCs in different domains.

A secure channel always involves a DC. Think of a secure channel as the enabler of secure communication between machines and their trusted authority in the same domain, and between the trusted authorities of different domains. Secure in this context means providing authentication of the requestor and confidentiality, integrity, and data-authentication services for the data sent across the channel.

Different Types of Secure Channel

Basically there are three types of secure channels. The first one is for communication between clients in a domain and domain controllers. This type of secure channel is established between a client computer and a domain controller in a domain.

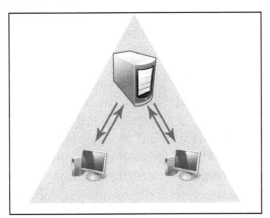

The second type of secure channel is responsible to establish a secure communication between domain controllers of a source domain and domain controllers of a trusted domain.

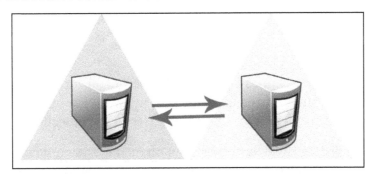

And the last one is responsible for establishing a secure path between domain controllers in the same domain.

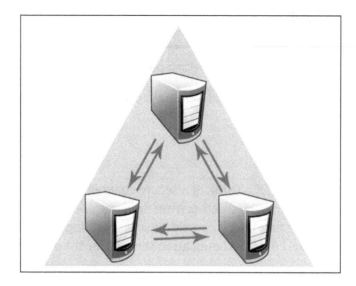

How Secure Channel Operates?

Different credentials are used during establishing a secure channel for each type. It is a misunderstanding, believed by many, that during the establishment of a secure channel, a user account is authenticated. The only account that is used in this process is the computer account of the requester. Since Active Directory has an automatic mechanism for computer accounts and their represented passwords.

Every computer account in Active Directory needs authentication and this requires a password. Once the computer is joined to a domain it will propose a password for its authentication in Active Directory. This mechanism is completely automated and Active Directory has no responsibility in this process. By default the machine account password change is initiated by computer itself every 30 days. However you can modify this value from Group Policy by navigating to *Computer Configuration → Windows Settings → Security Settings → Local Policies → Security Options → Domain* member: maximum machine account password age and specify your value. It is worth mentioning that computer accounts passwords do not expire in Active Directory. They are exempted from domain password policy.

The service responsible for establishing secure channel is NetLogon. When the computer is started and as soon as the Netlogon service becomes available it will start to establish a secure channel between the computer and domain controller. There are three important parameters which Netlogon will use during this process:

- ScavengeInterval: It determines how often the NetLogon service checks the password expiration on secure channels. Default value is 15 minutes. For an overview of other responsibilities of this parameter you can refer to the Useful Links section.

- MaximumPasswordAge: It determines how often the system changes the computer account password of the local computer. Default value is 30 days.

- DisablePasswordChange: You can prevent automatic password changes by setting the value of this entry to 1. Default value is 0.

If you need to change the above values, you can modify them using the methods below:

- DisablePasswordChange: HKLM $\rightarrow$ SYSTEM $\rightarrow$ CurrentControlSet $\rightarrow$ Services $\rightarrow$ NetLogon $\rightarrow$ Parameters Computer Configuration $\rightarrow$ windows Settings $\rightarrow$ Security settings $\rightarrow$ Local Policies $\rightarrow$ Security Options $\rightarrow$ Domain member: disable machine account Password changes.

- ScavengeInterval: HKLM $\rightarrow$ SYSTEM $\rightarrow$ CurrentControlSet $\rightarrow$ Services $\rightarrow$ NetLogon $\rightarrow$ Parameters Computer Configuration $\rightarrow$ Administrative Templates $\rightarrow$ System $\rightarrow$ Netlogon $\rightarrow$ Scavenge Interval.

- MaximumPasswordAge: HKLM $\rightarrow$ SYSTEM $\rightarrow$ CurrentControlSet $\rightarrow$ Services $\rightarrow$ NetLogon $\rightarrow$ Parameters Computer Configuration $\rightarrow$ windows Settings $\rightarrow$ Security settings $\rightarrow$ Local Policies $\rightarrow$ Security Options $\rightarrow$ Domain member: maximum machine account Password age.

When the NetLogon service starts, the ScavengeInterval service checks if the password is not older than MaximumPasswordAge. Otherwise it attempts to change the computer password. After finding a domain controller, client and server will create a secure channel by exchanging and validating challenge and response. The process is as follows:

- Client invokes the NetrServerReqChallanger() in order to request a challenge from the server. Also it sends a client challenge and computer name and domain controller name to the domain controller.

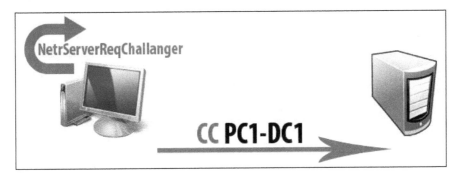

- Domain controller receives the request from the client and replies with his server challenge with NetrServerReqChallanger() to the client.

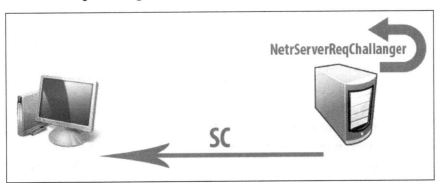

- At this point both client and domain controller generates a session key for secure channel.

- The client invokes NetrServerAuthenticate3() and generate a client response and send it to the domain controller.

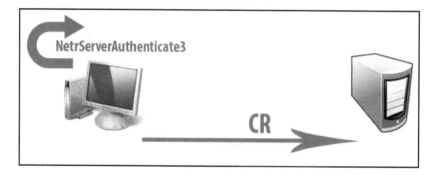

- The server receives the client response and will decide whether secure channel can be established or not based on client response and session key provided by both sides.

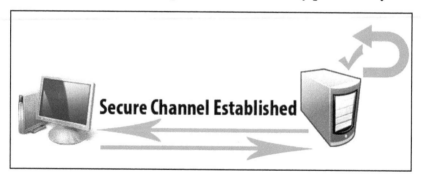

Broken Secure Channel

One of the most common problems indicating that you have a broken secure channel is the annoying *"the trust relationship between this workstation and the primary domain failed"* error. This error indicates that the machine is no longer able to establish a secure communication with a domain controller in its domain because the secret password which we talked about while ago is not set to the same value in domain controller. So as a result the authentication of computer account will fail due to this broken secure channel. But why this happens? There are quite many reasons behind this behavior. One of them is resetting the computer account in ADUC. When you reset your account, actually you just initiate a password change request but it is not replicated to the domain controller. So that is why you will not be able to logon after you reset a computer account. Deploy predefined images to the computer accounts is another reason for this.

Fixing the Broken Secure Channel

The the most user friendly solution in order to fix broken secure channel is to rejoin the computer into domain. It simply reestablishes the trust relationship to the domain. However it is a common solution for client computers, it is not practical when you face a broken secure channel between your CA server and domain due to impossibility of rejoining the certificate authority server. So in that case you have to choose another option. PowerShell v4.0 has a powerful CMDLET for automating this process with no need of rejoining the computer. You can run Reset-ComputerMachinePassword within a Powershell v4.0 console and have your secure channel fixed. The last option you have for restoring a broken secure channel is to use the old powerful Netdom command. You can use this tool in order to change the computer password and as a result the password will be synced on client and domain controller and you will face no issues related to secure channel. The key point in this solution is to have Kerberos Key Distribution Center service set as Manual and Disabled. After that you must remove the Kerberos cache either using a simple reboot or KerbTray.exe tool. Now you can reset the computer password using the command: netdom resetpwd → s:PDC Name → userd:Domain\User → password. As an example the command will look like this: netdom resetpwd → s:DC1 → userd:Contoso\administrator → password: Password Reboot the machine and enable the KDC service and have your broken secure channel fixed.

References

- Message-security: mozillazine.org, Retrieved 30 April, 2019

- Message-authentication-code-mac-algorithm: medium.com, Retrieved 29 June, 2019

- How-message-authentication-code-works: geeksforgeeks.org, Retrieved 14 July, 2019

- Mac , theory, eng: crypto-it.net, Retrieved 11 January, 2019

- Whats-secure-channel, windows-8: itprotoday.com, Retrieved 27 May, 2019

- Detailed-concepts-secure-channel-explained: microsoft.com, Retrieved 18 April, 2019

Cryptographic Protocols

The protocols which are used to perform security related functions and apply cryptographic methods are known as cryptographic protocols. Some of the common protocols are key exchange protocols and identification protocols. The topics elaborated in this chapter will help in gaining a better perspective about these cryptographic protocols.

A protocol is a set of actions that two or more entities need to perform in order to accomplish a task. All users take the actions step by step and successfully carry out the agreed procedure to the end.

Computers and other electronic devices use communications protocols to establish a connection and exchange data. Nowadays there are many protocols and communications standards which are recognized globally. Thanks to that, various different devices located in different places in the world may communicate with each other quite easily.

Cryptographic protocols are protocols that use cryptography. They have to guarantee that no entity will be able to gain more knowledge and access more privileges than it was designed in their algorithms. Cryptographic protocols include various types of encryption, message authentication or key agreement algorithms.

Arbitration Protocols

An additional entity, apart from communicating sides, takes part in arbitration protocols. The new entity is called an arbiter, and by definition, the arbiter is impartial, not interested in the communication and trusted by all the other sides. He acts like a bank officer, mediating in financial services.

Arbitration protocols simplify a lot of tasks which are performed by computers. The arbiter makes it easier to resolve disputes and exchange secret data safely. On the other hand, using arbitration protocols may sometimes be inconvenient:

- There is a need to find an arbiter, which may be located far from the other sides, and which would be trusted by all the other entities.

- The servers serving as arbiters must be financed and maintained.

- An arbiter is an obvious bottleneck of the transaction. A damaged, attacked or faulty arbiter is a serious problem for the communicating parties.

Most modern systems for transferring money, like credit cards and PayPal, require trusted intermediaries, like banks and credit card companies, to facilitate the transfer.

Dispute Protocols

A dispute protocol is a kind of arbitration protocol, in which the arbiter is involved only when it is really required. If there are not any problems, then the communicating parties perform the whole task and exchange information without the participation of the arbiter. On the other hand, if a problem occurs - an error, an unexpected circumstance or fraud - an arbiter is called for help. The arbiter has information and power to fix the situation.

Dispute protocols are cheaper and easier in use than arbitration protocols. Usually the fact of the arbiter's existence alone prevents fraud. Because the arbiter does not have to be involved in most communications, the major disadvantage of arbitration protocols is overcome.

Self-enforcing Protocols

In self-enforcing protocols the whole communication doesn't require trusted third parties. The algorithms are designed in a way that assures that any fraud attempt made by one side is immediately visible for others and they are able to prevent it, without suffering any loses.

Undoubtedly self-enforcing protocols have the largest number of advantages and they eliminate the need of involving additional entities. Unfortunately, no all operations can be carried out by using the protocols of this kind.

Attacking Protocols

In general, there are two types of attacks on protocols: passive and active.

- Passive attacks: The intruder may eavesdrop the communication but he is not able to interfere with the exchange of messages.

- Active attacks: The attacker tries to change the protocol - by sending new messages, modifying or removing the existing ones, or even altering the whole communication channel.

The main goal of a passive attack is only overhearing the communications. On the other hand, the goals of an active attack may vary, and the effects may usually be much more dangerous for the victims. In the most complex active attacks many intruders take part, attacking various points of the targeted system.

Key Exchange Protocol

Key exchange protocols are used in all secure communications. Virtual Private Networks, encrypted web traffic, SSH, all depend upon first exchanging a symmetric key. Despite this pivotal role in secure communications, many network security practitioners do not have a clear understanding of these protocols.

Diffie-Hellman

Diffie-Hellman, was the first publicly described asymmetric algorithm. This is a cryptographic protocol that allows two parties to establish a shared key over an insecure channel. In other words,

Diffie-Hellman is often used to allow parties to exchange a symmetric key through some unsecure medium, such as the internet. It was developed by Whitfield Diffie and Martin Hellman in 1976.

The Diffie-Hellman has two parameters called p and g. Parameter p is a prime number and parameter g (usually called a generator) is an integer less than p, with the following property: for every number n between 1 and p-1 inclusive, there is a power k of g such that n = gk mod p. Literally, g is able to generate all n's in the set of p to p-1 by raising g to some power k, mod p. To illustrate this concept, use the ubiquitous Alice and Bob examples. Alice generates a random private value a and Bob generates a random private value b. Both a and b are drawn from the set of integers. They derive their public values using parameters p and g and their private values. Alice's public value is ga mod p and Bob's public value is gb mod p. They exchange their public values.

Alice computes gab = (gb)a mod p, and Bob computes gba = (ga)b mod p.

Since,

gab = gba = k, Alice and Bob now have a shared secret key k.

This framework for establishing a shared key over an insecure medium is based on fundamental mathematics that makes it suitable for constructing efficient cryptographic systems with strong security properties. This is shown in figure below.

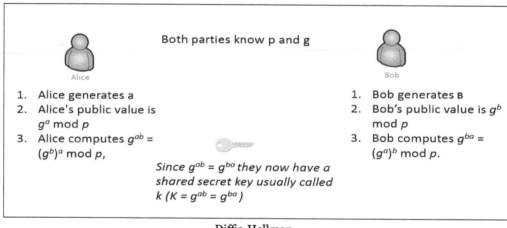

Both parties know p and g

Alice

1. Alice generates a
2. Alice's public value is g^a mod p
3. Alice computes g^{ab} = $(g^b)^a$ mod p,

Since $g^{ab} = g^{ba}$ they now have a shared secret key usually called k (K = g^{ab} = g^{ba})

Bob

1. Bob generates в
2. Bob's public value is g^b mod p
3. Bob computes g^{ba} = $(g^a)^b$ mod p.

Diffie-Hellman.

Diffie-Hellman was the first published asymmetric cipher and is widely used for key exchange. It is used in protocols such as IPSec and SSH to generate a shared key. There have been various improvements in Diffie-Hellman . Some, are significant departures from Diffie-Hellman, to minor modifications. Among the modifications to Diffie-Hellman are the addition of authentication.

Elgamal

It is based on the Diffie–Hellman key exchange. It was first described by Taher Elgamal in 1984. ElGamal is based on the Diffie-Hellman key exchange algorithm. It is used in some versions of PGP. The ElGamal algorithm has three components: the key generator, the encryption algorithm, and the decryption algorithm. Keep with the format we have used so far, that of using Alice and Bob.

Alice generates an efficient description of a multiplicative cyclic group G of order q with generator g. A cyclic group is a group that is generated by a single element, in this case that is the generator g. With a multiplicative cyclic group, each element can be written as some power of g.

Next,

Alice chooses a random from x from a set of numbers {0,...,q-1}.

Then, Alice computes h = gx. Remember g is the generator for the group and x is a random number from within the group. h, G, q, and g are the public key, x is the private key. If Bob wants encrypt a message m with the public key Alice generated, the following process is done:

Bob generates a random number y is chosen from {0,..,q-1}. Y is often called an 'ephemeral key'.

Next, Bob will calculate c1. That calculation is simple: c1 = g^y next a shared secret s =h^y is computed. The message m is converted to m' of G. Next Bob must calculate c2. That calculation is relatively easy: c2 = m' * s. Bob can now send c1 and c2 = as the encrypted text'.

To decrypt a message m with the public key the first person generated, the following process is done:

- The recipient calculates s = $c1^x$.

- The then the recipient calcualtes m' = c2 * s^{-1}.

- Finally, m' is converted back to the plain text m.

The structure should look somewhat similar to Diffie-Hellman . The algorithm has a similar basic structure.

ElGamal is based on the difficulty of solving the discrete logarithm problem within a cyclic group.

MQV

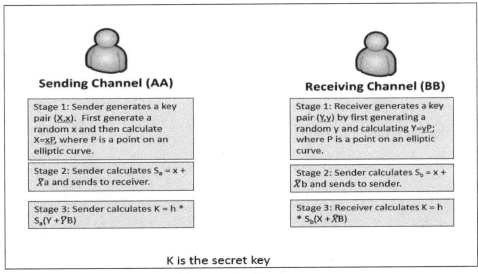

K is the secret key

Menezes–Qu–Vanstone.

Like ElGamal, MQV (Menezes–Qu–Vanstone) is a protocol for key agreement that is based on Diffie–Hellman. It was first proposed by Menezes, Qu and Vanstone in 1995, then modified in 1998. MQV is incorporated in the public-key standard IEEE P1363.

The primary advantage MQV has over Diffie-Hellman is that MQV is authenticated. Though there now exist variations of Diffie-Hellman that are authenticated, the original protocol was not. There are also variation of MQV that are based on an elliptic curve and are thus called Elliptic Curve MQV (ECMQV).

The Internet Key Exchange (IKEv1) Protocol, originally defined in RFC 2409, provides a method for creating keys used by IPsec tunnels. Protocol Security Descriptions for Media Streams (SDES), defined in RFC 4568, provides alternative methods for creating keys used to encrypt Real-time Transport Protocol (RTP) and Real-time Transport Control Protocol (RTCP) transactions.

IKEv1 Protocol

IKEv1 is specified by a series of RFCs, specifically RFCs 2401 through 2412. The most relevant are:

- RFC 2407: The Internet IP Security Domain of Interpretation for ISAKMP.

- RFC 2408: Internet Security Association and Key Management Protocol (ISAKMP).

- RFC 2409; The Internet Key Exchange (IKE).

- RFC 2412: Oakley Key Determination Protocol.

IKEv1 combines features of the Internet Security Association and Key Management Protocol (ISAKMP) and Oakley Key Determination Protocol in order to negotiate Security Associations (SA) for two communicating peers. IKEv1 also provides for key agreement using Diffie-Hellman.

IKEv1 uses two phases. Phase 1 is used to establish an ISAKMP Security Association for IKEv1 itself. Phase 1 negotiates the authentication method and symmetric encryption algorithm to be used. Phase 1 requires either six messages (main mode) or three messages (aggressive mode). Phase 2 negotiates the SA for two IPsec peers and is accomplished with three messages.

The initial IKEv1 implementation supports RFC 2409, Internet Key Exchange, and RFC 3706, A Traffic-based method of detecting dead internet key exchange (IKE) peers.

IKEv1 Configuration

IKEv1 configuration consists of five steps.

- Configure IKEv1 global parameters.

- Optionally, enable and configure Dead Peer Detection (DPD) Protocol.

- Configure IKEv1 interfaces.

- Configure IKEv1 Security Associations (SA).

- Assign the IKEv1 SA to an IPsec Security Policy.

IKEv1 Global Configuration

To configure global IKEv1 parameters:

- From superuser mode, use the following command sequence to access ike-config configuration mode. While in this mode, you configure global IKEv1 configuration parameters.

```
ORACLE# configure terminal

ORACLE(configure)# security

ORACLE(security)# ike

ORACLE(ike)# ike-config

ORACLE(ike-config)#
```

- Use the ike-version parameter to specify IKEv1.

- Use 1 to specify IKEv1 operations.

- Use the log-level parameter to specify the contents of the IKEv1 log.

Events are listed below in descending order of criticality.

- Emergency (most critical),

- Critical,

- Major,

- Minor,

- Warning,

- Notice,

- Info (least critical — the default),

- Trace (test/debug, not used in production environments),

- Debug (test/debug, not used in production environments),

- Detail (test/debug, not used in production environments).

In the absence of an explicitly configured value, the default value of info is used.

- Use the optional udp-port parameter to specify the port monitored for IKEv1 protocol traffic.

In the absence of an explicitly configured value, the default port number of 500 is used.

- Use the optional negotiation-timeout parameter to specify the maximum interval (in seconds) between Diffie-Hellman message exchanges.

In the absence of an explicitly configured value, the default specifies a 15 second timeout value.

- Use the optional event-timeout parameter to specify the maximum time (in seconds) allowed for the duration of an IKEv1 event, defined as the successful establishment of an IKE or IPsec Security Association (SA).

In the absence of an explicitly configured value, the default specifies a 60 second time span.

- Use the optional phase1-mode parameter to specify the IKE Phase 1 exchange mode.

During Phase 1 the IKE initiator and responder establish the IKE SA, using one of two available methods.

- Main mode: The default is more verbose, but provides greater security in that it does not reveal the identity of the IKE peers. Main mode requires six messages (3 requests and corresponding responses) to (1) negotiate the IKE SA, (2) perform a Diffie-Hellman exchange of cryptographic material, and (3) authenticate the remote peer.

- Aggressive mode: It is less verbose (requiring only three messages), but less secure in providing no identity protection, and less flexible in IKE SA negotiation.

In the absence of an explicitly configured value, the default (main mode) is used.

- Use the optional phase1-dh-mode parameter to specify the Diffie-Hellman Group used during IKE Phase 1 negotiation.

  - dh-group1: As initiator, propose Diffie-Hellman group 1 (768-bit primes, less secure).

  - dh-group2: As initiator, propose Diffie-Hellman group 2 (1024-bit primes, more secure).

  - first-supported: The default as responder, use the first supported Diffie-Hellman group proposed by initiator.

- If functioning as the IKE initiator, use the optional phase1-life-seconds parameter to specify the proposed lifetime (in seconds) for the IKE SA established during IKE Phase 1 negotiations.

Allowable values are within the range 1 through 999999999 (seconds) with a default of 3600 (1 hour).

This parameter can safely be ignored if functioning as a IKE responder.

- If functioning as the IKE responder, use the optional phase1-life-seconds-max parameter to specify the maximum time (in seconds) accepted for IKE SA lifetime during IKE Phase 1 negotiations.

Allowable values are within the range 1 through 999999999 (seconds) with a default of 86400 (1 day).

This parameter can safely be ignored if functioning as a IKE initiator.

- If functioning as the IKE initiator, use the optional phase2-life-seconds parameter to specify the proposed lifetime (in seconds) for an IPsec SA established during IKE Phase 2 negotiations.

Allowable values are within the range 1 through 999999999 (seconds) with a default of 28800 (8 hours).

This parameter can safely be ignored if functioning as a IKE responder.

- If functioning as the IKE responder, use the optional phase2-life-seconds-max parameter to specify the maximum time (in seconds) accepted for IPsec SA lifetime during IKE Phase 2 negotiations.

Allowable values are within the range 1 through 999999999 (seconds) with a default of 86400 (1 day).

This parameter can safely be ignored if functioning as a IKE initiator.

- Use the optional phase2-exchange-mode parameter to specify the Diffie-Hellman group used in Phase 2 negotiations.
    - dh-group1: Use Diffie-Hellman group 1 (768-bit primes, less secure).
    - dh-group2: Use Diffie-Hellman group 2 (1024-bit primes, more secure).
    - no-forward-secrecy: Use the same key as used during Phase 1 negotiation.
    - phase1-group: The default - use the same Diffie-Hellman group as used during Phase 1 negotiation.
- Use the shared-password parameter to specify the PSK (pre-shared key) used during authentication with the remote IKE peer.

The PSK is a string of ACSII printable characters no longer than 255 characters (not displayed by the ACLI).

This global PSK can be over-ridden by an interface-specific PSK.

- Use the optional dpd-time-interval parameter to specify the maximum period of inactivity before the DPD protocol is initiated on a specific endpoint.

Allowable values are within the range 1 through 999999999 (seconds) with a default of 0.

The default value, 0, disables the DPD protocol; setting this parameter to a non-zero value globally enables the protocol and sets the inactivity timer.

- Use done, exit, and verify-config to complete configuration of IKEv1 global parameters instance.

DPD Protocol Configuration

If you enabled the DPD protocol with the dpd-time-interval parameter, use the following procedure to create a DPD template, an operational set of DPD parameters, that you subsequently assign to one or more IKEv1 interfaces.

- Access the dpd-params configuration parameter.

```
ORACLE# configure terminal
ORACLE(configure)# security
ORACLE(security)# ike
ORACLE(ike)# dpd-params
ORACLE(dpd-params)#
```

- Name: It provide a unique identifier for this dpd-params instance.

- Max-loop: It specify the maximum number DPD peers examined every dpd-interval, whose value is established during IKv1 global configuration.

If CPU workload surpasses the threshold set by max-cpu-limit, this value is over-ridden by load-max-loop.

Allowable values are within the range 1 through 999999999 (endpoints) with a default of 100.

- Max-endpoints: It specify the maximum number of simultaneous DPD protocol negotiations supported when the CPU is not under load (as specified by the max-cpu-limit property).

If CPU workload surpasses the threshold set by max-cpu-limit, this value is over-ridden by load-max-endpoints.

Allowable values are within the range 1 through 999999999 (endpoints) with a default of 25.

- Max-cpu-limit": It specify a threshold value (expressed as a percentage of CPU capacity) at which DPD protocol operations are minimized to conserve CPU resources.

Allowable values are within the range 0, which disables DPD operations, through 100 (percent) with a default of 60.

- Load-max-loop: It specify the maximum number of endpoints examined every dpd-time-interval when the CPU is under load, as specified by the max-cpu-limit parameter.

Allowable values are within the range 1 through 999999999 (endpoints) with a default of 40. Ensure that the configured value is less than the value assigned to max-loop.

- Load-max-endpoints: It specify the maximum number of simultaneous DPD Protocol negotiations supported when the CPU is under load, as specified by the max-cpu-limit property.

Allowable values are within the range 1 through 999999999 (endpoints) with a default of 5. Ensure that the configured value is less than the value assigned to max-endpoints.

- Type done, exit, and verify-config to complete configuration of the DPD template instance.

IKEv1 Interface Configuration

To configure IKEv1 interface parameters:

- From superuser mode, use the following command sequence to access ike-config configuration mode. While in this mode, you configure IKEv1 interface parameters.

```
ORACLE# configure terminal

ORACLE(configure)# security

ORACLE(security)# ike

ORACLE(ike)# ike-interface

ORACLE(ike-interface)#
```

- Use the address parameter to specify the IPv4 address of the interface.

- Use the realm-id parameter to specify the realm that contains the IP address assigned to this IKEv1 interface.

- Use the ike-mode parameter to specify the operational mode, either responder (the default) or initiator.

- If DPD has been enabled at the global level, use the dpd-params-name parameter to assign a DPD template, an operational set of DPD parameters, to the current IKEv1 interface.

- If DPD has not been enabled, this parameter can be safely ignored.

- Use the optional shared-password parameter to assign an interface PSK.

This IKEv1-interface-specific value over-rides the global default value set at the IKE configuration level.

- Use done, exit, and verify-config to complete configuration of IKEv1 interface.

- Repeat above steps to configure additional IKEv1 interfaces.

IKEv1 Security Association Configuration

An IKEv1 SA identifies cryptographic material available for IPsec tunnel establishment. To configure IKEv1 SA parameters:

- From superuser mode, use the following command sequence to access ike-sainfo configuration mode. While in this mode, you configure global IKEv1 SAs.

```
ORACLE# configure terminal

ORACLE(configure)# security

ORACLE(security)# ike

ORACLE(ike)# ike-interface

ORACLE(ike-interface)#
```

- Use the required name parameter to provide a unique identifier for this ike-sainfo instance. The name enables the creation of multiple ike-sainfo instances.

- Use the security-protocol parameter to specify the IPsec security (authentication and encryption) protocols supported by this SA.

The following security protocols are available:

- Authentication Header (AH): The default value — as defined by RFC 4302, IP Authentication Header, which provides authentication integrity to include the mutual identification of remote peers, non-repudiation of received traffic, detection of data that has been altered in transit, and detection of data that has been replayed, that is copied and then re-injected into the data stream at a later time. Authentication services utilize the authentication algorithm specified by the auth-algo property.

- Encapsulating Security Payload (ESP) as defined by RFC 4303, IP Encapsulating Security Payload, which provides both authentication and privacy services. Privacy services utilize the encryption algorithm specified by the encryption-algo property.

- ESP-AUTH (also RFC 4303-based), which supports ESP's optional authentication.

- ESP-NULL (also RFC 4303-based) which proves NULL encryption. This option provides no privacy services, and is not recommended for production environments.

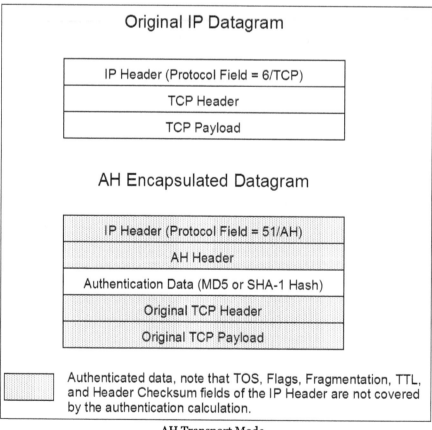

AH Transport Mode.

Original IP Datagram

IP Header (Protocol Field = 6/TCP)
TCP Header
TCP Payload

AH Encapsulated Datagram

New IP Header (Protocol Field = 51/AH)
AH Header
Authentication Data (MD5 or SHA-1 Hash)
Original IP Header
Original TCP Header
Original TCP Payload

Authenticated data, note that TOS, Flags, Fragmentation, TTL, and Header Checksum fields of the IP Header are not covered by the authentication calculation.

AH Tunnel Mode.

Original IP Datagram

IP Header (Protocol Field = 6/TCP)
TCP Header
TCP Payload

ESP Encapsulated Datagram

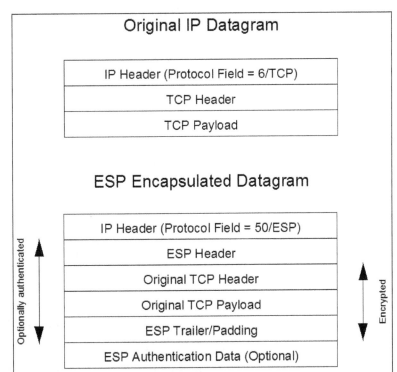

IP Header (Protocol Field = 50/ESP)
ESP Header
Original TCP Header
Original TCP Payload
ESP Trailer/Padding
ESP Authentication Data (Optional)

Optionally authenticated

Encrypted

ESP Transport Mode.

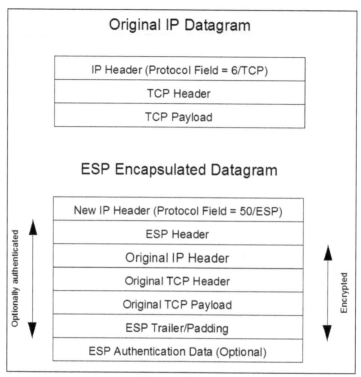

ESP Tunnel Mode.

```
ORACLE(ike-sainfo)# auth-algo md5

ORACLE(ike-sainfo)#
```

- Use the auth-algo parameter to specify the authentication algorithms supported by this SA.

The following authentication protocols are available:

- Message Digest Algorithm 5 (md5): As defined by RFC 1321, The MD5 Message-Digest Algorithm.

- Secure Hash Algorithm (sha): As defined by RFC 3174, Secure Hash Standard.

- Any (the default): It supports both MD5 and SHA-1.

```
ORACLE(ike-sainfo)# auth-algo md5

ORACLE(ike-sainfo)#
```

- Use the encryption-algo parameter to specify the encryption algorithms supported by this SA.

The following encryption protocols are available:

- Triple DES (3des): As defined by ANSI X.9.52 1998, Triple Data Encryption Algorithm Modes of Operation.

- Advanced Encryption Standard (aes): As defined by RFC 3565, Advanced Encryption Standard.

- NULL Encryption (null): As described in RFC 2410, *The NULL Encryption Algorithm and Its Use With IPsec.* This option provides no privacy services, and is not recommended for production environments.

- Any (the default): It supports all listed encryption protocols.

```
ORACLE(ike-sainfo)# encryption-algo aes

ORACLE(ike-sainfo)#
```

- Use the ipsec-mode parameter to specify the IPSec operational mode.

    - Transport mode (the default) provides a secure end-to-end connection between two IP hosts. Transport mode encapsulates the IP payload.

    - Tunnel mode provides VPN service where entire IP packets are encapsulated within an outer IP envelope and delivered from source (an IP host) to destination (generally a secure gateway) across an untrusted internet.

```
ORACLE(ike-sainfo)# ipsec-mode tunnel

ORACLE(ike-sainfo)#
```

- If ipsec-mode is tunnel, use the required tunnel-local-addr parameter to specify the IP address of the local IKEv1 interface that terminates the IPsec tunnel.

    - This parameter can safely be ignored if ipsec-mode is transport.

```
ORACLE(ike-sainfo)# tunnel-local-addr 192.169.204.14

ORACLE(ike-sainfo)#
```

- If ipsec-mode is tunnel, use the tunnel-remote-addr parameter to specify the IP address of the remote IKEv1 peer that terminates the IPsec tunnel.

Provide the remote IP address, or use the default wild-card value (*) to match all IP addresses.

This parameter can safely be ignored if ipsec-mode is transport.

```
ORACLE(ike-sainfo)# tunnel-remote-addr *

ORACLE(ike-sainfo)#
```

- Use done, exit, and verify-config to complete configuration of IKEv1 SA.

- Repeat above steps to configure additional IKEv1 SAs.

IPsec Security Policy Configuration

Use the following procedure to assign an IKEv1 SA to an existing IPsec Security Policy.

- From superuser mode, use the following command sequence to access ike-config configuration mode. While in this mode, you configure global IKEv1 configuration parameters.

```
ORACLE# configure terminal

ORACLE(configure)# security

ORACLE(security)# ipsec

ORACLE(ipsec)# security-policy

ORACLE(security-policy)#
```

- Use the required ike-sainfo-name parameter to assign an IKv1 SA to this IPsec Security Policy.

- Use done, exit, and verify-config to complete configuration of IPsec Security Policy.

Secure Real-time Transport Protocol

The Secure Real-Time Transport Protocol, as described in RFC 3711, *The Secure Real-time Transport Protocol (SRTP)*, provides a framework for the encryption and authentication of Real-time Transport Protocol (RTP) and RTP Control Protocol (RTCP) streams. Both RTP and RTCP are defined by RFC 3550, RTP: A Transport Protocol for Real-Time Applications.

Encryption ensures that the call content and associated signaling remains private during transmission. Authentication ensures that: (1) received packets are from the purported source, (2) packets are not been tampered with during transmission, and (3) a packet has not been replayed by a malicious server.

Protocol

While the RFC 3711 framework provides encryption and authentication procedures and defines a set of default cryptographic transforms required for RFC compliance, it does not specify a key management protocol to securely derive and exchange cryptographic keys. RFC4568, Protocol (SDP) Security Description for Media Streams, defines such a protocol specifically designed to exchange cryptographic material using a newly defined SDP crypto attribute. Cryptographic parameters are established with only a single message or in single round-trip exchange using the offer/answer model defined in RFC 3264.

Release S-C6.2.0 provides support for an initial SDP Security Descriptions (SDES) implementation that generates keys used to encrypt SRTP/SRTCP packets. Authentication of packets will be added to a subsequent release.

A sample SDP exchange is,

The SDP offerer sends:

```
v=0

o=sam 2890844526 2890842807 IN IP4 10.47.16.5

s=SRTP Discussion

i=A discussion of Secure RTP
```

```
u=http://www.example.com/seminars/srtp.pdf

e=marge@example.com (Marge Simpson)

c=IN IP4 168.2.17.12

t=2873397496 2873404696

m=audio 49170 RTP/SAVP 0

a=crypto:1 AES_CM_128_HMAC_SHA1_80

inline:WVNfX19zZW1jdGwgKCkgewkyMjA7fQp9CnVubGVz|2^20|1:4
```

The SDP answerer replies:

```
v=0

o=sam 2890844526 2890842807 IN IP4 10.47.16.5

s=SRTP Discussion

i=A discussion of Secure RTP

u=http://www.example.com/seminars/srtp.pdf

e=marge@example.com (Marge Simpson)

c=IN IP4 168.2.17.12

t=2873397496 2873404696

m=audio 49170 RTP/SAVP 0

a=crypto:1 AES_CM_128_HMAC_SHA1_80

inline:WVNfX19zZW1jdGwgKCkgewkyMjA7fQp9CnVubGVz|2^20|1:4
```

The media-level SDP attribute, crypto, describes the cryptographic suite, key parameters, and session parameters for the preceding unicast media line. The crypto attribute takes the form:

> a=crypto: tag crypto-suite key-parameter [session-parameters]

Tag

The tag field contains a decimal number that identifies a specific attribute instance. When an offer contains multiple crypto attributes, the answer uses the tag value to identify the accepted offer.

In the sample offer the tag value is 1.

Crypto-suite

The crypto-suite field contains the encryption and authentication algorithms, either AES_CM_128_HMAC_SHA1_80 orAES_CM_128_HMAC_SHA1_32.

The key-parameter field contains one or more sets of keying material for the selected crypto-suite and it has following format.

> "inline:" <key||salt> ["|" lifetime] ["|" MKI ":" length]

Inline is a method and specifies that the crypto material to be used by the offerer is transmitted via the SDP. The key||salt field contains a base64-encoded concatenated master key and salt.

Assuming the offer is accepted, the key || salt provides the crypto material used by the offerer to encrypt SRTP/SRTCP packets, and used by the answerer to decrypt SRTP/SRTCP packets.

Conversely the key||salt contained in the answer to the offer provides the crypto material used by the answerer to encrypt SRTP/SRTCP packets, and used by the offerer to decrypt SRTP/SRTCP packets.

The lifetime field optionally contains the master key lifetime (maximum number of SRTP or SRTCP packets encoded using this master key).

In the sample offer the lifetime value is 1,048, 576 (2^{20}) packets.

The MKI: length field optionally contains the Master Key Index (MKI) value and the MKI length.

The MKI is used only when the offer contains multiple keys; it provides a means to differentiate one key from another. The MKI takes the form of an integer, followed by its byte length when included in SRTP/SRTCP packets.

In the sample offer the MKI value is 1 with a length of 4 bytes.

The session-parameters field contains a set of optional parameters that may override SRTP session defaults for the SRTP and SRTCP streams.

- UNENCRYPTED_SRTP — SRTP messages are not encrypted.

- UNENCRYPTED_SRTCP — SRTCP messages are not encrypted.

- UNAUTHENTICATED_SRTP — SRTP messages are not authenticated.

When generating an initial offer, the offerer must ensure that there is at least one crypto attribute for each media stream for which security is desired. Each crypto attribute for a given media stream must contain a unique tag. The ordering of multiple crypto attributes is significant — the most preferred crypto suite is listed first.

Upon receiving the initial offer, the answerer must either accept one of the offered crypto attributes, or reject the offer in its entirety.

When an offered crypto attribute is accepted, the crypto attribute in the answer MUST contain the tag and crypto-suite from the accepted crypto attribute in the offer, and the key(s) the answerer will be using for media sent to the offerer.

The crypto-suite is bidirectional and specifies encryption and authentication algorithms for both ends of the connection. The keys are unidirectional in that one key or key set encrypts and decrypts traffic originated by the offerer, while the other key or key set encrypts and decrypts traffic originated by the answerer. The use of symmetric keying, where the same key is used for both encryption and decryption, mandates the key exchange between the offerer and the answerer.

Key exchange via text-based SDP is unacceptable in that malicious network elements could easily eavesdrop and obtain the plaintext keys, thus compromising the privacy and integrity of the encrypted media stream. Consequently, the SDP exchange must be protected by a security protocol such as IPsec or TLS.

Licensing and Hardware Requirements

SRTP/SRTCP support requires the presence of an IPsec NIU and an SSM (Security Service Module). No additional licences are required.

Operational Modes

SRTP topologies can be reduced to three basic topologies.

Single-ended SRTP Termination

Single-ended SRTP termination is illustrated in the following figure.

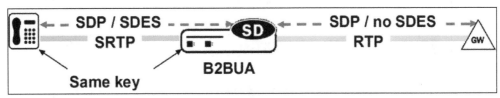

Single-ended SRTP Termination.

If SRTP is enabled for the inbound realm/interface, the Oracle Communications Session Border Controller handles the incoming call as specified by the Media Security Policy assigned to the inbound realm. If there is crypto attribute contained in the offer, the Oracle Communications Session Border Controller parses the crypto attributes and optional parameters, if any. If the offer contains a crypto attribute or attributes compatible with the requirements specified by the SDES profile assigned to the Media Security policy, it selects the most preferred compatible attribute. Otherwise, the Oracle Communications Session Border Controller rejects the offer. Before the SDP is forwarded to the called party, the Oracle Communications Session Border Controller allocates resources, established SRTP and SRTCP Security Associations and updates the SDP by removing the crypto attribute and inserting possibly NAT'ed media addresses and ports. At the same time, the original crypto attribute is also removed from the SDP.

Once the reply from the called party is received, the Oracle Communications Session Border Controller inserts appropriate crypto attribute(s) to form a new SDP, and forward the response back to the calling party.

Back-to-back SRTP Termination

Back-to-back SRTP termination is illustrated in the following figure.

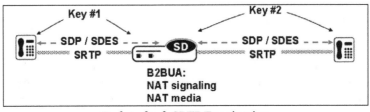

Back-to-back SRTP Termination.

Initial processing is similar to the single-ended termination. Before forwarding the request to the called party, the Oracle Communications Session Border Controller replaces the original crypto attribute with a new one whose crypto attribute conforms to the media security policy for the outbound realm/interface. Upon receiving the answer from the called party, the Oracle Communications Session Border Controller accepts or rejects it, again based upon conformity to the media security policy. If accepted, the Oracle Communications Session Border Controller replaces the original crypto attribute from the called party with its own to form a new SDP, which it forwards back to the calling party. At this point, SRTP media sessions are established on both sides for both calling and called parties.

SRTP Pass-thru

SRTP pass-thru is illustrated in the following figure.

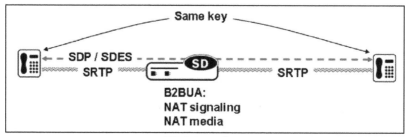

SRTP Pass-thru.

If the media security policy specifies pass-through mode, the Oracle Communications Session Border Controller does not alter the crypto attribute exchange between the calling and the called party; the attribute is transparently passed.

SDES Configuration

SDES configuration consists of the following steps:

- Create one or more SDES profiles which specify parameter values negotiated during the offer/answer exchange.

- Create one or more Media Security Policies that specify key exchange protocols and protocol-specific profiles.

- Assign a Media Security Policy to a realm.

- Create an interface-specific Security Policy.

SDES Profile Configuration

An SDES profile specifies the parameter values offered or accepted during SDES negotiation.

To configure SDES profile parameters:

- From superuser mode, use the following command sequence to access sdes-profile configuration mode.

```
ORACLE# configure terminal

ORACLE(configure)# security

ORACLE(security)# media-security

ORACLE(media-security)# sdes-profile

ORACLE(sdes-profile)#
```

- Use the required name parameter to provide a unique identifier for this sdes-profile instance. The name enables the creation of multiple sdes-profile instances.

- Use the crypto-suite parameter to select the encryption and authentication algorithms accepted or offered by this sdes-profile. Allowable values are:

  ○ AES_CM_128_HMAC_SHA1_80 (the default value).

  ○ It supports AES/128 bit key for encryption and HMAC/SHA-1 80-bit digest for authentication.

  ○ AES_CM_128_HMAC_SHA1_32.

  ○ It supports AES/128 bit key for encryption and HMAC/SHA-1 32-bit digest for authentication.

- Because SRTP authentication is not currently supported, ignore the srtp-auth parameter.

- Use the srtp-encrypt parameter to enable or disable the encryption of RTP packets.

  With encryption enabled, the default condition, the Oracle Communications Session Border Controller offers RTP encryption, and rejects an answer that contains an UNENCRYPTED_SRTP session parameter in the crypto attribute.

  With encryption disabled, the Oracle Communications Session Border Controller does not offer RTP encryption and includes an UNENCRYPTED_SRTP session parameter in the SDP crypto attribute; it accepts an answer that contains an UNENCRYPTED_SRTP session parameter.

- Use the srtcp-encrypt parameter to enable or disable the encryption of RTCP packets.

  With encryption enabled, the default condition, the Oracle Communications Session Border Controller offers RTCP encryption, and rejects an answer that contains an UNENCRYPTED_SRTCP session parameter in the crypto attribute.

  With encryption disabled, the Oracle Communications Session Border Controller does not offer RTCP encryption and includes an UNENCRYPTED_SRTCP session parameter in the SDP crypto attribute; it accepts an answer that contains an UNENCRYPTED_SRTCP session parameter.

- Use the mki parameter to enable or disable the inclusion of the MKI: length field in the SDP crypto attribute. The master key identifier (MKI) is an optional field within the SDP crypto attribute that differentiates one key from another. MKI is expressed as a pair of decimal numbers in the form: |mki:mki_length| where mki is the MKI integer value and mki_ length is the length of the MKI field in bytes. For hardware-based platforms, the length value can be up to 32 bytes. For software-based platforms, the length value is 4 bytes.

- The MKI field is necessary only in topologies that may offer multiple keys within the crypto attribute.

  ◦ Allowable values are enabled and disabled (the default).

  ◦ Enabled – an MKI field is sent within the crypto attribute (16 bytes maximum).

  ◦ Disabled – no MKI field is sent.

- Use done, exit, and verify-config to complete configuration of this SDES profile instance.

- Repeat above steps to configure additional SDES profiles.

Media Security Policy Configuration

Use the following procedure to create a Media Security Policy that specifies the role of the Oracle Communications Session Border Controller in the security negotiation. If the Oracle Communications Session Border Controller takes part in the negotiation, the policy specifies a key exchange protocol and SDES profile for both incoming and outgoing calls.

To configure media-security-policy parameters:

- From superuser mode, use the following command sequence to access media-sec-policy configuration mode.

```
ORACLE# configure terminal

ORACLE(configure)# security

ORACLE(security)# media-security

ORACLE(media-security)# media-sec-policy

ORACLE(media-sec-policy)#
```

- Use the required name parameter to provide a unique identifier for this media-sec-policy instance. The "name" enables the creation of multiple media-sec-policy instances.

- Use optional pass-thru parameter to enable or disable pass-thru mode. With pass-thru mode enabled, the User Agent (UA) endpoints negotiate security parameters between each other; consequently, the Oracle Communications Session Border Controller simply passes SRTP traffic between the two endpoints.

  With pass-thru mode disabled (the default state), the Oracle Communications Session Border Controller disallows end-to-end negotiation — rather the Oracle Communications Session Border Controller initiates and terminates SRTP tunnels with both endpoints.

- Use the outbound navigation command to move to media-sec-outbound configuration mode. While in this configuration mode you specify security parameters applied to the outbound call leg, that is calls sent by the Oracle Communications Session Border Controller.

- Use the protocol parameter to select the key exchange protocol. Select sdes for SDES key exchange.

- Use the profile parameter to specify the name of the SDES profile applied to calls sent by the Oracle Communications Session Border Controller.

- Use the mode parameter to select the real time transport protocol. Allowable values are rtp and srtp (the default). The "mode" identifies the transport protocol (RTP or SRTP) included in an SDP offer when this media-security-policy is in effect.

- Use the done and exit parameters to return to media-sec-policy configuration mode.

- Use the inbound navigation command to move to media-sec-inbound configuration mode. While in this configuration mode you specify security parameters applied to the inbound call leg, that is calls received by the Oracle Communications Session Border Controller.

- Use the protocol parameter to select the key exchange protocol. Select sdes for SDES.

- Use the profile parameter to specify the name of the SDES profile applied to calls received by the Oracle Communications Session Border Controller.

- Use the mode parameter to select the real time transport protocol. Allowable values are rtp and srtp (the default). The "mode" identifies the transport protocol (RTP or SRTP) accepted in an SDP offer when this media-security-policy is in effect.

- Use done, exit, and verify-config to complete configuration of this media security policy instance.

- Repeat above steps to configure additional media-security policies.

Assign the Media Security Policy to a Realm

To assign a media-security-policy to a realm:

- From superuser mode, use the following command sequence to access realm-config configuration mode. While in this mode, you assign an existing media-security-policy to an existing realm.

```
ORACLE# configure terminal

ORACLE(configure)# media-manager

ORACLE(media-manager)# realm-config

ORACLE(realm-config)# select

identifier:

1. access-12
```

```
...

...

selection: 1

ORACLE(realm-config)#
```

- Use the media-sec-policy parameter to assign the policy to the target realm.

- Use done, exit, and verify-config to complete assignment of the media-security-policy to the realm.

ACLI Example Configurations

The following section contain relevant sections of system configurations for basic operational modes.

Single-ended SRTP Termination Configuration

```
ORACLE# show running-config

...

...

...

sdes-profile

    name                    sdes1

    crypto-list             AES_CM_128_HMAC_SHA1_80

    srtp-auth               enabled

    srtp-encrypt            enabled

    srtcp-encrypt           enabled

    mki                     disabled

    key

    salt

    last-modified-by        admin@console

    last-modified-date      2009-11-16 15:37:13

media-sec-policy

    name                    msp2

    pass-through            disabled

    inbound

        profile             sdes1
```

```
        mode                srtp
        protocol            sdes
    outbound
        profile             sdes1
        mode                srtp
        protocol            sdes
    last-modified-by        admin@console
    last-modified-date      2009-11-16 15:37:51
...
...
...
realm-config
    identifier              peer
    description
    addr-prefix             192.168.0.0/16
    network-interfaces      M00:0
    mm-in-realm             enabled
    mm-in-network           enabled
    mm-same-ip              enabled
    mm-in-system            enabled
    bw-cac-non-mm           disabled
    msm-release             disabled
    qos-enable              disabled
    generate-UDP-checksum   disabled
    max-bandwidth           0
    fallback-bandwidth      0
    max-priority-bandwidth  0
    max-latency             0
    max-jitter              0
    max-packet-loss         0
    observ-window-size      0
    parent-realm
```

```
    dns-realm

    media-policy

    media-sec-policy          msp2

    in-translationid
...

...

...

    last-modified-by          admin@console

    last-modified-date        2009-11-10 15:38:19
```

Back-to-back SRTP Termination Configuration

```
ORACLE# show running-config

...

...

...

sdes-profile

    name                      sdes1

    crypto-list               AES_CM_128_HMAC_SHA1_80

    srtp-auth                 enabled

    srtp-encrypt              enabled

    srtcp-encrypt             enabled

    mki                       disabled

    key

    salt

    last-modified-by          admin@console

    last-modified-date        2009-11-16 15:37:13

media-sec-policy

    name                      msp2

    pass-through              disabled

    inbound

        profile               sdes1

        mode                  srtp
```

```
        protocol              sdes
    outbound
        profile               sdes1
        mode                  srtp
        protocol              sdes
    last-modified-by      admin@console
    last-modified-date    2009-11-16 15:37:51
...
...
...
realm-config
    identifier            peer
    description
    addr-prefix           192.168.0.0/16
    network-interfaces    M00:0
    mm-in-realm           enabled
    mm-in-network         enabled
mm-same-ip                enabled
    mm-in-system          enabled
    bw-cac-non-mm         disabled
    msm-release           disabled
    qos-enable            disabled
    generate-UDP-checksum disabled
    max-bandwidth         0
    fallback-bandwidth    0
    max-priority-bandwidth 0
    max-latency           0
    max-jitter            0
    max-packet-loss       0
    observ-window-size    0
    parent-realm
    dns-realm
```

```
      media-policy
      media-sec-policy      msp2
...
...
...
realm-config
      identifier            core
      description
      addr-prefix           172.16.0.0/16
      network-interfaces    M10:0
      mm-in-realm           enabled
      mm-in-network         enabled
      mm-same-ip            enabled
      mm-in-system          enabled
      bw-cac-non-mm         disabled
      msm-release           disabled
      qos-enable            disabled
      generate-UDP-checksum disabled
      max-bandwidth         0
      fallback-bandwidth    0
      max-priority-bandwidth 0
      max-latency           0
      max-jitter            0
      max-packet-loss       0
      observ-window-size    0
      parent-realm
      dns-realm
      media-policy
      media-sec-policy      msp2
      in-translationid
...
...
```

```
...
    last-modified-by              admin@console
    last-modified-date            2009-11-10 15:38:19
```

SRTP Pass-thru Configuration

```
ORACLE# show running-config

...

...

...

sdes-profile
    name                          sdes1
    crypto-list                   AES_CM_128_HMAC_SHA1_80
    srtp-auth                     enabled
    srtp-encrypt                  enabled
    srtcp-encrypt                 enabled
    mki                           disabled
    key
    salt
    last-modified-by              admin@console
    last-modified-date            2009-11-16 15:37:13
media-sec-policy
    name                          msp2
    pass-through                  enabled
    inbound
        profile                   sdes1
        mode                      srtp
        protocol                  sdes
    outbound
        profile                   sdes1
        mode                      srtp
        protocol                  sdes
    last-modified-by              admin@console
```

```
      last-modified-date              2009-11-16 15:37:51
...
...
...
realm-config
      identifier                      peer
      description
      addr-prefix                     192.168.0.0/16
      network-interfaces              M00:0
      mm-in-realm                     enabled
      mm-in-network                   enabled
      mm-same-ip                      enabled
      mm-in-system                    enabled
      bw-cac-non-mm                   disabled
      msm-release                     disabled
      qos-enable                      disabled
      generate-UDP-checksum           disabled
      max-bandwidth                   0
      fallback-bandwidth              0
      max-priority-bandwidth          0
      max-latency                     0
      max-jitter                      0
      max-packet-loss                 0
      observ-window-size              0
      parent-realm
      dns-realm
      media-policy
      media-sec-policy                msp2
...
...
...
realm-config
```

```
identifier                  core

description

addr-prefix                 172.16.0.0/16

network-interfaces          M10:0

mm-in-realm                 enabled

mm-in-network               enabled

mm-same-ip                  enabled

mm-in-system                enabled

bw-cac-non-mm               disabled

msm-release                 disabled

qos-enable                  disabled

generate-UDP-checksum       disabled

max-bandwidth               0

fallback-bandwidth          0

max-priority-bandwidth      0

max-latency                 0

max-jitter                  0

max-packet-loss             0

observ-window-size          0

parent-realm

dns-realm

media-policy

media-sec-policy            msp2

in-translationid

...

...

...

last-modified-by            admin@console

last-modified-date          2009-11-10 15:38:19
```

Security Policy

A Security Policy enables the Oracle Communications Session Border Controller to identify in-bound and outbound media streams that are treated as SRTP/SRTCP. The high-priority Security

Policy, p1, allows signaling traffic from source 172.16.1.3 to destination 172.16.1.10:5060. The lower-priority Security Policy, p2, matches media traffic with the same source and destination, but without any specific ports. Consequently, SIP signaling traffic (from local port 5060) go through, but the media stream will be handled by appropriate SRTP SA.

```
security-policy
    name                            p1
    network-interface               private:0
    priority                        0
    local-ip-addr-match             172.16.1.3
    remote-ip-addr-match            172.16.1.10
    local-port-match                5060
    remote-port-match               0
    trans-protocol-match            UDP
    direction                       both
    local-ip-mask                   255.255.255.255
    remote-ip-mask                  255.255.255.255
    action                          allow
    ike-sainfo-name
    outbound-sa-fine-grained-mask
        local-ip-mask               255.255.255.255
        remote-ip-mask              255.255.255.255
        local-port-mask             0
        remote-port-mask            0
        trans-protocol-mask         0
        valid                       enabled
        vlan-mask                   0xFFF
    last-modified-by                admin@console
    last-modified-date              2009-11-09 15:01:55

security-policy
    name                            p2
    network-interface               private:0
    priority                        10
    local-ip-addr-match             172.16.1.3
    remote-ip-addr-match            172.16.1.10
    local-port-match                0
```

```
    remote-port-match              0

    trans-protocol-match           UDP

    direction                      both

    local-ip-mask                  255.255.255.255

    remote-ip-mask                 255.255.255.255

    action                         ipsec

    ike-sainfo-name

    outbound-sa-fine-grained-mask

        local-ip-mask              0.0.0.0

        remote-ip-mask             255.255.255.255

        local-port-mask            0

        remote-port-mask           65535

        trans-protocol-mask        255

        valid                      enabled

        vlan-mask                  0xFFF

    last-modified-by               admin@console

    last-modified-date             2009-11-09 15:38:19
```

Modified ALCI Configuration Elements

The action parameter in security-policy configuration mode has been modified to accept additional values, srtp and srtcp.

- From superuser mode, use the following command sequence to access media-sec-policy configuration mode.

```
ORACLE# configure terminal

ORACLE(configure)# security

ORACLE(security)# ipsec

ORACLE(ipsec)# security-policy

ORACLE(security-policy)# action ?

<enumeration> action (default: ipsec)

ipsec, allow, discard, srtp, srtcp

ORACLE(security-policy)#
```

The show security command has been updated with an srtp option.

```
ORACLE# show security srtp

sad
```

```
spd

statistics

SRTP Statistics

status
```

The srtp option is similar to the ipsec option save for the sad sub-option that provides data for only SRTP SAs.

The show sa stats command has been updated with an srtp option.

```
ORACLE# show sa stats

<ENTER>      Show statistics summary of all Security Associations

<ike> Show statistics for IKE Security Associations

<ims-aka>    Show statistics for IMS-AKA Security Associations

<srtp>       Show statistics for SRTP Security Associations

sd# show sa stats srtp

20:06:24-114
```

SA Statistics	----	Lifetime ----	
	Recent	Total	PerMax
SRTP Statistics			
ADD-SA Req Rcvd	0	0	0
ADD-SA Success Resp Sent	0	0	0
ADD-SA Fail Resp Sent	0	0	0
DEL-SA Req Rcvd	0	0	0
DEL-SA Success Resp Sent	0	0	0
DEL-SA Fail Resp Sent	0	0	0
SA Added	0	0	0
SA Add Failed	0	0	0
SA Deleted	0	0	0
SA Delete Failed	0	0	0

Commitment Schemes

The functionality of a commitment scheme is commonly introduced by means of the following analogy. Suppose you need to commit to a certain value, but you do not want to reveal it right away. For example, the committed value is a sealed bid in some auction scheme. One way to do this is to write the value on a piece of paper, put it in a box, and lock the box with a padlock. The locked box is then given to the other party, but you keep the key. At a later time, you present the key to the other party who may then open the box, and check its contents.

An immediate application of commitment schemes is known as "coin flipping by telephone." Two parties, say A and B, determine a mutually random bit as follows. Party A commits to a random bit $b_A \in_R \{0, 1\}$ by sending a commitment on b_A to party B. Party B then replies by sending a random bit $b_B \in_R \{0, 1\}$ to A. Finally, party A opens the commitment and sends b_A to B. Both parties take $b = b_A \oplus b_B$ as the common random bit.

If at least one of the parties is honest, the resulting bit b is distributed uniformly at random, assuming that A and B cannot cheat when revealing their bits. Note that party B sees the commitment of A before choosing its bit b_B, so no information on bit b_A should leak from the commitment on b_A. Similarly, party A could try to influence the value of the resulting bit b (after seeing the bit b_B) by opening the commitment on b_A as a commitment on $1 - b_A$. Clearly, party A should not be able to "change its mind" in such a way.

Generating mutually random bits is a basic part of many protocols. Commitments are used as an auxiliary tool in many cryptographic applications, such as zero-knowledge proofs and secure multi-party computation.

A commitment scheme consists of two protocols, called commit and reveal, between two parties, usually called the sender and the receiver. In many cases, the protocols commit and reveal can be defined in terms of a single algorithm, requiring no interaction between the sender and receiver at all. Such commitment schemes are called non-interactive.

- Let commit: $\{0, 1\} k \times \{0, 1\}^* \to \{0, 1\}^*$ be a deterministic polynomial time algorithm, where k is a security parameter. A (non-interactive) commitment scheme consists of two protocols between a sender and a receiver:

- Commit Phase: A protocol in which the sender commits to a value $x \in \{0, 1\}^*$ by computing $C = $ commit (u, x), where $u \in_R \{0, 1\} k$, and sending C to the receiver. The receiver stores C for later use.

- Reveal Phase: A protocol in which the sender opens commitment $C = $ commit (u, x) by sending u and x to the receiver. The receiver computes commit (u, x) and verifies that it is equal to the previously received commitment.

In the special case that the committed value is a bit, that is, $x \in \{0, 1\}$, one speaks of a bit commitment scheme. The security requirements for a bit commitment scheme are the following.

The commitment must be binding, i.e., for any adversary $\mathcal{E}$, the probability of generating $u, u' \in \{0, 1\}^k$ satisfying commit $u, 0$ commit$(u'1)$ should be negligible (as a function of k). Furthermore, the commitment must be hiding, i.e., the distributions induced by commit (u, 0) and commit $(u, 1)$ (with $u \in R \{0, 1\}^k$) are indistinguishable.

Moreover, one makes the following distinctions. A commitment scheme is called computationally binding if the adversary E is restricted to be a p.p.t. algorithm. If no such restriction is made (in other words, the adversary may be unlimitedly powerful), the scheme is called information-theoretically binding. Similarly, if the distributions induced by commit (u, 0) and commit (u, 1) are computationally indistinguishable the scheme is called computationally hiding and the scheme is called information-theoretically hiding if these distributions are statistically (or even perfectly) indistinguishable. The security properties are easily extended to the case that x is an arbitrary bit string.

Note that the above security requirements only cover attacks by either the sender or the receiver. For example, suppose party A acts as the sender and party B acts as the receiver, and A sends a commitment C to B. Then there is no guarantee that B will notice if an attacker replaces C by a commitment $C' = \text{commit}(u', x')$ during the commit protocol, and replaces u, x by u', x' during the reveal protocol. Such attacks may be stopped by using an authenticated channel between A and B.

Using a Cryptographic Hash Function

Given a cryptographic hash function H, one obtains a bit commitment scheme simply by setting,

$$\text{commit}_0(u, x) = H(u, x),$$

where,

$$x \in \{0, 1\} \text{ and } u \in_R \{0, 1\}^k.$$

Collision-resistance of H guarantees that the committer cannot (efficiently) prepare u, x and $u', 1 - x$ with $H(u, x) = H(u', 1 - x)$. Hence, the scheme is binding.

Preimage resistance of H is necessary but not sufficient to guarantee that the value of x remains hidden (as well as the value of u). Rather, one needs to assume partial preimage resistance of H. In the random oracle model, the scheme is hiding as long as guessing a bit string of k + 1 bits is infeasible. Thus, we can say that the scheme is computationally binding and computationally hiding.

Using a Discrete Log Setting

Let $\langle g \rangle$ be a group of order n, where n is a large prime. Let $h \in_R \langle g \rangle \setminus \{1\}$ denote a random group element (such that logg h is not known to any party).

We define the following bit commitment scheme (known as "Pedersen's commitment scheme"):

$$\text{commit}_1(u, x) = g^u h^x,$$

where $u \in_R \mathbb{Z}_n$. This scheme is computationally binding (under the DL assumption), which can be seen as follows. Suppose it is computationally feasible to compute u, $u' \in Z_n$ such that $\text{commit1}(u, x) = \text{commit1}(u', 1 - x)$. That means that $g^u h g^u h^x = g u' h^{1-x}$, hence that $\log_g h = (u - u')/(1 - 2x)$. Since u, u', and x are all known, this means that the discrete log of h with respect to g would be computed.

On the other hand, the scheme is information-theoretically hiding, since the distribution of $g^u h^x$ is statistically independent of the value of x (and hence g^u and $g^u h$ are perfectly indistinguishable).

As a complementary bit commitment scheme, one may use the following ElGamal-like scheme:

$$\text{commit}_2 \left(u, x\right) = \left(g^u, h^{u+x}\right),$$

Where $u \in_R \mathbb{Z}_n$. This scheme is information-theoretically binding, since it is easily seen that there cannot even exist u, $u' \in \mathbb{Z}_n$ such that $\text{commit}_2 \left(u, x\right) = \text{commit}_2 \left(u', 1-x\right)$, for $x \in \{0, 1\}$.

On the other hand, this scheme is computationally hiding, since x can be computed as follows. Assuming that the DL problem is feasible, one may compute x from a given commitment $\text{commit}_2 \left(u, x\right) = \left(A, B\right)$, using the formula $x = \log_h B - \log_g A$. Note, however, that the DL assumption is not sufficient to guarantee that the scheme is hiding. We need to use the DDH assumption to ensure the hiding property, as solving for x given commit (u, x) is equivalent to solving the DDH problem.

Both commitment schemes remain secure when used for $x \in_R \mathbb{Z}_n$ instead of $x \in \{0,1\}$.

Impossibility Result

A natural question is whether there exists a commitment scheme which is both information theoretically binding and information-theoretically hiding. The following informal argument shows that such a scheme cannot exist.

Consider any bit commitment scheme which is information-theoretically binding. For such a scheme there cannot exist any u, u' such that $\text{commit}\left(u, 0\right) = \text{commit}\left(u', 1\right)$, because then the (unlimitedly powerful) sender would be able to compute both u and u', and open the commitment at its liking. However, if the sender commits to 0, say, using C = commit (u, 0) for some u, the (unlimitedly powerful) receiver will notice, by exhausting the finite set of possibilities, that there does not exist any u 0 with C = commit $(u', 1)$, hence the receiver knows that the committed bit must be 0.

Homomorphic Commitments

The basic security requirement for a commitment scheme are that it must be binding and hiding. Another relevant property of a commitment scheme is that it may be homomorphic. For the moment introduce the homomorphic property by means of an example. Consider Pedersen's commitment scheme, given by $\text{commit}_1 \left(u, x\right) = g^u h^x$, where $u \in_R \mathbb{Z}_n$ and $x \in \mathbb{Z}_n$. This scheme is additively homomorphic in the sense that:

$$\text{commit}_1 \left(u, x\right) \ \text{commit}_1 \left(u', x'\right) = \text{commit}_1 \left(u + u', x + x'\right),$$

where the multiplication on the left-hand side is in the group $\langle g \rangle$ and the additions on the right-hand side are in $\mathbb{Z}_n$. So, the product of two commitments is a commitment to the sum of the committed values.

Homomorphic properties turn out to be very useful, e.g., for achieving secure multiparty computation. As a concrete example, homomorphic commitments can be used as a building block for secure election schemes: very roughly, during the voting stage, voters put their votes into homomorphic commitments, and during the tallying stage, the votes are counted in a verifiable manner by taking the product of all commitments.

Identification Protocols

Identification protocols is between two parties where one party is called the verifier needs to get convinced that the other party, called the prover, is as claimed. A typical example is when a user wants to gain access to a computer account (secure login), or when someone needs to enter a secured room.

In general, identification protocols may be based on one or more of the following factors.

- What you are: Biometrics, such as fingerprints, iris scans, etc.

- What you have: Smart cards, SIM cards, or similar hardware tokens.

- What you know: Passwords, PIN codes, secret keys.

There are many, many cryptographic constructions of identification protocols. A general goal is to minimize the computational effort for the prover and the verifier. The security ranges from rather weak for password-based protocols to strong for zero-knowledge protocols and witness-hiding protocols.

The problem addressed by identification protocols is related to message authentication (e.g., by means of digital signatures) and also to authenticated key exchange.

Compared to message authentication, an important difference is that there is some notion of freshness to be fulfilled. On the other hand, compared to digital signatures, there is no such thing as non-repudiation: it is not required that the verifier is able to convince an outsider at a later point in time that a prover indeed successfully identified itself to the verifier. In other words, it is not a requirement that the prover gets an alibi from engaging in an identification protocol.

Compared to authenticated key exchange, the problem is easier as there is no requirement for actually establishing a secure (session) key.

An identification protocol is actually part of an identification scheme. An identification scheme consists of two protocols, called registration and identification, between two parties, called the prover and the verifier.

In a basic symmetric identification scheme, registration will end with both parties sharing a secret key, which both of them need to store securely. In a basic asymmetric identification scheme, registration will end with both parties sharing a public key, for which only the prover knows the private key. In more advanced schemes, also the verifier may have a private key. A major advantage of asymmetric schemes is that the prover may use its public key with several, possibly many, verifiers.

Attacks are considered on the identification protocol only. Hence, The registration protocol is performed in a secure environment. Furthermore, we consider only cryptographic attacks.

The basic security requirement for an identification protocol is that it stops impersonation attacks, that is, it should be impossible for an attacker to successfully identify itself as another party. We distinguish several passive and active impersonation attacks.

The main type of passive impersonation attack is eavesdropping on communication between a prover and a verifier in legal executions of the identification protocol. Another type of passive attack is a key-only attack for asymmetric schemes, in which the attacker tries to find the private key from the public key. However, ot be concerned with key-only attacks.

A simple form of active impersonation attack is a guessing attack, in which the attacker poses as the prover and hopes to make the right guesses, without knowing the prover's secret key or private key. The success rate of a guessing attack may be increased considerably by combining it with a cheating verifier attack, in which the attacker poses as a verifier and hopes to extract some useful information from the prover by deviating from the protocol.

Finally, the attacker may apply a man-in-the-middle attack: an honest prover V thinks it runs the identification protocol with verifier V^* but actually V^* relays all messages to a verifier V who thinks it runs the protocol with V. For example, one may identify itself to open a certain door X but the attacker will have you open another door Y (while you get the message that there was some malfunctioning at door X).

The man-in-the-middle attack is reminiscent of the so-called grandmaster chess attack, in which an amateur chess player tries to increase his or her rating by playing correspondence chess with two grandmasters at the same time. The amateur chess player will engage in a chess game with both grandmasters, playing white in one game and black in the other one. Once started, the amateur simply copies all moves from one grandmaster to the other one. As a result, the amateur will either win one game and lose the other one, or play two draws. In any event, the amateur's rating will increase considerably.

Password-based Schemes

The conventional way to login to a computer is to provide a user-id and a password. Upon registration it is ensured that the prover gets a unique user-id. The prover is also allowed to pick a password. During identification, the prover sends the user-id and password to the verifier.

A password scheme is a symmetric identification scheme, supposed to withstand guessing attacks. One may think of the password as a random bit string in $\{0, 1\}^k$. If the password is human-memorizable, the security parameter k is usually rather small, say k ≤ 20. Clearly, it is possible to withstand guessing attacks by taking k = 80, but then the password will be harder to memorize.

A password scheme does not withstand eavesdropping attacks at all. Once the password is intercepted, the scheme is broken.

One-way Hash Chains

Lamport's identification scheme provides a relatively easy way to stop eavesdropping attacks by using so-called (one-way) hash chains. A hash chain of length l is a sequence of values x_i, $0 \le i \le$, satisfying $x_{i+1} = H(x_i)$, for $0 \le i < \ell$, where $H : \{0, 1\}^* \to \{0, 1\}^k$ is a cryptographic hash function.

For registration, the prover picks $x_0 \in_R \{0, 1\}^k$, computes $x_\ell = H^\ell(x_0)$, and sends x_ℓ to the verifier. Both the prover and the verifier keep a counter i, initially $i = 0$. The prover stores x_0 for later use. The verifier keeps a variable v, which is initially set to x_ℓ.

For identification, the prover increments counter i, computes $x_{\ell-i} = H^{\ell-i}(x_0)$ and sends this value to the verifier. The verifier tests whether $H(x_{\ell-i}) = v$. If so, identification is successful and the verifier increments i and sets $v = x_{\ell-i}$; otherwise, the verifier discards the identification attempt.

Lamport's identification scheme thus requires the prover and the verifier to remain "in sync" (counter i), but unlike a completely symmetric scheme, the verifier does not need to store a secret key.

A key-only attack is infeasible. The scheme withstands eavesdropping attacks as interception of a value $x_{\ell-i}$ does not help the attacker in succeeding in any of the subsequent runs of the identification protocol.

Basic Challenge-response Protocols

Four basic challenge-response schemes.

It consists four basic challenge-response protocols. In each of these identification protocols, the verifier starts by sending a random challenge, which the prover answers by sending a response, which is then checked by the verifier. The schemes are summarized in figure. Consider eavesdropping attacks and cheating verifier attacks for each of the schemes.

Using Symmetric Encryption

Assume that prover and verifier share a symmetric key $K \in_R \{0,1\}^k$. Let E_K denote an encryption algorithm using key K, and let DK denote the corresponding decryption algorithm. Assume for simplicity that $E_K, D_K : \{0,1\}^k \to \{0,1\}^k$.

The identification protocol starts with the verifier sending a challenge $c \in_R \{0,1\}^k$, for which the prover is supposed to return the response $r = E_K(c)$. The verifier checks that indeed $D_K(r) = c$.

To withstand eavesdropping attacks an encryption scheme withstanding known-plaintext attacks must be used. To withstand cheating verifier attacks, the encryption scheme must withstand adaptive chosen-plaintext attacks.

Using Symmetric Authentication

Assume that prover and verifier share a symmetric key $K \in_R \{0,1\}^k$. Let $H : \{0,1\}^* \to \{0,1\}^k$ denote a cryptographic hash function.

The identification protocol starts with the verifier sending a challenge $c \in_R \{0,1\}^k$, for which the prover is supposed to return the response $r = H(K, c)$. The verifier checks that indeed $r = H(K, c)$.

In the random oracle model, the scheme withstands both eavesdropping and cheating verifier attacks.

Using Asymmetric Encryption

Assume that prover and verifier share a public key pk for which the prover knows the private key sk. Let E_{pk} denote an encryption algorithm using key pk, and let D_{sk} denote the corresponding decryption algorithm using key sk.

The verifier challenges the prover with $c = E_{pk}(M)$ with $M \in_R \{0,1\}^k$, for which the prover is supposed to produce response $r = D_{sk}(c)$. The verifier checks that indeed r = M holds.

To withstand eavesdropping attacks the encryption scheme must be semantically secure. To withstand cheating verifier attacks, the encryption scheme must withstand adaptive chosen-ciphertext attacks.

Using Asymmetric Authentication

Assume that prover and verifier share a public key pk for which the prover knows the private key sk. Let S_{sk} denote a signing algorithm using key sk, and let V_{pk} denote the corresponding verification algorithm using key pk.

The identification protocol starts with the verifier sending a challenge $c \in_R \{0,1\}^k$, for which the prover is supposed to return the response $r = S_{sk}(c)$. The verifier checks that indeed $V_{pk}(c, r)$ holds, that is, whether r is indeed a signature on message c under public key pk.

To withstand eavesdropping attacks the digital signature scheme must withstand knownmessage attacks. To withstand cheating verifier attacks, the digital signature scheme must withstand adaptive chosen-message attacks.

Zero-knowledge Identification Protocols

The schemes of zero-knowledge principle is when used with sufficiently strong encryption or authentication schemes. The cost of a digital signature scheme withstanding adaptive chosenmessage attack is quite high, though. In addition, the work for the prover for computing the response may be costly, in particular considering the work the prover needs to do strictly after receiving the challenge.

In this section consider zero-knowledge identification protocols, which will have the property that no matter what a cheating verifier does, it will not extract any useful information from the (honest) prover. More precisely, the term "zero-knowledge" refers to the fact that whatever information the cheating verifier learns from (interacting with) the prover, that information could have been generated by the cheating verifier on its own— without interacting with the prover at all. In other words, it is possible to show that the messages sent by the prover can be (efficiently) simulated without actually involving the prover. An honest verifier, however, will be convinced that the prover knows the private key, as required.

$$
\begin{array}{ll}
\textbf{Prover} & \textbf{Verifier} \\
(x = \log_g h) & \\
u \in_R \mathbb{Z}_n & \\
a \leftarrow g^u & \xrightarrow{\quad a \quad} \\
& \qquad c \in_R \{0, 1\} \\
& \xleftarrow{\quad c \quad} \\
r \leftarrow_n \begin{cases} u, & \text{if } c = 0 \\ u + x, & \text{if } c = 1 \end{cases} & \xrightarrow{\quad r \quad} \quad g^r = \begin{cases} a, & \text{if } c = 0 \\ ah, & \text{if } c = 1 \end{cases}
\end{array}
$$

Schnorr's zero-knowledge protocol.

Schnorr Zero-knowledge Protocol

As a first example of a zero-knowledge protocol we consider Schnorr's protocol for proving knowledge of a discrete logarithm.

Let $\langle g \rangle$ be a group of order n, where n is a large prime. Let $x \in_R \mathbb{Z}_n$ be the prover's private key, and let $h = g^x$ be the prover's public key. The verifier gets the public key h during the registration protocol. One iteration of Schnorr's identification protocol is given in figure. In total, k iterations are executed between the prover and the verifier, one after the other, where k is a security parameter. The three-flow structure of (one iteration of) Schnorr's protocol is typical of many zero-knowledge protocols; refer to the first message a as the announcement, the second message c is called the challenge, and the third message r is called the response.

We first discuss why Schnorr's protocol convinces the verifier that the prover indeed knows $x = \log_g h$. This property is called the soundness property. If the prover does not know x, the best the prover can do is prepare announcement a such that it knows response r either in the case c = 0 or in the case c = 1. To prepare for answering challenge c = 0, a cheating prover sets $a = g^u$, and sends r = u as response. And, to prepare for answering challenge c = 1, a cheating prover sets $a = g^u / h$, and sends the response r = u; then the verification $g^r = ah$ will hold.

The point is that the prover cannot prepare for answering both cases c = 0 and c = 1, without knowing the private key x. This follows from the following observation. Suppose that after sending announcement a, a prover is able to respond to both challenges c = 0 and c = 1 correctly. That is, the prover is able to produce two responses r_0 and r_1, which are correct for challenges c = 0 and c = 1, respectively. Then it follows that a, r_0, and r_1 satisfy.

$$g^{r_0} = a, \; g^{r_1} = ah,$$

which implies that,

$$h = g^{r_1 - r_0}$$

But this means that the prover actually knows x, since $x = r_1 - r_0 \bmod n$ holds.

Consequently, at each iteration of Schnorr's protocol a cheating prover "survives" with probability at most 50% essentially. Thus after k iterations, a cheating prover succeeds with probability at most 2^{-k} essentially.

Now, we discuss why Schnorr's protocol is zero-knowledge. A cheating verifier may engage many times in the identification protocol, obtaining a conversation (a; c; r) for each run of the protocol. Here, "many times" means at most $O(k^\gamma)$ times for some constant $\gamma \in \mathbb{N}$ (polynomially bounded in the security parameter k). The cheating verifier thus obtains many conversations (a; c; r). However, it turns out that the verifier may generate these conversations completely on its own, without interacting with the prover at all: the verifier may generate simulated conversations (a; c; r) that follow exactly the same distribution as the conversations (a; c; r) that occur in executions of the identification protocol with a real prover.

We first consider the zero-knowledge property for the case of an honest verifier $\mathcal{V}$, that is, the verifier picks c uniformly at random in $\{0, 1\}$ as prescribed by the protocol. Below, we present two p.p.t. algorithms, one for generating real conversations (following the protocol), and one for generating simulated conversations (deviating from the protocol).

Real conversations:

- Input: private key x,

- Output: conversation (a; c; r),

- $u \in_R \mathbb{Z}_n$,

- $a \leftarrow g^u$,

- $c \in_R \{0,1\}$,

- $r \leftarrow_n u + cx$,

- output (a; c; r).

Simulated conversations:

- Input: public key h,

- Output: conversation (a; c; r),

- $c \in_R \{0,1\}$,

- $r \in_R \mathbb{Z}_n$,

- $a \leftarrow g^r h^{-c}$,

- output $(a;\ c;\ r)$.

Both algorithms generate accepting conversations (a; c; r) uniformly at random, that is,

$$\Pr\left[(a;c;r)=(A;C;R)\right]=\frac{1}{2n} \quad \text{for any triple} \ \ (A;C;R)\in\langle g\rangle\times\{0,1\}\times\mathbb{Z}_n \ \ \text{satisfying} \ \ g^R=Ah^C.$$

The crux is that the real conversations are generated given access to the private key x, whereas the simulated conversations are generated given access to the public key h only.

Next, we consider the zero-knowledge property for the general case of any p.p.t. cheating verifier V^*. Use probabilistic Turing machine V^* as a rewindable black-box, which means: (i) that we access V^* in a black-box manner only, restricted to exchanging messages with V^* through its input and output tapes, and (ii) that we can rewind V^* to any prior configuration. The configuration of a probabilistic Turing machine is determined by the state of its finite control part, the contents of its tapes (including the random tape) as well as the positions of its tape heads. By rewinding V^* we can test it on several input values until a desired output value is obtained.

Real conversations:

- Input: private key x,
- Output: conversation (a; c; r),
- $u \in_R \mathbb{Z}_n,$
- $a \leftarrow g^u,$
- send a to V^*,
- receive $c \in \{0,\ 1\}$ from V^*,
- $r \leftarrow_n u + cx,$
- send r to V^*,
- output (a; c; r).

Simulated conversations:

- Input: public key h,
- Output: conversation (a; c; r),
- $c \in_R \{0,1\},$
- $r \in_R \mathbb{Z}_n,$
- $a \leftarrow g^r h^{-c},$
- send a to V^*,
- receive $c' \in \{0,\ 1\}$ from V^*,

- if $c \neq c'$ rewind $\mathcal{V}^*$ to point prior to receiving a,

- send r to $\mathcal{V}^*$,

- output (a; c; r).

The probability that $c = c'$ is exactly 1/2, since $c \in_R \{0, 1\}$. Hence, on average two iterations are required to generate a simulated conversation (a; c; r).

We can say that no matter what algorithm (or "strategy") a cheating verifier $\mathcal{V}^*$ follows in trying to extract useful information from the prover, the same algorithm can be used to generate identically distributed conversations without needing the cooperation of the prover. Whereas the real conversations are generated using the private key x as input, the simulated conversations are generated using only the public key h as input.

Schnorr Protocol

The protocol of Figure is a zero-knowledge protocol. However, as we have argued informally, the probability that a cheating prover succeeds is 50%. By using k sequential iterations of this protocol the zero-knowledge property is preserved, but the probability that a cheating prover succeeds becomes 2−k, which is negligible as a function of k.

The computational complexity of the resulting protocol is rather high, since both the prover and the verifier need to compute $O(k)$ exponentiations in the group $\langle g \rangle$. Therefore, Schnorr also proposed to use the variant given in figure (which is actually known as "Schnorr's protocol"). In this protocol, the verifier picks its challenge from a large range, say $c \in \mathbb{Z}_n$.

The soundness property of Schnorr's protocol can be analyzed similarly as above. Suppose that a prover is able to answer correctly at least two challenges c and c', with $c \neq c'$, after sending announcement a. That is, the prover is able to produce two valid conversations (a; c; r) and (a; c'; r'). Then it follows as before that the prover actually knows the discrete $\log x = \log_g h$.

Since,

$$g^r = ah^c, g^{r'} = ah^{c'}$$

implies that

$$h = g^{(r-r')/(c-c')}.$$

Therefore, intuitively, after sending announcement a, the prover can answer at most one challenge correctly, if the prover does not know the private key x. Since there are n possible values for the challenge, the probability of success is basically bounded above by 1/n, which is negligibly small.

$$
\begin{array}{ll}
\text{Prover} & \text{Verifier} \\
(x = \log_g h) & \\[1em]
u \in_R \mathbb{Z}_n & \\
a \leftarrow g^u & \\
& \xrightarrow{\quad a \quad} \\
& c \in_R \mathbb{Z}_n \\
& \xleftarrow{\quad c \quad} \\
r \leftarrow_n u + cx & \\
& \xrightarrow{\quad r \quad} \\
& g^r = ah^c
\end{array}
$$

Schnorr's identification protocol.

The zero-knowledge property can also be proved for Schnorr's protocol similarly as above for the case of an honest verifier $\mathcal{V}$. The distributions of the real conversations (generated using private key $x \in \mathbb{Z}_n$) and of the simulated conversations (generated using public key $h \in \langle g \rangle$ only) are, respectively:

$$\left\{ (a;c;r) : u, c \in_R \mathbb{Z}_n; \, a \leftarrow g^u ; r \leftarrow_n u + cx \right\}$$

$$\left\{ (a;c;r) : c, r \in_R \mathbb{Z}_n; \, a \leftarrow g^r h^{-c} \right\}$$

These distributions are identical, as each valid conversation (a; c; r) (satisfying $c, r \in \mathbb{Z}_n$ and $g^r = ah^c$ occurs with probability $1/n^2$ in both distributions.

In trying to simulate conversations for an arbitrary verifier $\mathcal{V}^*$, we run into a problem. We may use the same algorithm as before, first picking $c, r \in_R \mathbb{Z}_n$, setting $a = g^r h^{-c}$, feeding a to $\mathcal{V}^*$ and then hoping that the c' returned by $\mathcal{V}^*$ matches c. However, $\Pr[c = c'] = 1/n$ which is negligibly small, and it will take n tries on average to find a valid conversation this way. In other words, the running time of the simulator is $O(n)$, which is exponentially large.

Schnorr's protocol is sound and honest-verifier zero-knowledge. Although it cannot be proved zero-knowledge in general, no attacks are known for this protocol, hence it can be used as an identification protocol, if so desired.

How to obtain so-called Schnorr signatures from Schnorr's identification protocol. At this point, we remark that if one could prove that Schnorr's protocol is zero-knowledge then it would follow that Schnorr signatures can be forged. In a way it is therefore good that Schnorr's protocol is not zero-knowledge.

Guillou-Quisquater Protocol

The identification protocol by Guillou and Quisquater is similar to Schnorr's protocol, except that it is defined in an RSA setting instead of a DL setting.

Let $m = pq$ be an RSA modulus, that is, p and q are large, distinct primes of bit length k, for security parameter k. Let e be a positive integer satisfying $\gcd(e, \phi(m)) = 1$, where $\phi(m) = (p-1)(q-1)$. As an additional requirement for e we have that e is a large prime such that 1/e is negligible in security parameter k. For example, e may be a 128-bit prime.

Prover	Verifier
$(x = y^{1/e} \bmod m)$	
$u \in_R \mathbb{Z}_m^*$	
$a \leftarrow_m u^e$	
$\xrightarrow{\quad a \quad}$	
	$c \in_R \mathbb{Z}_e$
$\xleftarrow{\quad c \quad}$	
$r \leftarrow_m ux^c$	
$\xrightarrow{\quad r \quad}$	
	$r^e =_m ay^c$

Guillou-Quisquater's identification protocol.

Recall that the RSA problem is to compute $x = y^{1/e} \bmod m$ given $y \in \mathbb{Z}_m^*$, which is assumed to be hard for sufficiently large values of k. For Guillou-Quisquater's protocol, the private key of the prover is therefore a number $x \in \mathbb{Z}_m^*$, and the corresponding public key is $y = x^e \bmod m$. One can easily verify that the verifier indeed accepts if the prover follows the protocol, as we have (modulo m):

$$r^e = (ux^c)^e = u^e (x^e)^c = ay^c$$

The security properties of Guillou-Quisquater's protocol are as follows. The soundness property holds as the success probability of a cheating prover is basically bounded by 1/e for the following reason. Suppose that a prover is able to answer two distinct challenges $c, c' \in \mathbb{Z}_e$ correctly, after sending announcement a to the verifier. In other words, suppose a prover is able to produce two accepting conversations (a; c; r) and $(a; c'; r')$, with $c \neq c'$. Then we have (modulo m):

$$r^e = ay^c, \quad r'^e = ay^{c'},$$

which implies,

$$(r/r')^e = y^{c-c'}$$

To isolate y in this equation, $\gcd(e, c - c') = 1$, since e is prime and $c, c' \in \mathbb{Z}_e, c \neq c'$. By the extended Euclidean algorithm integers s, t can thus be computed efficiently satisfying $se + t(c - c') = 1$. Raising both sides of the equation to the power t we get:

$$(r/r')^{te} = y^t (c - c') = y^{1 - se},$$

hence,

$$y = \left(y^s \left(r / r' \right)^t \right)^e$$

Given accepting conversations $(a; c; r), (a; c'; r')$, where $c \neq c'$, the private key x can be computed as $x = y^s \left(r / r' \right)^t \bmod m$, where s, t satisfy $se + t(c - c') = 1$ (as obtained by the extended Euclidean algorithm).

The protocol is honest-verifier zero-knowledge, since the distributions of the real conversations (generated using private key $x \in \mathbb{Z}_m^*$) and of the simulated conversations (generated using public key $y \in \mathbb{Z}_m^*$ only) are identical:

$$\left\{ (a; c; r) : u \in_R \mathbb{Z}_m^*; c \in_R \mathbb{Z}_e; a \leftarrow_m u^e; r \leftarrow_m ux^c \right\},$$

$$\left\{ (a; c; r) : c \in_R \mathbb{Z}_e; r \in_R \mathbb{Z}_m^*; a \leftarrow_m r^e y^{-c} \right\}.$$

Each valid conversation $(a; c; r)$ (satisfying $c \in \mathbb{Z}_e, r \in \mathbb{Z}_m^*$ and $r^e =_m ay^c$) occurs with probability $1 / (e\phi(m))$.

Witness Hiding Identification Protocols

Schnorr's identification protocol is quite efficient, but it can be proved zero-knowledge only for an honest verifier. By using k iterations of Schnorr's protocol (with binary challenges), the resulting protocol is zero-knowledge for arbitrary verifiers, but, clearly, the computational complexity of the protocol also increases by a factor of k.

Witness hiding identification protocols strike a nice balance between security and efficiency. Consider a protocol that satisfies the soundness property. It follows that a prover can only be successful if it actually knows the complete private key. So, the only problem we need to care about is that a cheating verifier is not able to learn the complete private key. Therefore, an identification protocol is called witness hiding if a cheating verifier is not able to obtain the prover's private key by interacting with the prover.

If a protocol is witness hiding, it is not necessarily zero-knowledge (but the converse is always true). A cheating verifier may be able to extract some partial information on the private key, but the amount of information it is able to get is not sufficient for successful impersonation of the prover.

Okamoto Protocol

As before, let $\langle g \rangle$ be a group of order n, where n is a large prime. In addition, let $g_1, g_2 \in \langle g \rangle$s be given such that $\log_{g_1} g_2$ is not known to anybody. If g_1, g_2 are picked uniformly at random in $\langle g \rangle$ then $\log_{g_1} g_2$ is not known under the DL assumption. Let $x_1, x_2 \in_R \mathbb{Z}_n$ be the prover's private key, and let $h = g_1^{x_1} g_2^{x_2}$ be the prover's public key. Okamoto's protocol, may be viewed as a variation of Schnorr's protocol. The computational complexity of Okamoto's protocol and of Schnorr's protocol only differ by a constant factor.

Prover	Verifier

$$(h = g_1^{x_1} g_2^{x_2})$$

$$u_1, u_2 \in_R \mathbb{Z}_n$$
$$a \leftarrow g_1^{u_1} g_2^{u_2}$$

$$\xrightarrow{\quad a \quad}$$

$$c \in_R \mathbb{Z}_n$$

$$\xleftarrow{\quad c \quad}$$

$$r_1 \leftarrow_n u_1 + cx_1$$
$$r_2 \leftarrow_n u_2 + cx_2 \qquad \xrightarrow{\quad r_1, r_2 \quad}$$

$$g_1^{r_1} g_2^{r_2} = ah^c$$

Okamoto's identification protocol.

Also, Okamoto's protocol satisfies the same properties of soundness and honest-verifier zero-knowledgeness as Schnorr's protocol. The important difference is that Okamoto's protocol can be proved to be witness hiding.

We first note the following property. For a given public key h and given generators g_1, g_2 there are exactly n possible pairs $(x_1, x_2) \in \mathbb{Z}_n \times \mathbb{Z}_n$ satisfying $h = g_1^{x_1} g_2^{x_2}$. Since if one fixes any $x_1 \in \mathbb{Z}n$, the corresponding x_2 is uniquely defined by $x_2 = \log_{g_2}\left(h / g_1^{x_1}\right)$. Such a pair (x_1, x_2) is referred to as a witness.

The prover's private key is one such witness (x_1, x_2). A crucial property of Okamoto's protocol is that it is witness indistinguishable, as the conversations seen by an arbitrary, possibly cheating, verifier are (statistically) independent of the particular witness used by the prover.

To see that Okamoto's protocol is witness indistinguishable we argue as follows. Let $(a; c; r_1, r_2)$ be a conversation between an (honest) prover $\mathcal{P}_{(x_1, x_2)}$ using witness (x_1, x_2) and a possibly cheating verifier $\mathcal{V}^*$, and let u_1, u_2 be the corresponding random numbers used by $\mathcal{P}_{(x_1, x_2)}$. Now, consider another witness (x_1', x_2'). Then there exist unique values $u_1', u_2' \in \mathbb{Z}_n$ that yield the same conversation for a prover $\mathcal{P}_{(x_1', x_2')}$ using witness (x_1', x_2'):

$$u_1' \leftarrow_n u_1 + c\left(x_1 - x_1'\right),$$
$$u_2' \leftarrow_n u_2 + c\left(x_2 - x_2'\right).$$

Indeed,

$$a' = g_1^{u_1'} g_2^{u_2'} = g_1^{u_1} g_2^{u_2} \left(g_1^{x_1} g_2^{x_2}\right)^c / \left(g_1^{x_1'} g_2^{x_2'}\right)^c = a,$$

and (modulo n)

$$r_1' = u_1' + cx_1' = u_1 + c\left(x_1 - x_1'\right) + cx_1' = r_1,$$

$$r_2' = u_2' + cx_2' = u_2 + c\left(x_2 - x_2'\right) + cx_2' = r_2.$$

Phrased slightly differently: for each combination of a conversation $(a; c; r_1, r_2)$ between an honest prover $\mathcal{P}$ and a possibly cheating verifier $\mathcal{V}^*$, and a possible witness $\left(x_1', x_2'\right)$ satisfying $h = g_1^{x_1'} g_2^{x_2'}$, there exist unique u_1', u_2' satisfying $a = g_1^{u_1'} g_2^{u_2'}$, $r_1 =_n u_1' + cx_1'$, and $r_2 =_n u_2' + cx_2'$. This implies that Okamoto's protocol is witness indistinguishable.

Now, suppose that a cheating verifier $\mathcal{V}^*$ is able to find a witness $\left(x_1', x_2'\right)$ after interacting with a given prover $\mathcal{P}(x_1, x_2)$ polynomially many times. Since Okamoto's protocol is witness indistinguishable, it follows that the witness $\left(x_1', x_2'\right)$ found by will be equal to the witness used by $\mathcal{P}(x_1, x_2)$ with probability exactly equal to $1/n$. In other words, with probability close to 1, the two witnesses will be different.

However, now viewing the prover $\mathcal{P}(x_1, x_2)$ and the verifier $\mathcal{V}^*$ as one "big" p.p.t. algorithm $\mathcal{E}$, it follows that $\mathcal{E}$ is able to compute two pairs $(x_1, x_2) \neq \left(x_1', x_2'\right)$ satisfying:

$$h = g_1^{x_1} g_2^{x_2}, \quad h = g_1^{x_1'} g_2^{x_2'}.$$

But this implies that,

$$g_2 = g_1^{\left(x_1' - x_1\right)/\left(x_2' - x_2\right)}$$

hence that $\mathcal{E}$ computed $\log g_1 g_2$, which we assumed to be infeasible. Under the DL assumption, Okamoto's protocol is witness hiding, which means that no p.p.t. verifier is able to extract a prover's private key.

Zero Knowledge Proof

A zero-knowledge proof is one of the most abstract and fascinating concepts in applied cryptography today. From potentially being used in nuclear disarmament to providing anonymous and secure transactions for public blockchain networks, a zero-knowledge proof is a profound example of cryptographic innovation.

Zero Knowledge proofs can be used for identification. Identification schemes in general, then "traditional" secret-key and public-key schemes and finally zero-knowledge schemes. Identification schemes are methods by which a user may prove his or her identity without revealing knowledge that may be used by an eavesdropper to impersonate the user.

The traditional form of identification is by use of a secret key, password or pin, but this scheme is extremely insecure since they are easy to guess, for example, through an exhaustive search. Recently, biometric parameters like fingerprints, retinal scans or facial recognition are used, but they are not comfortable, and they give value to body parts, which can have many disadvantages. Another common scheme is using digital signatures and public-key cryptography. An identification scheme consists essentially of two separate stages:

- Initialization,

- Operation.

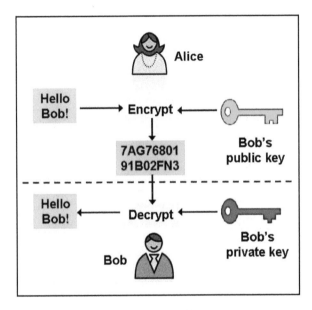

In public-key identification schemes, during the first stage each user generates a private key and a public key. A Trusted Authority is required to ensure the link between each user and his public key. At the end of the operation stage the verifier can accept or reject the identification.

A Zero Knowledge protocol must satisfy the three conditions:

- Completeness: If a statement is true and both parties follow the same protocol correctly, then the verifier naturally becomes convinced.

- Soundness: If statement is false, the verifier will almost certainly not be convinced (Probabilistically Checkable Proof constructions rely on repetition until probability of falsehood or plain coin flip luck approaches zero).

- Zero-knowledge: If the statement is true, no verifier learns anything other than the fact that the statement is true.

Types of Zero-knowledge Proof

- Intercative zero-knowledge proof: 1st invention, multiple messages between Prover and Verifier.

- Non-intercative zero-knowledge proof: Less interaction required between Prover and Verifier.

Data Exchange proofs reveal only the data that Alice wants to be revealed. In this case, the minimum balance instead of the actual one. In effect what Alice is proving is that "I, Alice, have the knowledge of my statement of balance (as of a certain date and time) signed by the bank that you, the auction house, have trust in. Using that knowledge, I prove to you that I have at least the amount you are looking for."

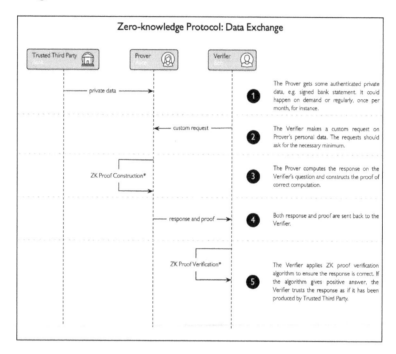

Thus, ZKPs allow Alice to satisfy the wishes of a verifier (the auction house) without exposing information the details of her private life to neither the verifier or the mutually trusted source of information (the bank).

ZKP Advantages

- Zero knowledge transfer as the name suggest.

- Computational efficiency - No Encryption.

- Based on problem like discrete logarithms and integer factorization.

- No degradation of the protocol.

Zk-snark

Data privacy is the most important thing now days. Let's talk about the ZK-SNARK. As the name suggest *ZK* stands for Zero-Knowledge and *SNARK* stand for "Succinct Non-Interactive Argument of Knowledge". Zk-snark is an acronym for 'Zero-Knowledge Succinct Non-Interactive Argument of Knowledge'.

- Zero-knowledge: If the statement is true, a verifier does not learn anything beyond the fact that the statement is true.

- Succint: It indicates that the zero-knowledge proof can be verified quickly. This includes proofs with statements that are large. With previous zero-knowledge protocols, the prover and the verifier had to engage in multiple rounds of communication in order to validate a proof.

- Non-interactive: It means that the verifier does not have to interact with the Prover in order to validate a zero-knowledge proof. Instead, the Prover can publish their proof in advance, and a verifier can ensure its correctness.

- Argument of knowledge: A computationally sound proof: soundness holds against the Prover that leverages polynomial-time, i.e. bounded computation. The proof cannot be constructed without access to the witness (the private input needed to prove the statement).

- Zk- Snark Transaction: In incorporating zk-SNARKS into the Zcash blockchain, the function that determines the correctness of a transaction, in accordance with consensus rules, must return the answer of whether or not that transaction is valid, without disclosing any of the information with which it performed calculations. This is accomplished by encoding some Zcash consensus rules into zk-SNARKs themselves.

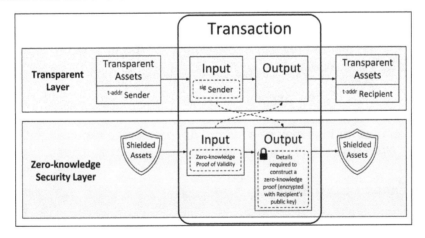

Zcash uses Zk-snarks to prove that the conditions for a valid transaction have been satisfied without revealing any crucial information about the addresses or values involved. The sender of a shielded transaction constructs a proof to show that, with high probability:

- The input values sum to the output values for each transaction.

- The sender proves that they have the private keys of the input, which gives a user the authority to spend.

- The private spending keys of the input are cryptographically linked to a signature that pertains to the entire transaction, in a manner in which a transaction cannot be modified by a party who did not know these private keys.

The Transport Layer

Transport Layer Security (TLS) is a protocol that provides security for communication over the Internet. TLS encrypts segments of network connections, in order to provide confidentiality when communicating via the Internet.

Working of TLS

A TLS session begins with a handshake. The client first sends the server a hello message that lists the client's supported capabilities. The server responds back with its own hello message, with its choice of one of the available listed capabilities, to ensure the client and the server will be able to speak the same language.

The server then sends its certificate, which contains its public key, and may request a certificate from the client if client authentication is required. The client checks to see if it's a valid certificate, and sends its own back if necessary.

The client then sends a random number that has been encrypted with the server's public key. After this number is decrypted by the server, the client and server will have a common key that can be used to the send and receive data that only the pair of them can understand. Both the client and server then send messages notifying the other that all further communication will be encrypted and both send final messages that are actually encrypted, ending the handshake and allowing encrypted data exchange to begin. While this may seem like a lengthy process, a TLS/SSL handshake in most cases takes less than a second.

Whether you need to use TLS/SSL depends on your organization's activities. For organizations involved in health services or payment processing, using a security protocol such as TLS/SSL to encrypt network communications may be a federal or commercial requirement. For other organizations, using TLS/SSL might simply be a good idea.

How TLS Increases Email Security?

TLS ensures that no third party may eavesdrop or tamper with any message. TLS is the successor to the Secure Sockets Layer (SSL).

Implementing TLS

TLS implementation varies greatly depending on the server it is to be installed on, please see instructions pertaining to your software/hardware vendor. A common step that would apply to all implementations would be to acquire a digital certificate for each server. These certificates may be from a Certificate Authority, or self-signed.

References

- Protocols, theory, eng: crypto-it.net, Retrieved 21 July, 2019

- Lecturenotes, cryptographicprotocols, berry: win.tue.nl, Retrieved 13 July, 2019

- Zero-knowledge-proof-improving-privacy-for-a-blockchain: altoros.com, Retrieved 1 June, 2019

- Introduction-to-zero-knowledge-proof-the-protocol-of-next-generation-blockchain, coinmonks: medium.com, Retrieved 23 June, 2019

Cryptographic Algorithms

The set of detailed and complex mathematical instructions which are used to encrypt or decrypt data are known as cryptographic algorithms. Some of its types are symmetric-key algorithms and asymmetric-key algorithms. The diverse aspects of these cryptographic algorithms have been thoroughly discussed in this chapter.

An encryption algorithm is a formula or instructions series that converts a plaintext readable message into an unreadable cipher text. Algorithms use advanced mathematics and one or more encryption keys to make it relatively easy to encode a message but virtually impossible to decode without knowing the keys. Algorithms often involve multiple layers of encryption and can require additional random and sequential one-time values that prevent attacks and duplicate results.

AWS cryptography tools and services that encrypt data support secure algorithms that are publicly vetted. Some tools and services, like AWS Key Management Service (AWS KMS) use a particular algorithm. AWS KMS uses the Advanced Encryption Standard (AES) algorithm in Galois/Counter Mode (GCM) with 256-bit secret keys. Other tools and services offer multiple algorithms and key sizes but recommend a secure default choice.

Symmetric-key Algorithms

Symmetric algorithm is a cryptographic algorithm that uses the same key to encrypt and decrypt data. These algorithms are designed to be very fast and have a large number of possible keys. The best symmetric key algorithms offer excellent secrecy; once data is encrypted with a given key, there is no fast way to decrypt the data without possessing the same key.

Symmetric key algorithms can be divided into two categories: block and stream. Block algorithms encrypt data a block (many bytes) at a time, while stream algorithms encrypt byte by byte (or even bit by bit).

Cryptographic Strength of Symmetric Algorithms

Different encryption algorithms are not equal. Some systems are not very good at protecting data, allowing encrypted information to be decrypted without knowledge of the requisite key. Others are quite resistant to even the most determined attack. The ability of a cryptographic system to protect information from attack is called its *strength*. Strength depends on many factors, including:

- The secrecy of the key.

- The difficulty of guessing the key or trying out all possible keys (a key search). Longer keys are generally more difficult to guess or find.

- The difficulty of inverting the encryption algorithm without knowing the encryption key (breaking the encryption algorithm).

- The existence (or lack) of back doors, or additional ways by which an encrypted file can be decrypted more easily without knowing the key.

- The ability to decrypt an entire encrypted message if you know how a portion of it decrypts (called a known plaintext attack).

- The properties of the plaintext and knowledge of those properties by an attacker. For example, a cryptographic system may be vulnerable to attack if all messages encrypted with it begin or end with a known piece of plaintext. These kinds of regularities were used by the Allies to crack the German Enigma cipher during World War II.

As part of proving the strength of an algorithm, a mathematician can show that the algorithm is resistant to specific kinds of attacks that have been previously shown to compromise other algorithms. Unfortunately, even an algorithm that is resistant to every known attack is not necessarily secure, because new attacks are constantly being developed.

From time to time, some individuals or corporations claim that they have invented new symmetric encryption algorithms that are dramatically more secure than existing algorithms. Generally, these algorithms should be avoided. As there are no known attack methods against the encryption algorithms that are in wide use today, there is no reason to use new, unproven encryption algorithms that might have flaws lurking in them.

Key Length with Symmetric Key Algorithms

Among those who are not entirely familiar with the mathematics of cryptography, key length is a topic of continuing confusion. The short keys can significantly compromise the security of encrypted messages because an attacker can merely decrypt the message with every possible key to decipher the message's content. But while short keys provide comparatively little security, extremely long keys do not necessarily provide significantly more practical security than keys of moderate length. That is, while keys of 40 or 56 bits are not terribly secure, a key of 256 bits does not offer significantly more real security than a key of 168 bits, or even a key of 128 bits.

To understand this apparent contradiction, it is important to understand what is really meant by the words *key length*, and how a brute force attack actually works.

Inside a computer, a cryptographic key is represented as a string of binary digits. Each binary digit can be a 0 or a 1. Thus, if a key is 1 bit in length, there are two possible keys: 0 and 1. If a key is 2 bits in length, there are four possible keys: 00, 01, 10, and 11. If a key is 3 bits in length, there are eight possible keys: 000, 001, 010, 011, 100, 101, 110, and 111. In general, each added key bit doubles the number of keys. The mathematical equation that relates the number of possible keys to the number of bits is:

number of keys = 2 (number of bits).

If you are attempting to decrypt a message and do not have a copy of the key, the simplest way to decrypt the message is to do a brute force attack. These attacks are also called key search attacks, because they involve trying every possible key to see if a specific key decrypts the message. If the key is selected at random, then on average, an attacker will need to try half of all the possible keys before finding the actual decryption key.

Fortunately, for those of us who depend upon symmetric encryption algorithms, it is a fairly simple matter to use longer keys. Each time a bit is added, the difficulty for an attacker attempting a brute force attack doubles.

The first widely used encryption algorithm, the DES, used a key that was 56 bits long. At the time that the DES was adopted, many academics said that 56 bits was not sufficient: they argued for a key that was twice as long. But it has been conjectured that the U.S. National Security Agency did not want a cipher with a longer key length widely deployed, most likely because such a secure cipher would significantly complicate its job of international surveillance. To further reduce the impact that the DES would have on its ability to collect international intelligence, U.S. corporations were forbidden from exporting products that implemented the DES algorithm.

The NSA operates a worldwide intelligence surveillance network. This network relies, to a large extent, on the fact that the majority of the information transmitted electronically is transmitted without encryption. The network is also used for obtaining information about the number of messages exchanged between various destinations, a technique called *traffic analysis*. Although it is widely assumed that the NSA has sufficient computer power to forcibly decrypt a few encrypted messages, not even the NSA has the computer power to routinely decrypt all of the world's electronic communications.

In the early 1990s, a growing number of U.S. software publishers demanded the ability to export software that offered at least a modicum of security. As part of a compromise, a deal was brokered between the U.S. Department of Commerce, the National Security Agency, and the Software Publisher's Association. Under the terms of that agreement, U.S. companies were allowed to export mass-market software that incorporated encryption, provided that the products used a particular encryption algorithm and the length of the key was limited to 40 bits. At the same time, some U.S. banks started using an algorithm called Triple-des (basically, a threefold application of the DES algorithm) to encryp some financial transactions. It has a key size of 168 bits.

In October 2000, the National Institute of Standards and Technology (NIST) approved the Rijndael encryption algorithm as the new U.S. Advanced Encryption Standard. Rijndael can be used with keys of 128, 192, or 256 bits. The algorithm's extremely fast speed, combined with its status as the government-chosen standard, means that it will likely be preferable to the DES, Triple-des, and other algorithms in the future.

So how many bits is enough? That depends on how fast the attacker can try different keys and how long you wish to keep your information secure. As table shows, if an attacker can try only 10 keys per second, then a 40-bit key will protect a message for more than 3,484 years. Of course, today's computers can try many thousands of keys per second and with special-purpose hardware and software, they can try hundreds of thousands. Key search speed can be further improved by running the same program on hundreds or thousands of computers at a time. Thus, it's possible to search a million keys per second or more using today's technology. If you have the ability to search a million keys per second, you can try all 40-bit keys in only 13 days.

If a key that is 40 bits long is clearly not sufficient to keep information secure, how many bits are necessary? In April 1993, the Clinton Administration introduced the Clipper encryption chip as part of its Escrowed Encryption Initiative (EEI). This chip used a key that was 80 bits long. As table shows, an 80-bit key is more than adequate for many applications. If you could search a billion keys per second, trying all 80-bit keys would still require 38 million years. Clipper was widely criticized not because of the key length, but because the Clipper encryption algorithm was kept secret by the National Security Agency, and because each Clipper chip came with a "back door" that allowed information encrypted by each Clipper chip to be decrypted by the U.S. government in support of law enforcement and intelligence needs.

Table: Estimated success of brute force attacks (for different numbers of bits in the key and number of keys that can be tried per second).

Length of key	Keys searched per second	Postulated key-searching technology	Approximate time to search all possible keys
40 bits	10	10-year-old desktop computer.	3,484 years
40 bits	1,000	Typical desktop computer today.	35 years
40 bits	1 million	Small network of desktops.	13 days
40 bits	1 billion	Medium-sized corporate network.	18 minutes
56 bits	1 million	Desktop computer a few years from now.	2,283 years
56 bits	1 billion	Medium-sized corporate network.	2.3 years
56 bits	100 billion	DES-cracking machine.	8 days
64 bits	1 billion	Medium-sized corporate network.	585 years
80 bits	1 million	Small network of desktops.	38 billion years
80 bits	1 billion	Medium-sized corporate network.	38 million years
128 bits	1 billion	Medium-sized corporate network.	10^{22} years
128 bits	1 billion billion (1 x 10^{18})	Large-scale Internet project in the year 2005.	10,783 billion years
128 bits	1 x 10^{23}	Special-purpose quantum computer in the year 2015.	108 million years
192 bits	1 billion	Medium-sized corporate network.	2 x 10^{41} years
192 bits	1 billion billion	Large-scale Internet project in the year 2005.	2 x 10^{32} years
192 bits	1 x 10^{23}	Special-purpose quantum computer in the year 2015.	2 x 10^{27} years
256 bits	1 x 10^{23}	Special-purpose quantum computer in the year 2015.	3.7 x 10^{46} years
256 bits	1 x 10^{32}	Special-purpose quantum computer in the year 2040.	3.7 x 10^{37} years

- Computing speeds assume that a typical desktop computer in the year 2003 can execute approximately 1 billion instructions per second. This is roughly the speed of a 1 Ghz Pentium III computer.

- In 1997, a 40-bit RC4 key was cracked in only 3.5 hours.

- In 2000, a 56-bit DES key was cracked in less than 4 days.

Increasing the key size from 80 bits to 128 bits dramatically increases the amount of effort to guess the key. As the table shows, if there were a computer that could search a billion keys per second, and if you had a billion of these computers, it would still take 10,783 billion years to search all possible 128-bit keys. As our Sun is likely to become a red giant within the next 4 billion years and, in so doing, destroy the Earth, a 128-bit encryption key should be sufficient for most cryptographic uses, assuming that there are no other weaknesses in the algorithm used.

Lately, there has been considerable interest in the field of quantum computing. Scientists postulate that it should be possible to create atomic-sized computers specially designed to crack encryption keys. But while quantum computers could rapidly crack 56-bit DES keys, it's unlikely that a quantum computer could make a dent in a 128-bit encryption key within a reasonable time: even if you could crack 1×10^{23} keys per second, it would still take 108 million years to try all possible 128-bit encryption keys.

It should be pretty clear at this point that there is no need, given the parameters of cryptography and physics as we understand them today, to use key lengths that are larger than 128 bits. Nevertheless, there seems to be a marketing push towards increasingly larger and larger keys. The Rijndael algorithm can be operated with 128-bit, 192-bit, or 256-bit keys. If it turns out that there is an as-yet hidden flaw in the Rijndael algorithm that gives away half the key bits, then the use of the longer keys might make sense. Why you would want to use those longer key lengths isn't clear, but if you want them, they are there for you to use.

Common Symmetric Key Algorithms

There are many symmetric key algorithms in use today, as shown in Table.

Table: Common symmetric encryption algorithms.

Algorithm	Description	Key Length	Rating
Blowfish	Block cipher developed by Schneier.	1-448 bits	Λ
DES	DES adopted as a U.S. government standard in 1977.	56 bits	§
IDEA	Block cipher developed by Massey and Xuejia.	128 bits	Λ
MARS	AES finalist developed by IBM.	128-256 bits	$\varnothing$
RC2	Block cipher developed by Rivest.	1-2048 bits	W
RC4	Stream cipher developed by Rivest.	1-2048 bits	Λ, §
RC5	Block cipher developed by Rivest and published in 1994.	128-256 bits	$\varnothing$
RC6	AES finalist developed by RSA Labs.	128-256 bits	$\varnothing$
Rijndael	NIST selection for AES, developed by Daemen and Rijmen.	128-256 bits	W
Serpent	AES finalist developed by Anderson, Biham, and Knudsen.	128-256 bits	$\varnothing$
Triple-des	A three-fold application of the DES algorithm.	168 bits	L
Twofish	AES candidate developed by Schneier.	128-256 bits	$\varnothing$

Key to ratings:

- Excellent algorithm Ω is widely used and is believed to be secure, provided that keys of sufficient length are used.

- Algorithm Λ appears strong but is being phased out for other algorithms that are faster or thought to be more secure.

- Algorithm ∅ appears to be strong but will not be widely deployed because it was not chosen as the AES standard.

- Use of § algorithm is no longer recommended because of short key length or mathematical weaknesses. Data encrypted with this algorithm should be reasonably secure from casual browsing, but would not withstand a determined attack by a moderately-funded attacker.

Data Encryption Standard

The Data Encryption Standard (DES) was adopted as a U.S. government standard in 1977 and as an ANSI standard in 1981. The DES is a block cipher that uses a 56-bit key and has several different operating modes depending on the purpose for which it is employed. The DES is a strong algorithm, but today the short key length limits its use. Indeed, in 1998 a special-purpose machine for "cracking DES" was created by the Electronic Frontier Foundation (EFF) for under $250,000. In one demonstration, it found the key to an encrypted message in less than a day in conjunction with a coalition of computer users around the world.

Triple-des

Triple-des is a way to make the DES dramatically more secure by using the DES encryption algorithm three times with three different keys, for a total key length of 168 bits. Also called "3DES," this algorithm has been widely used by financial institutions and by the Secure Shell program (ssh). Simply using the DES twice with two different keys does not improve its security to the extent that one might at first suspect because of a theoretical plaintext attack called *meet-in-the-middle*, in which an attacker simultaneously attempts encrypting the plaintext with a single DES operation and decrypting the ciphertext with another single DES operation until a match is made in the middle. Triple-des avoids this vulnerability.

Blowfish

Blowfish is a fast, compact, and simple block encryption algorithm invented by Bruce Schneier. The algorithm allows a variable-length key, up to 448 bits, and is optimized for execution on 32- or 64-bit processors. The algorithm is unpatented and has been placed in the public domain. Blowfish is used in the Secure Shell and other programs.

International Data Encryption Algorithm

The International Data Encryption Algorithm (IDEA) was developed in Zurich, Switzerland, by James L. Massey and Xuejia Lai and published in 1990. IDEA uses a 128-bit key. IDEA is used by the popular program PGP to encrypt files and electronic mail. Unfortunately, wider use of IDEA has been hampered by a series of software patents on the algorithm, which are currently held by Ascom-Tech AG in Solothurn, Switzerland.

Although we are generally in favor of intellectual property protection, we are opposed to the concept of software patents, in part because they hinder the development and use of innovative software by individuals and small companies. Software patents also tend to hinder some forms of experimental research and education.

RC2

This block cipher was originally developed by Ronald Rivest and kept as a trade secret by RSA Data Security. The algorithm was revealed by an anonymous Usenet posting in 1996 and appears to be reasonably strong (although there are some particular keys that are weak). RC2 allows keys between 1 and 2,048 bits. The RC2 key length was traditionally limited to 40 bits in software that was exported to allow for decryption by the U.S. National Security Agency.

The 40-bit "exportable" implementation of SSL actually uses a 128-bit RC2 key, in which 88 bits are revealed, producing a "40-bit secret." Netscape claimed that the 88 bits provided protection against *codebook attacks*, in which all 2^{40} keys would be precomputed and the resulting encryption patterns stored. Other SSL implementors have suggested that using a 128-bit key in all cases and simply revealing 88 bits of the key in exportable versions of Navigator made Netscape's SSL implementation easier to write.

RC4

This stream cipher was originally developed by Ronald Rivest and kept as a trade secret by RSA Data Security. This algorithm was also revealed by an anonymous Usenet posting in 1994 and appears to be reasonably strong. RC4 allows keys between 1 and 2,048 bits. The RC4 key length was traditionally limited to 40 bits in software that was exported.

RC5

This block cipher was developed by Ronald Rivest and published in 1994. RC5 allows a user-defined key length, data block size, and number of encryption rounds.

Rijndael (AES)

This block cipher was developed by Joan Daemen and Vincent Rijmen, and was chosen in October 2000 by the National Institute of Standards and Technology to be the U.S.'s new Advanced Encryption Standard. Rijndael is an extraordinarily fast and compact cipher that can use keys that are 128, 192, or 256 bits long.

In September 2002, Bruce Schneier's Crypto-Gram Newsletter reported on a series of academic papers that have found weaknesses or points of attack in the Rijndael cipher (as well as several others). Although Schneier takes pains to point out that these attacks are currently highly theoretical and potentially impossible to implement, the history of cryptography suggests that AES may not be remembered as the last best cryptosystem.

Attacks on Symmetric Encryption Algorithms

If you are going to use cryptography to protect information, then you must assume that people who you do not wish to access your information will be recording your data, and, if they determine it is encrypted, may try to decrypt it forcibly. To be useful, your cryptographic system must be resistant to this kind of direct attack.

Whitfield Diffie has pointed out that if your data is not going to be subjected to this sort of direct attack, then there is no need to encrypt it.

Attacks against encrypted information fall into three main categories. They are:

- Key search (brute force) attacks,
- Cryptanalysis,
- Systems-based attacks.

Brute Force Attacks

The simplest way to attack an encrypted message is simply to attempt to decrypt the message with every possible key. Most attempts will fail, but eventually one of the tries will succeed and either allow the cracker into the system or permit the ciphertext to be decrypted. These attacks, illustrated in figure are called key search or brute force attacks.

There's no way to defend against a key search attack because there's no way to keep an attacker from trying to decrypt your message with every possible key.

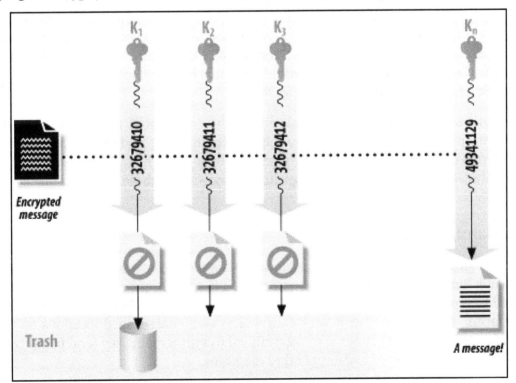

A key search attack.

Key search attacks are not very efficient. And, as we showed earlier, if the chosen key is long enough, a key search attack is not even feasible. For example, with a 128-bit key and any conceivable computing technology, life on Earth will cease to exist long before even a single key is likely to be cracked.

On the other hand, many key search attacks are made considerably simpler because most users pick keys based on small passwords with printable characters. For a 128-bit key to be truly secure, all 128 bits must be randomly chosen. That is, there must be 2^{128} distinct keys that could possibly be used to encrypt the data. If a "128-bit key" is actually derived from a password of four lower-case letters, then even though the key appears to be 128 bits long, there are really only 26 x 26 x 26 x 26, or 456,976 different keys that could actually be used. Instead of a 128-bit key, a key that is chosen from four lower-case letters has an effective key length between 18 bits and 19 bits. This is because $2^{18} = 262,144$, while $2^{19} = 524,288$.

From this simple analysis, it would appear that any of the strong algorithms described earlier with a 128-bit key length should be sufficient for most cryptographic needs both now and forever more. Unfortunately, there are a number of factors that make this solution technically, legally, or politically unsuitable for many applications.

Cryptanalysis

If key length were the only factor determining the security of a cipher, everyone interested in exchanging secret messages would simply use codes with 128-bit keys, and all cryptanalysts (people who break codes) would have to find new jobs. Cryptography would be a resolved branch of mathematics, similar to simple addition.

What keeps cryptography interesting is the fact that most encryption algorithms do not live up to our expectations. Key search attacks are seldom required to divulge the contents of an encrypted message. Instead, most encryption algorithms can be defeated by using a combination of sophisticated mathematics and computing power. The result is that many encrypted messages can be deciphered without knowing the key. A skillful cryptanalyst can sometimes decipher encrypted text without even knowing the encryption algorithm.

A cryptanalytic attack can have two possible goals. The cryptanalyst might have ciphertext and want to discover the plaintext, or might have ciphertext and want to discover the encryption key that was used to encrypt it. (These goals are similar but not quite the same.) The following attacks are commonly used when the encryption algorithm is known, and these may be applied to encrypted files or Internet traffic:

Known Plaintext Attack

In this type of attack, the cryptanalyst has a block of plaintext and a corresponding block of ciphertext. Although this may seem an unlikely occurrence, it is actually quite common when cryptography is used to protect electronic mail (with standard headers at the beginning of each message), standard forms, or hard disks (with known structures at predetermined locations on the disk). The goal of a known plaintext attack is to determine the cryptographic key (and possibly the algorithm), which can then be used to decrypt other messages.

Chosen Plaintext Attack

In this type of attack, the cryptanalyst has the subject of the attack (unknowingly) encrypt chosen blocks of data, creating a result that the cryptanalyst can then analyze. Chosen plaintext attacks are simpler to carry out than they might appear. For example, the subject of the attack might be a radio link that encrypts and retransmits messages received by telephone. The goal of a chosen plaintext attack is to determine the cryptographic key, which can then be used to decrypt other messages.

Differential Cryptanalysis

This attack, which is a form of chosen plaintext attack, involves encrypting many texts that are only slightly different from one another and comparing the results.

Differential Fault Analysis

This attack works against cryptographic systems that are built in hardware. The device is subjected to environmental factors (heat, stress, radiation) designed to coax the device into making mistakes during the encryption or decryption operation. These faults can be analyzed, and from them the device's internal state, including the encryption key or algorithm, can possibly be learned.

Differential Power Analysis

This is another attack against cryptographic hardware in particular, smart cards. By observing the power that a smart card uses to encrypt a chosen block of data, it is possible to learn a little bit of information about the structure of the secret key. By subjecting the smart card to a number of specially chosen data blocks and carefully monitoring the power used, it is possible to determine the secret key.

Differential Timing Analysis

This attack is similar to differential power analysis, except that the attacker carefully monitors the time that the smart card takes to perform the requested encryption operations.

The only reliable way to determine if an algorithm is strong is to hire a stable of the world's best cryptographers and pay them to find a weakness. This is the approach used by the U.S. National Security Agency. Unfortunately, this approach is beyond the ability of most cryptographers, who instead settle on an alternative known as peer review.

Peer review is the process by which most mathematical and scientific truths are verified. First, a person comes up with a new idea or proposes a new theory. Next, the inventor attempts to test his idea or theory on his own. If the idea holds up, it is then published in an academic journal or otherwise publicized within a community of experts. If the experts are motivated, they might look at the idea and see if it has any worth. If the idea stands up over the passage of time, especially if many experts try and fail to disprove the idea, it gradually comes to be regarded as truth.

Peer review of cryptographic algorithms and computer security software follows a similar process. As individuals or organizations come up with a new algorithm, the algorithm is published. If the algorithm is sufficiently interesting, cryptographers or other academics might be motivated to find flaws in it. If the algorithm can stand the test of time, it might be secure, pending some new mathematical discovery or technique being developed.

It's important to realize that simply publishing an algorithm or a piece of software does not guarantee that flaws will be found. The Wireless Encryption Protocol (WEP) encryption algorithm used by the 802.11 networking standard was published for many years before a significant flaw was found in the algorithm the flaw had been there all along, but no one had bothered to look for it.

The peer review process isn't perfect, but it's better than the alternative: no review at all. Do not trust people who say they've developed a new encryption algorithm but also say that they don't want to disclose how the algorithm works because such disclosure would compromise the strength of the algorithm. In practice, there is no way to keep an algorithm secret: if the algorithm is being used to store information that is valuable, an attacker will purchase (or steal) a copy of a program that implements the algorithm, disassemble the program, and figure out how it works. True cryptographic security lies in openness and peer review, not in algorithmic secrecy.

In the case of the RC2 and RC4 encryption algorithms, the attackers went further and published source code for the reverse-engineered algorithms.

Systems-based Attacks

Another way of breaking a code is to attack the cryptographic system that uses the cryptographic algorithm, without actually attacking the algorithm itself.

One of the most spectacular cases of a systems-based attack was the VC-I video encryption algorithm used for early satellite TV broadcasts. For years, video pirates sold decoder boxes that could intercept the transmissions of keys and use them to decrypt the broadcasts. The VC-I encryption algorithm was sound, but the system as a whole was weak. This case also demonstrates the fact that when a lot of money is at stake, people will often find the flaws in a weak encryption system, and those flaws will be exploited.

Many of the early attacks against Netscape's implementation of SSL were actually attacks on Netscape Navigator's implementation, rather than on the SSL protocol itself. In one published attack, researchers David Wagner and Ian Goldberg at the University of California at Berkeley discovered that Navigator's random number generator was not really random. It was possible for attackers to closely monitor the computer on which Navigator was running, predict the random number generator's starting configuration, and determine the randomly chosen key using a fairly straightforward method. In another attack, the researchers discovered that they could easily modify the Navigator program itself so that the random number generator would not be executed. This entirely eliminated the need to guess the key.

Covert channels are another concern. The U.S. Department of Defense's 1985 Trusted Computer System Evaluation Criteria define a covert channel as "any communication channel that can be exploited by a process to transfer information in a manner that violates the system's security policy." For example, even if an attacker cannot decrypt encrypted email messages, he may be able to gain information by examining the message sender, recipient, timing, path through the network, character set encoding, or other features that are often overlooked by those concerned about message confidentiality or integrity alone.

Asymmetric Key Algorithms

AWS services typically support RSA and Elliptic Curve Cryptography (ECC) asymmetric algorithms.

An encryption scheme is called asymmetric if it uses one key to encrypt and a different, but mathematically related, key to decrypt. It must be computationally infeasible to determine one key if the only thing one knows is the other key. Therefore, one key can be distributed publicly while the related key is kept secret and secure. Together the keys are referred to as a key pair. The key that's publicly distributed is called the public key and the key that's kept secret is called the private key.

Another more common name for asymmetric encryption is public-key cryptography. Public key cryptography is typically based on mathematical problems that are relatively easy to perform but cannot be easily reversed. These include factoring a large integer back into its component prime numbers and solving the elliptic curve discrete logarithm function. The RSA algorithm is based on the practical difficulty of factoring the product of two large prime numbers. Elliptic curve cryptography is based on the difficulty of finding the discrete logarithm of a random point on an elliptic curve given a publicly known point.

Berlekamp–Massey Algorithm

The Berlekamp-Massey algorithm is an algorithm for determining the linear complexity of a finite sequence and the feedback polynomial of a linearfeedback shift register (LFSR) of minimal length which generates this sequence. This algorithm is due to Massey, who showed that the iterative algorithm proposed in 1967 by Berlekamp for decoding BCH codes can be used for finding the shortest LFSR that generates a given sequence.

Let $\mathbb{K}$ be an arbitrary field. Given a linearly recurrent sequence, denoted by $S(x) = \sum_{i=0}^{\infty} a_i x^i$, $a_i \in \mathbb{K}$.

We wish to compute its minimal polynomial, denoted by $P(x)$. Recall that if $P(x)$ is given by $P(x) = \sum_{i=0}^{d} p_i x^i$ denotes such polynomial, then $P(x)$ is the polynomial of the smallest degree such that $\sum_{i=0}^{d} p_i a_{j+i} = 0$, for all j in $\mathbb{N}$.

Let suppose that the minimal polynomial of $S(x)$ has degree bound n. Under such hypothesis, the Berlekamp-Massey Algorithm only requires the first $2n$ coefficients of $S(x)$ in order to compute the minimal polynomial. Such coefficients define the polynomial $S = \sum_{i=0}^{2n-1} a_i x^i$.

The usual interpretation of the Berlekamp-Massey Algorithm for obtaining $P(x)$ is expressed in pseudocode in Algorithm.

In practice, we must apply the simplification of the extended Euclidean Algorithm given in, to find exactly the Berlekamp-Massey Algorithm. Such simplification is based on the fact that initial R_0 is equal to x^{2n}.

Although Algorithm is not complicated, it seems to be no easy to find a direct and transparent explanation for the determination of the degree of P. We think there is a little confusion with the different definitions of minimal polynomial and with the different ways of defining the sequence.

Algorithm: The Usual Berlekamp-Massey Algorithm

Input: $n \in \mathbb{N}$. The first $2n$ coefficients of a linearly recurrent sequence defined over $\mathbb{K}$, given by the list $[a_0; a_1, \ldots, a_{2n-1}]$. The minimal polynomial has degree bound n.

Output: The Minimal Polynomial P of the Sequence

Start

Local variables: $R, R_0, R_1, V, V_0, V_1, Q$: polynomials in x,

    # initialization

$$R_0 := x^{2n}; R_1 := \sum_{i=0}^{2n-1} a_i x^i; V_0 = 0; V_1 = 1;$$

    # loop

while $n \le deg(R_1)$ do,

    $(Q;R) :=$ quotient and remainder of R_0 divided by R_1;

    $V := V_0 - QV_1$;

    $V_0 := V_1; V_1 := V; R_0 := R_1; R_1 := R$;

    end while

    # exit

    $d := \max\left(\deg(V_1); 1 + \deg(R_1)\right); P := x^d V_1(1 = x);$ Return $P := P = \text{leadcoeff}(P)$.

End.

Some Good Reasons to Modify the Usual Algorithm

By the one hand, as it can be observed at the end of Algorithm, we have to compute the (nearly) reverse polynomial of V_1, in order to obtain the right polynomial. The following example helps us to understand what happens:

$$n = d = 3;$$

$$S = a_0 + a_1 x + a_2 x^2 + a_3 x^3 + a_4 x^4 + a_5 x^5 = 1 + 2x + 7x^2 - 9x^3 + 2x^4 + 7x^5,$$

Algorithm $\left(3, [1, 2, 7, -9, 2, 7]\right) \Rightarrow P = x + x^2 + x^3,$

with,

$$V_1 = v_0 + v_1 x + v_2 x^2 = 49/67\left(1 + x + x^2\right),$$

and R such that $S V_1 = R \bmod x^6$, $\deg(R) = 2$,

which implies that,

$$
\begin{aligned}
\mathrm{coeff}\left(S\ V_1, x, 3\right) &= a_1 v_2 + a_2 v_1 + a_3 v_0 = 2v_2 + 7v_1 - 9v_0 = 0, \\
\mathrm{coeff}\left(S\ V_1, x, 4\right) &= a_2 v_2 + a_3 v_1 + a_4 v_0 = 7v_2 - 9v_1 + 2v_0 = 0, \\
\mathrm{coeff}\left(S\ V_1, x, 5\right) &= a_3 v_2 + a_4 v_1 + a l v_0 = -9v_2 + 2v_1 + 7v_0 = 0.
\end{aligned}
$$

Hence, the right degree of P is given by the degree of the last R_1 plus one because x divides P. Observe that $a_0 v_2 + a_1 v_1 + a_2 v_0 = 490 = 676 \neq 0$. We would like to obtain directly the desired polynomial from V_1.

Moreover, by the other hand, in Algorithm all the first $2n$ coefficients are required to start the usual algorithm, where n only provides a degree bound for the minimal polynomial. Consequently, it may be possible that the true degree of P is much smaller that n and so, less coefficients of the sequence are required to obtain the wanted polynomial.

So it is a more natural, efficient and direct way to obtain P. The idea is to consider the Polynomial $\hat{S} = \sum_{i=0}^{2n-1} a_i x^{2n-1-i}$ as the initial R_1. Observe that in this case, using the same notation as in Algorithm, the same example shows that it is not necessary to reverse the polynomial V_1 at the end of the algorithm.

$$n = d = 3,$$

$$
\hat{S} = a_0 x^5 + a_1 x^4 + a_2 x^3 + a_3 x^2 + a_4 x + a_5 = x^5 + 2x^4 + 7x^3 - 9x^2 + 2x^1 + 7,
$$

Algorithm $\left(3, [1, 2, 7, -9, 2, 7]\right) \Rightarrow P = x + x^2 + x^3,$

with,

$$
V_1 = v_0 + v_1 x + v_2 x^2 + v_3 x^3 = -9/670\left(x + x^2 + x^3\right),
$$

and R such that $\hat{S} V_1 = R \bmod x^6$, $\deg(R) = 2$.

Which implies that,

$$
\begin{aligned}
\mathrm{coeff}\left(\hat{S}\ V_1, x, 3\right) &= a_2 v_0 + a_3 v_1 + a_4 v_1 = -9v_1 + 2v_2 + 7v_3 = 0, \\
\mathrm{coeff}\left(\hat{S}\ V_1, x, 4\right) &= a_1 v_0 + a_2 v_1 + a_3 v_2 + a_4 v_3 = 7v_1 - 9v_2 + 2v_3 = 0, \\
\mathrm{coeff}\left(\hat{S}\ V_1, x, 5\right) &= a_0 v_0 + a_1 v_1 + a_2 v_2 + a_3 v_3 = 2v_1 + 7v_2 + 9v_0 = 0.
\end{aligned}
$$

Furthermore, when $n \gg \deg(P)$, the algorithm can admit a lazy evaluation. In other words, the algorithm can be initiated with less coefficients than $2n$ and if the outcome does not provide the wanted polynomial, we increase the number of coefficients but remark that it is not necessary to initiate again the algorithm because we can take advantages of the computations done before. We will explain this application of the algorithm.

Next, we introduce the modified Berlekamp-Massey Algorithm in pseudocode (Algorithm):

Algorithm: Modified Berlekamp-Massey Algorithm

Input: $n \in \mathbb{N}$. The first $2n$ coefficients of a linearly recurrent sequence defined over $\mathbb{K}$, given by the list $[a_0; a_1, \ldots, a_{2n-1}]$. The minimal polynomial has degree bound n.

Output: The minimal polynomial P of the sequence.

Start:

Local variables: $R, R_0, R_1, V, V_0, V1, Q$: polynomials in x; $m = 2n - 1$; integer.

    # initialization

$$m := 2n - 1; \ R_0 := x^{2n}; \ R_1 := \sum_{i=0}^{M} a_{m-i} \, x^i; \ V_0 = 0; \ V_1 = 1;$$

    # loop

while $n \leq \deg(R_1)$ do,

    $V := V_0 - QV_1;$
    $V_0 := V_1; V_1 := V; R_0 := R_1; R_1 := R;$

    end while

    # exit

    Return $P := V_1 = \mathrm{lc}(V_1);$

End.

Now we prove the result. Let $\underline{a} = (a_n)_{n \in \mathbb{N}}$ be an arbitrary list and $i, r, p \in \mathbb{N}$. Let $H^{\underline{a}}_{i,r,p}$ denote the following Hankel matrix of order $r \times p$,

$$H^{\underline{a}}_{i,r,p} = \begin{bmatrix} a_i & a_{i+1} & a_{i+2} & \cdots & a_{i+p-1} \\ a_{i+1} & a_{i+2} & & & a_{i+p} \\ a_{i+2} & & & & \\ \vdots & & & & \vdots \\ a_{i+r-1} & a_{i+r} & \cdots & \cdots & a_{i+r+p-2} \end{bmatrix}$$

and let $P^{\underline{a}}(x)$ be the minimal polynomial of $\underline{a}$.

Proposition Let $\underline{a}$ be a linearly recurrent sequence. If $\underline{a}$ has a generating polynomial of degree $\leq n$, then the degree d of its minimal polynomial Pa is equal to the rank of the Hankel matrix,

$$
H_{i,r,p}^{\underline{a}} =
\begin{bmatrix}
a_0 & a_1 & a_2 & \cdots & a_{n-2} & a_{n-1} \\
a_1 & a_2 & & \cdot\cdot\cdot & a_{n-1} & a_n \\
a_2 & & \cdot\cdot\cdot & \cdot\cdot\cdot & \vdots & \vdots \\
\vdots & & \cdot\cdot\cdot & \cdot\cdot\cdot & \vdots & \vdots \\
a_{n-2} & a_{n-1} & \cdots & \cdots & a_{2n-2} & a_{2n-1} \\
a_{n-1} & a_n & \cdots & \cdots & a_{2n-1} & a_{2n-2}
\end{bmatrix}
$$

The coefficients of $P^{\underline{a}}(x) = x^d - \sum_{i=0}^{d-1} g_i x^i \in \mathbb{K}[x]$ are provided by the unique solution of the linear system,

$$ H_{0,d,d}^{\underline{a}} \, G = H_{1,d,1}^{\underline{a}}, $$

that is,

$$
\begin{bmatrix}
a_0 & a_1 & a_2 & \cdots & a_{d-1} \\
a_1 & a_2 & & \cdot\cdot\cdot & a_d \\
a_2 & & \cdot\cdot\cdot & \cdot\cdot\cdot & \vdots \\
\vdots & & \cdot\cdot\cdot & \cdot\cdot\cdot & \vdots \\
a_{d-1} & a_d & \cdots & \cdots & a_{2d-2}
\end{bmatrix}
\begin{bmatrix}
g_0 \\ g_1 \\ g_2 \\ \vdots \\ g_{d-1}
\end{bmatrix}
=
\begin{bmatrix}
a_d \\ a_{d+1} \\ a_{d+2} \\ \vdots \\ a_{2d-1}
\end{bmatrix}
$$

As an immediate corollary of Proposition, we have the following result.

Using the notation of Proposition, a vector $Y = (p_0, \ldots, p_n)$ is solution of,

$$ H_{0,n,n+1}^{\underline{a}} \, Y = 0 $$

that is,

$$
\begin{bmatrix}
a_0 & a_1 & a_2 & \cdots & a_{n-1} & a_n \\
a_1 & a_2 & & \cdot\cdot\cdot & a_n & a_{n+1} \\
a_2 & & \cdot\cdot\cdot & \cdot\cdot\cdot & \vdots & \vdots \\
\vdots & & \cdot\cdot\cdot & \cdot\cdot\cdot & \vdots & \vdots \\
a_{n-1} & a_n & \cdots & \cdots & a_{2n-2} & a_{2n-1}
\end{bmatrix}
\begin{bmatrix}
p_0 \\ p_1 \\ p_2 \\ \vdots \\ p_{n-1} \\ p_n
\end{bmatrix}
= 0
$$

If and only if the polynomial $P(x) = \sum_{i=0}^{n} p_1 x^i \in \mathbb{K}[x]$ is multiple of $P^{\underline{a}}(x)$.

By Proposition the dimension of $\mathrm{Ker}\left(H_{0,n,n+1}^{\underline{a}}\right)$ is $n-d$. For $0 \le j \le n-1$, let C_j denote the jth column of $H_{0,n,n+1}^{\underline{a}}$, that is $C_j = H_{j,n,1}^{\underline{a}} = \left[a_j, a_{j+1}, \ldots, a_{n+j-1}\right]^t$. Since $P^{\underline{a}}(x)$ is a generating polynomial of $\underline{a}$, for $d \le j \le n-1$, we obtain that,

$$C_j - \sum_{1=j-d}^{j-1} g_{i-j-d} C_i = 0.$$

Thus the linear independent columns $[-g_0,\ldots,-g_{d-1},1,0,\ldots,0]^t,\ldots,[0,\ldots,0;-g_0,\ldots,-g_{d-1},1]^t$ define a basis of Ker $\left(H^a_{0,n,n+1}\right)$. Therefore, $Y = (p_0,\ldots,p_n)$ verifies $H^a_{0,n,n+1} Y = 0$ if and only if the polynomial $P(x) = \sum_{i=0}^{n} p_i x^i$ is a multiple of $P^a(x)$.

If we consider $m = 2n - 1$ and $\hat{S} = \sum_{i=0}^{m} a_{m-i} x^i$, by applying above given equation we obtain:

$$\exists R; U \in K[x]$$

such that,

$$\deg(R) < n; \deg(P) \leq n$$

and

$$P(x)S(x) + U(x)x^{2n} = R(x).$$

Hence, it turns out that finding the minimal polynomial of a is equivalent to solving above equation for the minimum degree of P. Moreover, it's well known that,

- The extended Euclidean Algorithm, with x^{2n} and $\hat{S}$, provides an equality as above equation when the first remainder of degree smaller than $< n$ is reached. Let denote such remainder by R_k,

- If we consider other polynomials $P'(x), U'(x)$ and $R'(x)$ such that $P'(x)\hat{S}(x) + U'(x)x^{2n}$ $= R'(x)$ and $\deg(R')$ $\deg(R$ $)$, then $\deg(P') \geq \deg(P)$ and $\deg(U') \geq \deg(U)$.

That proves that the modification of Berlekamp-Massey Algorithm is right.

Lazy Evaluation

The modified Berlekamp-Massey Algorithm admits a lazy evaluation, which may be very useful in solving the following problem.

Let $f(x) \in K[x]$ be a squarefree polynomial of degree n. Let B be the universal decomposition algebra of $f(x)$, let A be a quotient algebra of B and $a \in A$. Thus, A is a zero–dimensional algebra given by,

$$A \simeq K[X_1,\ldots,X_n]/\langle f_1,\ldots,f_n\rangle,$$

where $f_1,\ldots,f_n$ define a Gröbner basis. The aim is to compute the minimal polynomial of a, or at least, one of its factors. However, the dimension of A, denoted by m, over K as vector space is normally too big to manipulate matrices of order m. Therefore, we apply the idea of Wiedemann's Algorithm, by computing the coefficients of a linearly recurrent sequence, $a_t = \phi(x^t)$, where ϕ is a linear form over A. Moreover, since the computation of x^t is usually very expensive and the minimal polynomial is likely to have degree smaller than the dimension, we are interested in computing the smallest possible number of coefficients in order to get the wanted polynomial.

Hence, we first choose $l < m$. We start Algorithm with l and $\left[\phi\left(x^0\right),\ldots,\phi\left(x^{2l-1}\right)\right]$ as input, obtaining a polynomial as a result. Now, we test if such a polynomial is the minimal one. If this is not the case, we choose again another $l', < l < l' \leq m$, and we repeat the process with $2\,l'$ coefficients. However, in this next step, it is possible to take advantages of all the quotients computed before (with the exception of the last one), such that Euclidean Algorithm starts at $R_0 = U_0 x^{2l'} + V_0 \sum_{i=0}^{2l'-1}\left(\phi\left(x^{2l'-1-i}\right)x^i\right)$

and $R_1 = U_1 x^{2l'} + V_1 \sum_{i=0}^{2l'-1}\left(\phi\left(x^{2l'-1-i}\right)x^i\right)$, where U_0, V_0, U_1 and V_1 are Bezout coefficients computed in the previous step. Manifestly, repeating this argument again and again, we obtain the minimal polynomial.

The following pseudocode tries to facilitate the understanding of the lazy version of Berlekamp-Massey Algorithm.

Obviously, the choice of l is not unique. Here we have started at $l = m/4$, adding two coefficients in every further step. In practice, the particular characteristics of the given problem could help to choose a proper l and the method of increasing it through the algorithm. Of course, the simplification of the Euclidean Algorithm in must be considered to optimize the procedure.

Algorithm: The lazy Berlekamp-Massey Algorithm

Input: $m \in N, C \in K^n$, G: Gröbner basis, $a \in A$. The minimal polynomial has degree bound m.

Output: The minimal polynomial P of a,

Start:

Local variables:

   l, i: integers, $R, R_{-1}; R_0; R_1, V, V_{-1}, V_0, V_1, U, U_{-1}, U_0, U_1, S_0, S_1, Q$: polynomials in $x, L; W$: lists, validez;

   # initialization

   $l = \left[m/4\right]$;

   $L := [1;\ a]; W := [1; Value(a;C)]$;

   $S_0 := x^{2l}; S_1 = W[1]x^{2l-1} + W[2]x^{2l-2}$;

   # loop

   for i from 3 to $2l$ do

$$L[i] := \text{normalf}\left(L[i-1]a, G\right); V[i] := Value\left(L[i], C\right); S_1 = S_1 + V[i]x^{2l-i};$$

end for,

$$R_0 := S_0; R_1 := S_1; V_0 = 0; V_1 = 1; U_0 = 1; V_1 = 0;$$
loop

while $l \leq \deg\left(R_1\right)$ do,

$$(Q;R) := \text{quotient and remainder of } R_0 \text{ divided by } R_1;$$

$$V := V_0 - QV_1; U := U_0 - QU_1; U_{-1} := U_0; V_{-1} := V_0;$$

$$V_0 := V_1; V_1 := V; U_0 := U_1; U_1 := U; R_0 := R_1; R_1 := R;$$

end while,

$$\text{validez} := \text{Subs}\left(x = a; V_1\right);$$

loop

while validez $\neq 0$ do,

$$l := l + 1;$$

loop

for i from $2l - 1$ to $2l$ do,

$$L[i] := \text{normalf}\left(L[i-1]a; G\right);$$

$$W[i] := Value\left(L[i]; C\right);$$

end for,

$$S_0 = x^2 S_0; S_1 = x^2 S_1 + W[2l - 1]x + W[2l];$$

$$R_0 := U_{-1}S_0 + V_{-1}S_1; R_1 := U_0 S_0 + V_0 S_1;$$

$$U_1 := U_0; V_1 := V_0; U_0 := U_{-1}; V_0 := V_{-1};$$

loop

while $l \leq deg\left(R_1\right)$ do,

$$(Q, R) := \text{quotient and remainder of } R_0 \text{ divided by } R_1;$$

$$V := V_0 - QV_1; U := U_0 - QU_1; U_{-1} := U_0; V_{-1} := V_0;$$

$$V_0 := V_1; V_1 := V; U_0 := U_1; U_1 := U; R_0 := R_1; R_1 := R;$$

end while,

$$\text{validez} := \text{Subs}\left(x = a, V_1\right)$$

end while,

exit

Return $P := V_1 / \text{leadcoeff}\left(P\right).$

End.

Encryption Algorithms for Information Security

Encryption algorithms are commonly used in computer communications, including FTP transfers. Usually they are used to provide secure transfers. If an algorithm is used in a transfer, the file is first translated into a seemingly meaningless cipher text and then transferred in this configuration; the receiving computer uses a key to translate the cipher into its original form. So if the message or file is intercepted before it reaches the receiving computer it is in an unusable (or encrypted) form.

Detailed Description of Common Encryption Algorithms

The generation, modification and transportation of keys have been done by the encryption algorithm. There are many cryptographic algorithms available in the market to encrypt the data. The strength of encryption algorithm heavily relies on the computer system used for the generation of keys.

Rivest Shamir Adleman

Rivest Shamir Adleman (RSA) is designed by Ron Rivest, Adi Shamir, and Leonard Adleman in 1978. It is one of the best known public key cryptosystems for key exchange or digital signatures or encryption of blocks of data. RSA uses a variable size encryption block and a variable size key. It is an asymmetric (public key) cryptosystem based on number theory, which is a block cipher system. It uses two prime numbers to generate the public and private keys. These two different keys are used for encryption and decryption purpose. Sender encrypts the message using Receiver public key and when the message gets transmit to receiver, then receiver can decrypt it using his own private key. RSA operations can be decomposed in three broad steps; key generation, encryption and decryption. RSA have many flaws in its design therefore not preferred for the commercial use. When the small values of p & q are selected for the designing of key then the encryption process becomes too weak and one can be able to decrypt the data by using random probability theory and side channel attacks. On the other hand if large p & q lengths are selected then it consumes more time and the performance gets degraded in comparison with DES. Further, the algorithm also requires of similar lengths for p & q, practically this is very tough conditions to satisfy. Padding techniques are required in such cases increases the system's overheads by taking more processing time. Figure illustrates the sequence of events followed by RSA algorithm for the encryption of multiple blocks.

Key Generation Procedure

Choose two distinct large random prime numbers p & q such that $p \neq q$.

- Compute $n = p \times q$.

- Calculate: phi $(n) = (p-1) \ (q-1)$.

- Choose an integer e such that $1 < e < \text{phi}(n)$.

- Compute d to satisfy the congruence relation d × e = 1 mod phi (n); d is kept as private key exponent.

- The public key is (n, e) and the private key is (n, d). Keep all the values d, p, q and phi secret.

Encryption

- Plaintext: P < n,

- Ciphertext: C= P^e mod n.

Decryption

- Ciphertext: C,

- Plaintext: P=C^d mod n.

Data Encryption Standard

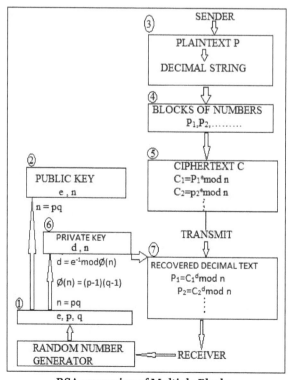

RSA processing of Multiple Blocks.

DES is one of the most widely accepted, publicly available cryptographic systems. It was developed by IBM in the 1970s but was later adopted by the National Institute of Standards and Technology (NIST), as Federal Information Processing Standard 46 (FIPS PUB 46). The Data Encryption Standard (DES) is a block Cipher which is designed to encrypt and decrypt blocks of data consisting of 64 bits by using a 64-bit key.

Although the input key for DES is 64 bits long, the actual key used by DES is only 56 bits in length. The least significant (right-most) bit in each byte is a parity bit, and should be set so that there are always an odd number of 1s in every byte. These parity bits are ignored, so only the seven most significant bits of each byte are used, resulting in a key length of 56 bits. The algorithm goes through 16 iterations that interlace blocks of plaintext with values obtained from the key. The algorithm transforms 64-bit input in a series of steps into a 64-bit output. The same steps, with the same key are used for decryption. There are many attacks and methods recorded till now those exploit the weaknesses of DES, which made it an insecure block cipher. Despite the growing concerns about its vulnerability, DES is still widely used by financial services and other industries worldwide to protect sensitive on-line applications.

The flow of DES Encryption algorithm is shown in figure. The algorithm processes with an initial permutation, sixteen rounds block cipher and a final permutation (i.e. reverse initial permutation).

Triple DES

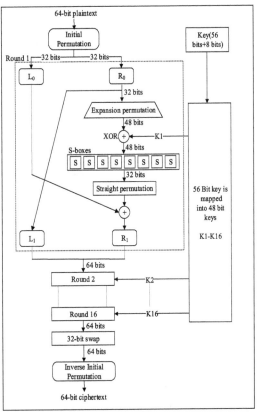

General Depiction of DES.

3DES or the Triple Data Encryption Algorithm (TDEA) was developed to address the obvious flaws in DES without designing a whole new cryptosystem. Data Encryption Standard (DES) uses a

56-bit key and is not deemed sufficient to encrypt sensitive data. 3-DES simply extends the key size of DES by applying the algorithm three times in succession with three different keys. The combined key size is thus 168 bits (3 times 56). TDEA involves using three 64-bit DEA keys (K1, K2, K3) in Encrypt-Decrypt- Encrypt (EDE) mode, that is, the plain text is encrypted with K1, then decrypted with K2, and then encrypted again with K3. The standards define three keying options.

- Option 1, the preferred option, employs three mutually independent keys $K1 \neq K2 \neq K3 \neq K1$. It gives keyspace of $3 \times 56 = 168$ bits.

- Option 2 employs two mutually independent keys and a third key that is the same as the first key $(K1\,K2 \text{ and } K3 = K1)$. This gives keyspace of $2 \times 56 = 112$ bits.

- Option 3 is a key bundle of three identical keys $(K1 = K2 = K3)$. This option is equivalent to DES Algorithm.

In 3-DES the 3-times iteration is applied to increase the encryption level and average time. It is a known fact that 3DES is slower than other block cipher methods.

Advanced Encryption Standard

AES is the new encryption standard recommended by NIST to replace DES in 2001. AES algorithm can support any combination of data (128 bits) and key length of 128, 192, and 256 bits. The algorithm is referred to as AES-128, AES-192, or AES-256, depending on the key length. During encryptiondecryption process, AES system goes through 10 rounds for 128-bit keys, 12 rounds for 192-bit keys, and 14 rounds for 256-bit keys in order to deliver final cipher-text or to retrieve the original plain-text. AES allows a 128 bit data length that can be divided into four basic operational blocks. These blocks are treated as array of bytes and organized as a matrix of the order of 4×4 that is called the state. For both encryption and decryption, the cipher begins with an AddRoundKey stage. However, before reaching the final round, this output goes though nine main rounds, during each of those rounds four transformations are performed; 1) Sub-bytes, 2) Shiftrows, 3) Mix-columns, 4) Add round Key. In the final (10th) round, there is no Mix-column transformation. Figure shows the overall process. Decryption is the reverse process of encryption and using inverse functions: Inverse Substitute Bytes, Inverse Shift Rows and Inverse Mix Columns.

Each round of AES is governed by the following transformations:

Substitute Byte Transformation

AES contains 128 bit data block, which means each of the data blocks has 16 bytes. In sub-byte transformation, each byte (8-bit) of a data block is transformed into another block using an 8-bit substitution box which is known as Rijndael Sbox.

Shift Rows Transformation

It is a simple byte transposition, the bytes in the last three rows of the state, depending upon the row location, are cyclically shifted. For 2nd row, 1 byte circular left shift is performed. For the 3rd and 4th row 2-byte and 3-byte left circular left shifts are performed respectively.

Mixcolumns Transformation

This round is equivalent to a matrix multiplication of each Column of the states. A fix matrix is multiplied to each column vector. In this operation the bytes are taken as polynomials rather than numbers.

Addroundkey Transformation

It is a bitwise XOR between the 128 bits of present state and 128 bits of the round key. This transformation is its own inverse.

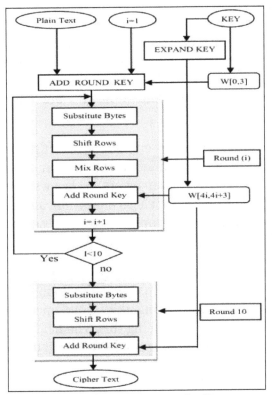

AES (Advanced Encryption Standard) process.

Double Ratchet Algorithm

The Double Ratchet Algorithm was developed by Trevor Perrin and Moxie Marlinspike, and is used in Open Whisper Systems Signal package. The method implements perfect forward secrecy for communications, with a triple Diffie-Hellman method for authentication and ECDHE for perfect forward secrecy. It is used in a number of systems including with Signal. The two parties exchange encrypted messages based on a shared secret key. They create a new set of keys every Double Ratchet message. In this way earlier keys cannot be calculated from the ones that follow. They also send Diffie-Hellman public values with their messages, and and the results of the Diffie-Hellman calculations are then mixed together into the derived keys. The protocol is useful for making sure that a hack on one set of keys does not lead to a hack on the rest of the keys. In the following we will create two names (a and b), and the a will encrypt two messages for b, and b will encrypt one message for a.

Within Signal we see the implementation of a double ratchet system which is able to generate a new encryption key for every message, and where a breach of any of the keys does not promise the previously used ones.

An important concept in defending against a breach of the trust infrastructure is to implement key exchange methods (FS). With this a comprise of the long-term keys will not compromise any previous session keys. For example, if we send the public key of the server to the client, and then the client sends back a session key for the connection which is encrypted with the public key of the server, then the server will then decrypt this and determine the session. A leakage of the public key of the server would cause all the sessions which used this specific public key to be compromised. FS thus aims to overcome this by making sure that all the sessions keys could not be compromised, even though the long-term key was compromised. The problem with using the RSA method to pass keys is that a breach of the long keys would breach the keys previously used for secure communications.

Another important concept is where is key is ephemeral. With some key exchange methods, the same key will be generated if the same parameters are used on either side. This can cause problems as an intruder could guess the key, or even where the key was static and never changed. With ephemeral methods a different key is used for each connection, and again, the leakage of any long-term would not cause all the associated session keys to be breached. The problem with the core Diffie-Hellman method is that the keys are not ephemeral, so we should avoid it in generating keys.

Signal, though, builds forward secrecy into their systems with a double ratchet method, and where each key will not lead to a breach of the previous ones. The double ratchet concept was created by Trevor Perrin and Moxie Marlinspike. In hashing, this is implemented by taking a secret ("A"), and then adding a value of zero to it and then hashing this. The next hash is then o secret with a one added to it, and so on. A breach of one of the hashed values will not reveal the original secret, and it will not be possible to guess the next key.

Within the double ratchet method, we have an on-going renewal system and where the session keys are only ever short-lived. For this it uses the Elliptic Curve Diffie-Hellman (ECDH) key exchange method and a hashing method for deriving the keys - this gives it a "double" ratchet.

The two parties exchange encrypted messages based on a shared secret key. They create a new set of keys for every Double Ratchet message. In this way earlier keys cannot be calculated from the ones that follow. They also send Diffie-Hellman public values with their messages, and and the results of the Diffie-Hellman calculations are then mixed together into the derived keys. The protocol is useful for making sure that a hack on one set of keys does not lead to a hack on the rest of the keys. In the following we will create two names (a and b), and then a will encrypt two messages for b, and b will encrypt one message for a:

```
Name 1:      Bob

Name 2:      Alice
```

```
Bob keys are:

Identity key (Public key):        tkUbaj1VwEIwi0kYRlWbl+0Don8WSgKOfbvij6+RT3c=

->Identity key (Private key):     hIHdPPYfiF5eEoqXhAIOq1H5qy2VIJToadn1azjk96Q=

Ratchet key (Public key):         7P3yOKPcAX5rVnQkQCmmGfQdo0mi4GL33Yy7DpFMbU0=

-> Ratchet key (Private key):     QYHS9FrJQ59VRDVqdwsDDVEbaaPp3myA+vUl3MTdC2Y=

Handshake Public key:             a/xifzSbU5wSwF8CFh+xP2ybY7jG/gKoY7dW0DTOHhA=

->Handshake Private key:          lSvv3TRFq7xuHxeTjQDqXQc2+UOALDDNJmRXnoDCUBA=
```

```
Encrypted message1 a->b:    2cuNbhbPkpcIck3j+9m76bUIr4X2cJdZSOARpGTzKPV3cs1NU-
rytT+CiNkgXVtJ2KEOzChxOeqLYoBjP11WW/UsSnkhFUkFH2So2iEXutBDHzlYExvQ9MCVkRkH-
6FaCnvpyPFvW5B6R+YUIok5CuZr0G9hI1Zqgcb0CRnZh0Nm4otP3f3A==
```

```
Encrypted message2 a->b: efj2axgAmcBuyjkDzKARlaNzu5MzWqqqd0T9OZH/hW5Oy5JCQH1PN3/
fYHu3lwU3N1gthhnGzHtJhlmq06pzXRcTJrhN5xlvsxAl+1K6t08QnD8Ev8myq1Ou719YySagwYRP-
BvZVo36GmFvN+qM05//weZtTFeL1fR2FZ1FMyjRR2+WiYjFzuE1AOw==
```

```
Encrypted message3 b->a:  H1gex6vZi0KTPywWK9XzVKmGiP2515XgYrM1Gx+kwq6JY8cQSLIK-
SHOjexqJhOR8MoGQs9IVX3aKbZkPRcKknsczl/jAdTav9ooFUe5c0XmJFWQEqwRkPgdpxFdbNmbM-
m7CwBne/6pyb7OfHEmzLUY+MYNLpF3dDwN6SOJFQTjzYe5eVaflBTrJn55TD
```

```
b decrypt:   The quick

b decrypt:   brown fox jumps

a decrypt:   over the lazy dog
```

A mechanical ratchet only moves forward for one step at a time. In cryptography, a ratchet method allows for future states to be calculated but only if you know an original seed value. It is not possible to calculate previous states from the current state. Typically this is done with a one-way-function such as a hash with a seed value and a salt.

For if we wanted to generate four ratchet values based a master key of "AlicePassword" (and using an HMAC hash, and were Alice will with an interactive hash of 0, 1, 2 and 3):

```
H0(AlicePassword) ≡ HMAC(AlicePassword, 0x00)

H1(AlicePassword) ≡ HMAC(AlicePassword, 0x01)

H2(AlicePassword) ≡ HMAC(AlicePassword, 0x02)

H3(AlicePassword) ≡ HMAC(AlicePassword, 0x03)
```

Each key is thus derived from the original seed. By observing H0(AlicePassword), it would not be possible to determine the next in the sequence (H1(AlicePassword)). As she sends messages, she creates an iterative hash for each one.

With the double racket method, Bob and Alice use their own outbound session - with a ratchet and elliptic curve key exchange - to encrypt messages.

The ratchet can only go forwards (and not backwards) and derives a unique key for each message. Ed25519 elliptic curve signatures are then used to prove authenticity. The value of the ratchet and the Ed25519 public key are shared with the other parties in the conversation.

Initially, Alice and Bob each create three Elliptic Curve key pairs (Identity, Ratchet and Handshaking).

The keys will then be derived from these. Bob, for example, exposes thre three public keys to Alice, but keeps his private keys for the generation of the shared secret key for the messages that Alice send to him. This key exchange will only be for the messages flowing between Alice and himself.

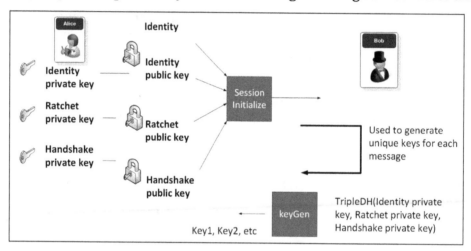

Coding

The following is some sample code:

```
import sys

import binascii

from pyaxo import Axolotl


name1='bob'

name2='alice'

m1='hello'

m2='goodbye'

m3='nice'


a = Axolotl(name1, dbpassphrase=None)

b = Axolotl(name2, dbpassphrase=None)
```

```
print "Name 1:\t",name1

print "Name 2:\t",name2


print "\n",name1," keys are:"


print "Identity key (Public key):\t\t",binascii.b2a_base64(a.state['DHIs']),

print "->Identity key (Private key):\t\t",binascii.b2a_base64(a.state['DHIs_
priv']),


print "Ratchet key (Public key):\t\t",binascii.b2a_base64(a.state['DHRs']),

print "-> Ratchet key (Private key):\t\t",binascii.b2a_base64(a.state['DHRs_
priv']),


print "Handshake Public key:\t\t",binascii.b2a_base64(a.handshakePKey),

print "->Handshake Private key:\t\t",binascii.b2a_base64(a.handshakeKey)



# initialize their states
a.initState(name2, b.state['DHIs'], b.handshakePKey, b.state['DHRs'], verify=-
False)

b.initState(name1, a.state['DHIs'], a.handshakePKey, a.state['DHRs'], verify=-
False)


msg0 = a.encrypt(m1)

msg1 = a.encrypt(m2)

msg2 = b.encrypt(m3)

print 'Encrypted message1 a->b: ',binascii.b2a_base64(msg0)

print 'Encrypted message2 a->b: ',binascii.b2a_base64(msg1)

print 'Encrypted message3 b->a: ',binascii.b2a_base64(msg2)

print 'b decrypt: ', b.decrypt(msg0)

print 'b decrypt: ', b.decrypt(msg1)

print 'a decrypt: ', a.decrypt(msg2)
```

```
a.saveState()

b.saveState()
```

Common Scrambling Algorithm

The Common Scrambling Algorithm (CSA) is used to encrypt streams of video data in the Digital Video Broadcasting (DVB) system. The algorithm cascades a stream and a block cipher, apparently for a larger security margin.

The DVB Common Scrambling Algorithm is an ETSI-specified algorithm for securing MPEG-2 transport streams such as those used for digitally transmitted Pay-TV. It was adopted by the DVB consortium in May 1994, the exact origin and date of the design is unclear. Until 2002, the algorithm was only available under a Non-Disclosure Agreement from an ETSI custodian. This NDA disallowed and still disallows licensees to implement the algorithm in software for "security reasons". The little information that was then available to the public is contained in an ETSI Technical Report and patent applications. This changed in the fall of 2002, when a Windows program called FreeDec appeared which implemented the CSA in software. It was quickly reverse-engineered and details were disseminated on a web site.

For keying the CSA, so called control words are used. These control words are provided by a conditional access mechanism, which generates them from encrypted control messages embedded in the transport stream. Conditional access mechanisms vary between broadcasters and can be more easily changed than the actual scrambling algorithm. Examples for commonly used conditional access mechanisms are Irdeto, Betacrypt, Nagravision, CryptoWorks etc. A new common key is usually issued every 10–120 seconds. The great relevance of CSA lies in the fact that every encrypted digital Pay-TV transmission in Europe is secured using this algorithm. A practical break of CSA would thus affect all broadcasters and could not be remedied by changing the conditional access mechanism.

The scrambling algorithm can be seen as the layering of two cryptographic primitives: a 64-bit block cipher and a stream cipher. Both ciphers employ a common key; the stream cipher uses an additional 64-bit nonce.

Cascading the Block and the Stream Cipher

The scrambling algorithm can be seen as a cascade of a block cipher and a stream cipher. Both ciphers use the same 64-bit key K, which is called the common key. We will now describe how the block and the stream cipher are combined. Figure depicts the descrambling process.

For scrambling the payload of an m-byte packet, it is divided into blocks (DB_i) of 8 bytes each. If an adaption field was used, it is possible that the length of the packet is not a multiple of 8 bytes. Thus the last block is n < 8 bytes long and shall be called residue.

The sequence of 8-byte blocks is encrypted in reverse order with the block cipher in CBC mode, whereas the residue is left untouched. The last output of the chain IB_0 is then used as a nonce for the stream cipher. The first m bytes of keystream generated by the stream cipher are XORed to the encrypted blocks $(IB_i)_{i \geq 1}$ followed by the residue.

Stream Cipher

The stream cipher is built of two feedbackshift-registers and a combiner with memory. The overall layout is shown in figure. The registers p, q and c are bit registers. All other registers are 4 bit wide.

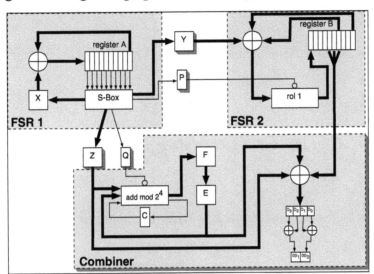

The stream cipher.

The stream cipher operates in one of two modes. The first one is the initialization mode in which the starting state of the cipher is set up. The second one is the generating mode in which the cipher produces two pseudo-random bits per clock cycle.

Key Schedule

The cipher uses the common key K and the first scrambled block of the transport stream SB_0 as a nonce to set up the initial state. At first all registers of the cipher are set to o. Then the common key $K = k_0, \ldots, k_{63}$ is loaded into the shift registers $A := a_{0,j}, \ldots, a_{9,j}$ and $B := b_{0,j}, \ldots, b_{9,j}$ with $0 \le j \le 3$ according to the following rule:

$$a_{i,j} = \begin{cases} k_{4 \cdot i + j} & i \le 7 \\ 0 & \text{else} \end{cases}$$

$$b_{i,j} = \begin{cases} k_{32 + 4 \cdot i + j} & i \le 7 \\ 0 & \text{else} \end{cases}$$

In the following a_i and b_i denote the 20 4-bit registers $a_{i,0}, \ldots, a_{i,3}$ and $b_{i,0}, \ldots, b_{i,3}$ respectively.

Hereafter the cipher is in initialization mode. It uses SB_0 and the feedback register D as input and performs 32 clock cycles to calculate the starting state. The inputs for feedback shift registers 1 and 2 are derived from SB_0:

$$(I^A, I^B) := \begin{cases} (SB_0 \ div \ 2^4, SB_0 \ mod \ 2^4) & \text{in state } t_i, i \in \{-31, -29, \ldots\}) \\ (SB_0 \ mod \ 2^4, SB_0 \ div 2^4) & \text{else} \end{cases}$$

Thus in every odd cycle number I^A is the high nibble of SB_0 whereas   is the low nibble. In even cycles the nibbles are used the other way round. See below for the equations which update the internal cipher state.

Generation Mode

- Feedback shift register: The feedback a_0' of shift register A is calculated as,

$$a_0' := \begin{cases} a_9 \oplus X & \text{if not in init mode} \\ a_9 \oplus X \oplus D \oplus I^A & \text{else} \end{cases}$$

The next value A' for register A is then given by,

$$A' := \left(a_0', a_0, \ldots, a_8 \right)$$

- Feedback shift register: The feedback b_0' of shift register B is given by,

$$b_0' := \begin{cases} b_6 \oplus b_9 \oplus Y & \text{if not in init mode} \\ b_6 \oplus b_9 \oplus Y \oplus I^B & \text{else} \end{cases}$$

and the new value B' for B is,

$$B' := \begin{cases} \left(b_0', b_0, \ldots, b_8 \right) & p = 0 \\ \left(rol\left(b_0' \right), b_0, \ldots, b_8 \right) & \text{else} \end{cases}$$

- Other registers: New values for the other registers, namely X, Y, Z, p and q are derived from seven 5×2 S-Boxes. Table shows which bits from shift-register A are used as input for the S-Boxes and how the new register values are constructed. The S-Boxes itself are shown in table. Table gives an algebraic description of the S-Boxes, with a being the most significant input bit and e the least significant.

- Combiner: The stream cipher uses a combiner with memory to calculate two bits of output per clock. The memory of the combiner consists of registers E, F and c. In each cycle a new state for these registers is determined according to:

$$(E, F)' := \begin{cases} (E, F) & q = 0 \\ \left(f, E + Z + c \bmod 2^4 \right) & \text{else} \end{cases}$$

c is unchanged if $q = 0$. Otherwise it is 1 if $E + Z + c \geq 2^4$ and 0 else.

The output of the generator is calculated by $D_2 \oplus D_3 \| D_0 \oplus D_1$ where $D := E \oplus Z \oplus B^{out}$ with B^{out} given by,

$$B_3^{out} := b_{2,0} \oplus b_{5,1} \oplus b_{6,2} \oplus b_{8,3}$$

$$B_2^{out} := b_{5,0} \oplus b_{7,1} \oplus b_{2,3} \oplus b_{3,2}$$

$$B_1^{out} := b_{4,3} \oplus b_{7,2} \oplus b_{3,0} \oplus b_{4,1}$$

$$B_0^{out} := b_{8,2} \oplus b_{5,3} \oplus b_{2,1} \oplus b_{7,0}$$

Block Cipher

CSA employs an iterated block cipher that operates bytewise on 64-bit blocks of data and uses a 64-bit key, the common key K. Each round of the cipher employs the same round transformation ϕ, which takes an 8-byte vector along with a single byte of the expanded key as input and outputs an 8-byte vector. This round transformation is applied 56 times. One could also lump together 8 successive rounds of the cipher into a round function ϕ' and describe a 7-round cipher which uses 64-bit subkeys; however we feel that the description we give below is more natural and easier to comprehend.

- The Key Schedule: Let ρ be the bit permutation on 64-bit strings which is defined in table. The expanded key $K^E = \left(k_0^E, \ldots, k_{447}^E \right)$ consists of a total of 448 bits which are recursively computed as follows:

$$k_{0,\ldots,63}^E = k_{0,\ldots,63}$$

$$k_{64i,\ldots,64i+63}^E = \rho \left(k_{64(i-1),\ldots,64i-1}^E \right) \oplus 0 \times 0i0i0i0i0i0i0i0i \qquad 1 \leq i \leq 6$$

where the expression $0 \times 0i0i0i0i0i0i0i0i$ is to be interpreted as a hexadecimal constant. The key schedule is entirely GF(2)-linear.

- The Round Function: At the core of the round transformation ϕ are the nonlinear functions f and f'. These are distinct permutations on the set of all byte values and can be seen as the S- Boxes of the cipher.

Table: S-Box input and generation of new register values.

S_1	$a_{3,0}$	$a_{0,2}$	$a_{5,1}$	$a_{6,3}$	$a_{8,0}$
S_2	$a_{1,1}$	$a_{2,2}$	$a_{5,3}$	$a_{6,0}$	$a_{8,1}$
S_3	$a_{0,3}$	$a_{1,0}$	$a_{4,1}$	$a_{4,3}$	$a_{5,2}$
S_4	$a_{2,3}$	$a_{0,1}$	$a_{1,3}$	$a_{3,2}$	$a_{7,0}$
S_5	$a_{4,2}$	$a_{3,2}$	$a_{5,0}$	$a_{7,1}$	$a_{8,2}$
S_6	$a_{2,1}$	$a_{3,1}$	$a_{4,0}$	$a_{6,2}$	$a_{8,3}$
S_7	$a_{1,2}$	$a_{2,0}$	$a_{6,1}$	$a_{7,2}$	$a_{7,2}$

X	$S_{4,0}$	$S_{3,0}$	$S_{2,1}$	$S_{1,1}$
Y	$S_{6,0}$	$S_{5,0}$	$S_{4,1}$	$S_{3,1}$
Z	$S_{2,0}$	$S_{1,0}$	$S_{6,1}$	$S_{5,1}$
P	$S_{7,1}$			
q	$S_{7,0}$			

Table: Key bit permutation.

i	0	1	2	3	4	5	6	7	8	9	10	11	12	13	14	15
p(i)	17	35	8	6	41	48	28	20	27	53	61	49	18	32	58	63
i	16	17	18	19	20	21	22	23	24	25	26	27	28	29	30	31
p(i)	23	19	36	38	1	52	26	0	33	3	12	13	56	39	25	40
i	32	33	34	35	36	37	38	39	40	41	42	43	44	45	46	47
p(i)	50	34	51	11	21	47	29	57	44	30	7	24	22	46	60	16
i	48	49	50	51	52	53	54	55	56	57	58	59	60	61	62	63
p(i)	59	4	55	42	10	5	9	43	31	62	45	14	2	37	15	54

Both permutations have maximum cycle length and are related to each other by a bit permutation σ, i.e. $f' = \sigma \circ f$. This bit permutation maps bit 0 to 1, bit 1 to 7, bit 2 to 5, bit 3 to 4, bit 4 to 2, bit 5 to 6, bit 6 to 0 and bit 7 to 3. Table above for the actual values described by f.

Let $S = (s_0, \ldots, s_7)$ be the vector of bytes representing the internal state of the block cipher in an arbitrary round. The function ϕ taking the internal state S from round i to round $i+1$ can then be defined as,

$$\phi(s_0, \ldots, s_7, k) = (s_1, s_2 \oplus s_0, s_3 \oplus s_0, s_4 \oplus s_0, s_5, s_6 \oplus f'(k \oplus s_7), s_7, s_0 \oplus f(k \oplus s_7))$$

whereas for decrypting a block of ciphertext we need the inverse function:

$$\phi^{-1}(s_0, \ldots, s_7, k) = (s_7 \oplus f(s_6 \oplus k), s_0,$$
$$s_7 \oplus s_1 \oplus f(s_6 \oplus k), s_7 \oplus s_2 \oplus f(s_6 \oplus k),$$
$$s_7 \oplus s_3 \oplus f(s_6 \oplus k), s_4, s_5 \oplus f'(s_6 \oplus k), s_6)$$

Encrypting a plaintext $P = (p_0, \ldots, p_7)$ is accomplished by,

$$S^0 = P$$
$$S^r = \phi\left(S^{r-1}, \left(k^E_{8r}, \ldots, k^E_{8r+7}\right)\right) \quad 1 \le r \le 56$$
$$C = S^{56}$$

which yields the ciphertext $C = (c_0, \ldots, c_7)$. For decrypting this ciphertext the following sequence of operations needs to be carried out:

$$S^0 = C$$
$$S^r = \phi\left(S^{r-1}, \left(k^E_{448-8r}, \ldots, k^E_{455-8r}\right)\right) \quad 1 \le r \le 56$$
$$C = S^{56}$$

Analysis of the Stream Cipher

In the following we denote with t_0 the stream cipher's state after the initialization. That means t_{-31} is the initial state, in which the common key is loaded in the registers A and B respectively. Given this notation we define a full cycle to be the smallest number $l_w := j - i$ for which the values of all registers in state t_i are equal to the values in t_j. Also we define a small cycle to be the smallest number $l_s := j - i$ when the values of X and A in state t_i are equal to the values in t_j.

The CSA stream cipher's state consists of 103 bits. This means that the maximum period length is 2^{103}. For cryptographic purposes, one would expect the cycle to go through a minimum of 2^{80} states. Using Floyd's cycle-finding algorithm however, we observed that after a relatively short preperiod there exist only a few different cycle lengths for different key/nonce combinations; all of these have a length of $l_w < 109$, which of course is much smaller than 2^{80}. When comparing the set of states in several cycles with the same length which where generated by different key/nonce pairs, one notices that these are disjunct; many different cycles with length l_w exist.

On the other hand, taking only A and X in account shows that if two cycles have the same length l_w then l_s is equal too. Moreover the sequence of states in feedback-shift-register 1 is equal. This means that if l_w is equal for two cycles then the registers A and X for these cycles are going through the same values.

We conducted a total of 10^5 experiments with random key/nonce pairs to determine the most probable period lengths for the state transition function operating on register A. Table shows some small cycle lengths l_s together with the number of times $n(l_s)$ we observed a cycle of this length in our test and $a(l_s)$ the average length of the pre-period for a given cycle length.

Table: Probability distribution for small cycles.

$n(l_s)$	l_s	$a(l_s)$
36106	22778	152854.6
24196	97494	83098.3
18054	121992	27726.2
15171	42604	65556.8
3244	25802	17643.8
1495	108	21051.6
131	2391	3138.5

In 1.6% of all cases we observed cycle lengths not listed in the above table. For each of these the probability of occurrence must be lower than 0.2%. This observation leads to the following attack:

- Calculate a table T with the states of the small cycles,

- For every state in T do,

- Test if the state is correct,

- Reconstruct the remaining registers,

- End for.

It remains to show how one can determine if the state is correct and how the remaining registers can be reconstructed.

Finding the Correct Value for FSR1

The trivial method of finding the correct value for FSR1 is to simply try all possible values. That means that one searches through all states which belong to one of the small cycles. Summing up the number of states in table shows that in 98.4% of all cases testing 313, 169 possibilities is sufficient; this is far less than the 2^{44} possible values for A and X.

Reconstructing the Remaining Registers

The stream cipher's output is calculated by XORing Z, E and B^{out}. Since we can now consider A to be known,   is fully determined. For all possible 2^9 values of E, F and c do the following:

Consider all bits of B at clock cycle t as variables with values in GF(2). Generate a system of equations describing the two output bits at clock cycle $t + k$ as linear equations of bits of these variables. This system is linear since the additional inputs for the feedback shift register are fully determined by A and hence are known. In other words: for every state of A a system of linear equations that fully describes B with respect to B^{out} exists. Therefore this system can be efficiently solved using Gaussian elimination. If the system is inconsistent then the guess for E, F and c was wrong and has to be altered.

The last step of the attack is to determine which of the possible solutions for the linear equations system is the correct one. This has to be done because different values for E, F and c may lead to a solution of the system. The correct value can be determined simply by running the keystream generator with the calculated state and checking if the output corresponds to the actual output of the generator.

Some of the generated equations are linearly dependent. Experimentally we derived that for finding a unique solution to the system described above, 60 equations are sufficient.

For carrying out the attack one thus needs to solve approximately $2^{19} \cdot 2^9 = 2^{28}$ systems of linear equations, each of which contains 60 equations in 40 unknowns. Experiments showed that this can be done in less than an hour on a 1.25 GHz PowerPC G4. We stress that our attack leaves much room for improvement. It might be possible to increase our chances at guessing the correct value for A from statistical deviation in the output of the stream cipher. But already our unoptimized version shows that the stream cipher can be broken in a very short time. Also, this attack is well suited to parallelization.

Analysis of the Block Cipher

We note that the round function ϕ is a weak permutation. Given the inputs x_1, x_2 and outputs $y_1 = \phi(x_1, k)$ and $y_2 = \phi(x_2, k)$ of a single round it is trivial to determine the round subkey k. The key schedule however seems to make the cipher resistant against slide attacks.

Linear Approximation of the S-boxes

The maximum bias of both S-Boxes is $\dfrac{17}{128}$. Trying to find a linear path through several rounds of the cipher we see that the number of active S-Boxes in the path increases exponentially in the number of rounds. Because of this fact and the high number of rounds, the authors believe that classical linear cryptanalysis poses not threat to the cipher.

Polynomial Interpolation of the S-boxes

We have interpolated the S-Boxes as polynomials over fields $GF(2^8) = GF(2)[X]/m(X)$ for all $m \in GF(2)[X]$ with $\deg(m) = 8$ and m irreducible. The resulting polynomials are all dense and of maximum degree. Interpolating bit traces of the S-Boxes results in polynomials consisting of 117–137 terms. Two of them are of degree 8, the other 6 of degree.

Thus we conclude that both representations are not useful for algebraic cryptanalysis of the cipher.

References

- Concepts-algorithms, userguide, latest, crypto: aws.amazon.com, Retrieved 19 May, 2019

- Reference work entry: springer.com, Retrieved 3 August, 2019

- The-berlekamp-massey-algorithm-revisited: researchgate.net, Retrieved 8 August, 2019

- Ratchet, encryption: asecuritysite.com, Retrieved 9 May, 2019

Permissions

We would like to thank the editorial team for lending their expertise to make the book truly unique. They have played a crucial role in the development of this book. Without their invaluable contributions this book wouldn't have been possible. They have made vital efforts to compile up to date information on the varied aspects of this subject to make this book a valuable addition to the collection of many professionals and students.

This book was conceptualized with the vision of imparting up-to-date and integrated information in this field. To ensure the same, a matchless editorial board was set up. Every individual on the board went through rigorous rounds of assessment to prove their worth. After which they invested a large part of their time researching and compiling the most relevant data for our readers.

The editorial board has been involved in producing this book since its inception. They have spent rigorous hours researching and exploring the diverse topics which have resulted in the successful publishing of this book. They have passed on their knowledge of decades through this book. To expedite this challenging task, the publisher supported the team at every step. A small team of assistant editors was also appointed to further simplify the editing procedure and attain best results for the readers.

Apart from the editorial board, the designing team has also invested a significant amount of their time in understanding the subject and creating the most relevant covers. They scrutinized every image to scout for the most suitable representation of the subject and create an appropriate cover for the book.

The publishing team has been an ardent support to the editorial, designing and production team. Their endless efforts to recruit the best for this project, has resulted in the accomplishment of this book. They are a veteran in the field of academics and their pool of knowledge is as vast as their experience in printing. Their expertise and guidance has proved useful at every step. Their uncompromising quality standards have made this book an exceptional effort. Their encouragement from time to time has been an inspiration for everyone.

The publisher and the editorial board hope that this book will prove to be a valuable piece of knowledge for students, practitioners and scholars across the globe.

Index

Printed in the USA
CPSIA information can be obtained
at www.ICGtesting.com
JSHW051411221024
72173JS00006B/1341